# Transformations
## at the Edge of the World

—∾—

Publication of this book was made possible by
a gift from Terry Koonce of Houston, Texas.

—∾—

Forming
Global Christians
through the
Study Abroad
Experience

# Transformations
## at the Edge of the World

Ronald J. Morgan and Cynthia Toms Smedley,
editors

Abilene Christian University Press

Abilene, Texas

**TRANSFORMATIONS AT THE EDGE OF THE WORLD**
*Forming Global Christians through the Study Abroad Experience*

ACU
PRESS

Copyright 2010 by Ronald J. Morgan and Cynthia Toms Smedley

ISBN 978-0-89112-047-6

Printed in the United States of America

Scripture taken from the HOLY BIBLE, NEW INTERNATIONAL VERSION®. Copyright © 1973, 1978, 1984 Biblica. Used by permission of Zondervan. All rights reserved.

LIBRARY OF CONGRESS CATALOGING-IN-PUBLICATION DATA
Transformations at the edge of the world : forming global Christians through the study abroad experience / Ronald J. Morgan and Cynthia Toms Smedley, editors.
    p. cm.
ISBN 978-0-89112-047-6
1. Foreign study--United States. 2. Christian college students--United States. 3. Church colleges--United States. I. Morgan, Ronald J. (Ronald Jay), 1958- II. Smedley, Cynthia Toms, 1975-
LB2376.T63 2010
370.116--dc22
                        2009049231

Cover design by Jennette Munger
Interior text design by Sandy Armstrong

For information contact:
Abilene Christian University Press
1626 Campus Court
Abilene, Texas 79601

1-877-816-4455 toll free
www.abilenechristianuniversitypress.com

10 11 12 13 14 15 / 7 6 5 4 3 2 1

# Dedications

## Ron

To Janine—You continue to be
a deeply transformative agent in my life

## Cynthia

To Michael, my partner on the journey

# Table of Contents

## Part I:
## The Journey Inward

## Part II:
## Inward Journey to Outward Living: Community Teacher

## Part III:
## Coming Face to Face with the Social Other:
## Bridging Intercommunal Divides

## Part IV:
## The Year of the Lord's Good Favor:
## Cultivating Solidarity with the Global Poor

# Contributors

**Karen M. Andrews** (Ph.D. in English and American Literature, Claremont Graduate University) is associate professor of urban studies and English at the San Francisco Urban Program of Westmont College. She has taught urban studies, English electives, and independent study tutorials on the Urban Program since 1997. Her academic and personal interests have recently focused on human trafficking.

**John Barbour**, professor of religion at St. Olaf College, received his Ph.D. in religion and literature from the University of Chicago Divinity School. His most recent book is *The Value of Solitude: The Ethics and Spirituality of Aloneness in Autobiography* (2004). He has led seven St. Olaf College January terms to off-campus locations, as well as two five-month programs: The Global Program (2001–02) and Term in Asia (2008–09).

**Brad Berky** (M.Div., Fuller Theological Seminary and doctoral work at Graduate Theological Union, Berkeley) has been faculty coordinator of student internships at the San Francisco Urban Program of Westmont College since 1990 and is a 1982 Urban alum. He teaches a weekly practicum and independent studies. He also holds a B.A. from Gordon College.

**Don J. Briel** holds the Koch Chair in Catholic Studies and the director of the Center for Catholic Studies at the University of St. Thomas in St. Paul, Minnesota. He holds a doctorate in Catholic theology from the University of Strasbourg. His publications have focused on the character and promise of Christian higher education, the thought of John Henry Newman, and the role of Catholic Studies in the Catholic university.

**Kenneth E. Bussema** is vice president for student programs for the Council for Christian Colleges & Universities. He holds an Ed.D. in counseling psychology from Northern Arizona University and has worked in Christian higher education for over thirty-five years. Prior to joining the CCCU, Ken served as professor of psychology and director of off-campus programs at Dordt College and has a variety of cross-cultural experiences that include working for five years on the Navajo Reservation. His publications include several articles that reflect his interests in faith development, identity formation, and the role of spirituality in recovery from mental illness.

**Mary Docter** (Ph.D. in Hispanic Languages and Literatures, UCLA) is professor of Spanish at Westmont College, where she teaches courses in Spanish language and composition, Hispanic cultures, Latin American literature, and cross-cultural studies. Besides her current work on study abroad with Dr. Laura Montgomery, she has several publications in her other area of research, contemporary Latin American poetry.

**Chris Elisara** (Ph.D., Biola University) founded the Creation Care Study Program (CCSP) in 2002 with his wife Tricia. For a native New Zealander with a passion for climbing and God's creation on the one hand, and God's justice, compassion, and the transformative power of education on the other, directing CCSP has been a dream vocation. Whereas Dr. Elisara's published work focuses on environmental education, most of his extra creative energy is funneled into producing award-winning films.

**Lon Fendall** was director of the Center for Global Studies at George Fox University until 2009. His academic positions have included dean of the faculty at Wilmington College (OH), vice president of academic affairs at Tabor College (KS), and dean of undergraduate studies at George Fox. Among the books he has authored and co-authored are *Stand Alone or Come Home; At Home With the Poor;* and *Practicing Discernment Together.*

**David P. Holt** received an M.A. in government at the Claremont Graduate School and his Ph.D. in comparative politics of the Middle East at the University of Chicago. For nearly a decade, he has lived, worked, or traveled to many countries of the Middle East, including Turkey, Syria, Lebanon, Jordan, Israel, Morocco, Tunisia, Iran, and select Palestinian areas. He has published in the areas of foreign policy and ethnicity.

**Janine Paden Morgan** (Ph.D., Fuller Theological Seminary) is chaplain and instructor in Bible, Ministry and Missions for Abilene Christian University's ACU in Oxford program. Raised in Italy, Janine has been active in cross-cultural ministry and education in Europe and Latin America. Her research and teaching reflect her interests in religious ritual, spiritual formation, and the relationship between Christianity and human cultures.

**Scott E. McClelland** (Ph.D. in New Testament, University of Edinburgh, Scotland) has been director of the San Francisco Urban Program of Westmont College since 2006. Scott also teaches and writes on the Emergent Church. With wife Louise, he co-pastors Grace Community Church of San Francisco and is an adjunct professor for Fuller Theological Seminary (Northern California). Scott also holds degrees from Westminster Theological Seminary and Wheaton College.

**Thomas J. Meyers** (Ph.D. in Sociology, Boston University) is associate academic dean, director of international education, and professor of sociology at Goshen College. His research has focused on the Old Order Amish. Recent publications include *Plain Diversity*, co-authored by Steven Nolt (Johns Hopkins University Press, 2007). He has lived and worked in the Caribbean and West Africa. In his current position, he has established semester programs in Asia, Africa, and Latin America.

**Laura M. Montgomery** is a professor of anthropology at Westmont College. She holds an M.A. and Ph.D. from Michigan State University and a B.A. from Wheaton College. She teaches courses on cultural anthropology, Latin America, and cross-cultural communication. Her publications focus on agricultural change and development policy in Mexico, short-term medical missions, and the role of gender in shaping the academic and life choices of college students.

**Ronald J. Morgan** (Ph.D., UC-Santa Barbara) is associate professor of history and director of ACU in Oxford for Abilene Christian University. Ron has worked in cross-cultural Christian ministries (Brazil) and international education (England, Germany). His publications include *Spanish American Saints and the Rhetoric of Identity, 1600–1810* and several articles on Roman Catholic history and Christian spirituality.

**John E. Skillen** (Ph.D., Duke University) is professor of English at Gordon College and director of the Gordon in Orvieto program, which he established in 1998 with colleagues from the art department. Under his leadership, the Orvieto program has become a multifaceted Studio for Art, Faith and History, hosting conferences, art exhibits, theatrical and musical performances, retreats, and graduate-level seminars.

**Richard Slimbach** (Ph.D. in International Education, UCLA) is founder of the Global Studies Program at Azusa Pacific University (APU). His passion is to design cross-cultural programs that integrate traditional and alternative (experiential, service-based) pedagogies, and that foster in students a profound sense of responsibility for the fate of the poor and the planet. He is the author of *Becoming World Wise* (Stylus Publishers, 2010).

**Andrea Smith Shappell** (M.A., theology, Notre Dame) is an assistant director, Center for Social Concerns of the University of Notre Dame, and director, Theological Reflection and the Summer Service Learning Program (SSLP). She is an associate professional specialist, concurrent in theology. Previous publications include editorial work on *Doing the Truth in Love* by Michael Himes and *Compassion* (2nd ed.) by McNeill, Morrison, and Nouwen.

**Cynthia Toms Smedley** (M.S., Boston University) is director of educational immersions at the University of Notre Dame's Center for Social Concerns. Cynthia taught at Tsinghua University's Center for Overseas Academic and Cultural Exchange (Beijing, China) and was the associate director of the Uganda Studies Program (Mukono, Uganda). She and her husband, Michael, have been greatly influenced by their work with NGOs such as Hope International and ChildVoice International.

# Acknowledgments

The two editors of this volume acknowledge that many important influences—spiritual, educational, and social—have helped shape our desire to pursue this book project. The project reflects our love for God, our students, and the global human family, as well as the work we do as Christian scholars and educators.

Both of us wish to offer special thanks to Heidi Nobles, our managing editor. Her tireless efforts and wise counsel helped us to see the forest from the trees and kept the project on track. We also wish to thank C. Leonard Allen, director of ACU Press, for believing in this project. We offer praise to all those who collaborated on this volume; not only for their thoughtful essays, but also for the energy and commitment they continue to bring to the formation of global Christians. Finally, we recognize that this project would not exist, nor be as interesting, without the helpful input and anonymous contributions of our students. We tip our hat to you and we consider it a privilege to work with you daily—the transformations we see in you, and your transformative work in the world, get us out of bed in the morning.

Ron—I wish to thank those who have had significant spiritual influence on my life: my parents, Page and Joyce Morgan; the Paden family; members of the Rio mission team; my childhood congregation, the A&M Church of Christ; friends at Santa Barbara Community Church; and Brazilian and British Christians. There are those who shaped my global and international outlook, including Mrs. Kitty Worley, who transmitted her love not only for the Spanish language, but also for Latin American peoples. More recently, the leadership of Dr. Dwayne Van Rheenen, Dr. Kevin Kehl, and Mr. Stephen Shewmaker at Abilene Christian University has allowed me to create programs that form students spiritually and globally. My wife Janine and our co-worker Jacqueline Holton Morrison, along with a variety of visiting faculty members, have made major contributions to those same goals.

**Cynthia** wishes to thank the team of people that kept her spiritually and emotionally grounded during this project: colleagues at the Center for Social Concerns; Friday Night Home Group; Katie and Adam MacLeod; Chad and Sue Toms; Julie and Tim Poludniak; Bethany Deamer; Karla Klockenteger; Kathy Smarrella; Angelina Baglini and Jake Griswold, the world's most capable student workers; and Meredith Whitnah, who edited my drafts and helped to refine my thinking on our daily lake walks. Finally, a very special thanks to Monte and Linda Unger, who encouraged this neophyte toward the joy of writing; Ken Bussema (who originally connected Ron and me for this project); Clarice and Jerry Smedley, who joyfully watched the boys while I shirked off to write; to my parents, Debbie and Eugene Toms, who lovingly instilled authentic faith in our family, and taught me the value of education and living life to the fullest every day; and finally, to my biggest fan and encourager, Michael—your love and partnership is more than this sojourner deserves. I am so blessed to do this life with you.

# Foreword

**KEN BUSSEMA**

Vice President of the Council for Christian Colleges and Universities

"Find yourself somewhere else!" I liked the catchy slogan so I put the poster in a prominent place by my office inviting students to consider off-campus study opportunities. The slogan's double meaning appealed to me as it captured two important motivations for traveling away from the home campus. The "get away from here" aspect taps into that part of our human psyche that yearns for adventure and discovery, to find out what's on the other side, over the next hill, or across the next sea. Traveling away from home in pursuit of new experiences, perspectives, and knowledge has become an established educational strategy for preparing the next generation of global citizens.

Perhaps more importantly, the poster also suggests that journeys away from "home" have the potential to be transformative experiences. From a variety of perspectives, the university years are understood to be critical years in a person's developmental journey—a vulnerable, yet opportune time for the transition from dependency on ways of thinking rooted in family, childhood and social group to critically examined, refitted, and tested patterns of one's own. Finding oneself somewhere else, testing one's sense of identity through the lens of different places, peoples, and customs, may indeed be the most significant discovery of the journey.

This year more than two hundred and fifty thousand U.S. students will venture abroad to earn academic credits. My own organization, the Council for Christian Colleges & Universities, has reached the milestone of serving more than ten thousand students in our BestSemester programs. Looking ahead over the next ten years, the U.S. government and educational agencies are posed to greatly expand study abroad opportunities with the goal of sending one million American college students each year to study in locations across the globe. We can make a convincing case for supporting study abroad as a venue to meet common educational objectives such as global awareness, cultural enrichment, or political expediencies. However, as higher education professionals, we must also press the question of whether all of this travel really does have the significant impact, both personally and culturally, that my marketing poster claimed.

Will the mere experience of jumping on a plane, train, or bus provide transformative opportunities? Can some travel be better or worse than other travel? And specifically for those of us in faith-based higher education, what impact does the journey have on students' faith and worldview? These questions and others, especially when the costs of higher education are under close scrutiny, demand our attention. We need to demonstrate not only that the study abroad opportunities we offer and support are effective in achieving our institutional missions and providing personally meaningful growth experiences for our students, but also that they contribute to ongoing transformation for the broader global community. *Transformations at the Edge of the World* takes on many of these important questions, providing both compelling examples of quality programming and fresh insights for effective culture crossing. Sharing the collective expertise of experienced educators in articulating both the rationale for their particular programs as well as lessons learned from traveling with students across the globe, this volume will inspire and instruct, while helping us all appreciate the contours of faith-informed sojourns.

Each contributor embraces a dynamic understanding of the nature of faith and the experience of traveling away from home as both an individual and communal activity of making meaning. Recognizing our human rootedness and dependence on relationships, tradition and culture, often unexamined and uncritically accepted as truth, the authors explore the developmentally critical process of taking some distance from these moorings to examine, test, challenge and perhaps reshape in order to more authentically "own" one's commitments and convictions. It is interesting to note how comfortable the contributors are with the language of journey, sojourn, and discovery as essential components of the students' personal growth and understanding. The authors recognize, often in distinctive ways, the transformative dimensions of these dynamic encounters, which require both distancing and engagement. The authors thus create the teachable moments from times of disequilibrium and experiences beyond the reach of established frames of reference, thereby creating personal and collective space and tolerance for incomplete answers. These ingredients are familiar to those acquainted with the language and thinking of faith development and spiritual formation writers and they serve well as word pictures of the experience and process of the journey. What I enjoy most in these descriptions is the contributors' shared appreciation for the uniquely personal way each participant must wrestle to achieve their own insights and answers to fundamental questions of identity, group membership, and vocation. More importantly, the authors argue convincingly that willingness to serve the global community as agents of reconciliation, justice, and shalom is the primary catalyst in real student transformation. Reading this volume convinces me that study abroad experiences, affording rich opportunities to discover self, other, and God, are more important today than ever.

October 2009

# Introduction

CYNTHIA TOMS SMEDLEY

The clouds unleashed a torrent of rainfall into the warm afternoon air of equatorial Uganda. Kate and I exchanged nervous glances as our program vehicle rumbled over potholes and prickly vegetation, scrambling to convert a heavily traveled footpath into a makeshift road. Over the years, I had grown accustomed to the rainy season showers and even grew to welcome them. Our final destination, an orphanage just beyond the village settlement, suddenly seemed a lofty goal.

I was tempted to suggest that Kate forgo her service project hours for the week and make them up at a later time. But I had come to know Kate over the past two months, and I was certain that my concern would be met with her characteristic fortitude and determination. As one of the more mature students in the group, Kate came to East Africa hoping to better understand her faith by encountering the people and cultures across the globe from her arid Southern Arizona home. Her sights were set on graduate school, and she often sought counsel on how to make her studies more relevant. During one afternoon conversation, Kate told me, "A lot of my friends are talking about how they want to change the world. At this point, I just want to get in touch with it." It was plain to see that Kate had "a teachable spirit."

Kate's youthful zeal gave me personal resolve, and I squinted through the rain-streaked windshield and steadied my hands on the wheel. Long minutes passed before the thatched-roof huts came into focus. I steered the Land Rover into a clearing as two bony dogs braved the rain to announce our arrival. Kate reached for the truck's handle, and then paused to release a deep sigh. I could tell she had been thinking hard about something for most of our trip.

"What's on your mind, Kate?" I asked. Kate's eyes remained focused on the floor of the car as she replied, "You know, I have been thinking really hard about how to help the children. They need soap, shampoo, and other basic hygiene and health products. So yesterday, I asked Momma Ruth if it would be okay to gather resources and make health kits for each hut." As Kate talked, her voice began to crack. I allowed her to continue, even though I was quite sure I knew what she was going to say. As I turned to face her, I could see tears beginning to well in her eyes. She continued, "Momma Ruth said no, that I should not take the time to make hygiene kits. I don't understand why. How could providing these kids with health products and soap be a bad idea?" Kate's voice trailed off as she spoke these last words.

The air in the truck grew thick. The best teachers will tell you that a certain stillness enters the air when a teachable moment cracks the space between mentor and student. In a setting such as this, words often carry great weight and are received more readily than when they are spoken in concrete buildings or ivory towers.

Sensing the potential, I carefully explained to Kate that last year's students brought similar projects to the farm. They made health boxes in the fall, and in the spring, they started a chicken farm. Unfortunately, the chickens did not survive more than a month or two—and she was already considering another run of hygiene kits. "It's not that these initiatives were not helpful, or even welcomed," I continued, "but they were not what the community or Momma Ruth really wanted. They certainly helped for a time, but students spent all of their time at the orphanage *doing* good work—and they missed out on an opportunity to practice *being* present and giving the children their full attention." Kate's face was moving from confusion to total bewilderment. Her gaze swept upward from the floor until our eyes met and I could sense her deep frustration. So much of her training in development studies and sociology was about how to effectively vault people out of poverty—and here she was, finally able to help and feeling like her efforts were thwarted. "Kate, it's never wrong to help," I said. "But, good intention is only part of the criteria for truly serving others, especially when we are reaching across cultures."

Kate and I talked for well over an hour as the rain poured around our makeshift classroom. We discussed the different value systems that exist between our individualist culture in the U.S. and the collectivist culture in Uganda. We reflected on a few points that had come out in our class readings. We even talked about how the story of Mary and Martha could be interpreted anew now that she could view Scripture with African lenses. But the real epiphany came when I asked Kate why she was so deeply disappointed by not being able to live out her version of helping the children. How could she be frustrated when it was clear that the orphanage wanted her relationship of solidarity over her efforts to change their condition? I encouraged her to look deep inside and find out what motivated her to the action of helping. I challenged her to consider whether God was most pleased with her faithfulness as a Christian or her effectiveness as an incarnational servant? These questions cut deep to the heart of how Kate viewed God, her faith, and the global community. She did not emerge from our discussions that day with definite answers, but she gained a better understanding of the big questions. Namely, the question of how she was called to be an agent of change in the world in the midst of such difficult circumstances.

Each year, thousands of students just like Kate venture to what the editors of this volume are calling the edge of the world. For us, "the edge of the world" is not necessarily a place of physical remoteness or a region of economic marginality. Instead, we conceive of it as a place of personal transformation, the point of convergence between an individual's spiritual development and commitment to global engagement. As Kate discovered, the medium of study abroad invokes shifts in faith interpretation, knowledge paradigm, and cultural familiarity. For this reason, Christian institutions of higher learning are moving beyond campus borders to nurture spiritual transformations and form globally conscious Christians. This book examines cultural immersion pedagogy as an extension of the Christian higher education mission and efforts by program leaders to shape a generation whose Christian faith informs their approaches to global issues, and whose global commitments shape their faith.

## Universities Unbound

The globalization of American Christianity presents new challenges for faith-based higher education. In an increasingly connected and complex world, training a generation of leaders as actors on the world stage is paramount. As Jon Wergin noted recently in the foreword to *Putting Students First*, "Faith based institutions do more than just educate the mind, they help students define their vocation, their calling, and their place in the world—'the place where their deep gladness meets the world's deep need' (Buechner)."[1]

To that end, Christian higher education should aim to deliver a truly *holistic* education, one that connects knowledge with action and head with heart.[2] A stance such as this would ensure a thriving Christian intelligentsia, as well as the formation of moral conscience. By definition, the *intelligentsia* enables people to engage in creative labor directed toward cultural development and dissemination of knowledge.[3] If Christians are to have cultural relevance and global influence, they must enter into all matters of intellectual discourse. For graduates of faith-based institutions, this translates into relevant contributions to cross-national discourse and embracing what historian Mark Noll describes as the effort "to think within a specifically Christian framework— across the whole spectrum of modern learning."[4]

The latter task, formation of conscience, has been described as a never-ending search that every person must undertake in order to determine what is a worthy and virtuous endeavor.[5] The Catholic Catechism states, "The education of conscience guarantees freedom and engenders peace of heart. Conscience formulates its judgments according to reason, in conformity with the true good willed by the wisdom of the Creator."[6] In students, formation of conscience invites self-awareness, social interdependence, empathy with the cultural "other," and a growing commitment to social responsibility. By developing these two facets of holistic education—a desire in students for a "life of the mind," and conscience formation—Christian institutions embrace the mission of helping students align their spiritual commitments (or "deep gladness") with the deep needs of the human community.

Today, our connectedness to the human community extends across the globe. Therefore, education and formation must stretch beyond traditional national borders. Recently, a number of faith-based higher education institutes have introduced language of global engagement into their institutional mission statement. For example, Abilene Christian University's vision statement includes teaching students to think "critically, globally, and missionally." Crichton College encourages students to "grow spiritually, and change their world." Eastern Mennonite University's mission to "educate students to serve and lead in a global context" reflects a long-standing paradigm that is alive and working to continuously shape their campus. And these examples are only a small cross section of the newly emerging global-mindedness of the university without borders. The contributors of this volume further expand on this movement, all representing extensions of their universities' missions.

Departures from faith-based campuses and church-related universities should not signify a pause in spiritual growth. Rather, the journey should afford students continuous transformative learning in a new social and cultural context. Kate's college experiences helped her develop spiritually long before she stepped off the plane in East Africa. During her formative years as a freshman and sophomore on her home campus, class material helped her understand the dialectical relationship between sociology and development. That intellectual foundation prepared her to ask deep questions of her faith understanding and to desire to engage the other in the world. Her desire to interact with this knowledge in a personal way led her to Uganda, where the immersion experience further refined her questions. Through continuing the university mission, study abroad leaders help to form globally conscious Christians and invite students into a deeper understanding of themselves, their faith, and their world.

## Students without Borders

Today's generation of students are globally minded. In the book entitled, *Millennials Rising: The Next Great Generation*, Howe & Strauss note, "Much as American Millennials share a *national* location in history, kids around the world today share a *global* one, based on both cultural and family trends as well as changes in geopolitics and technology. Are they a global generation? Indeed . . . ."[7] They are the evolutionary product of global outreach within American churches. Sociologist Robert Wuthnow notes, "At least a quarter of churchgoers said they had heard sermons in the past year on such topics as poverty and the environment. In another study, three-quarters of self-identified Christians said the United States should be actively involved in world affairs."[8] This reality is reflected in study abroad numbers, which have increased by nearly 150% over the past decade, from 84,000 in 1998 to more than 240,000 in 2007.[9] Despite a recent downturn in the economy and weakened U.S. dollar, study abroad professionals are predicting growth at an even faster rate in the coming years.[10] By learning foreign languages, experiencing other cultures, and better understanding the international economic system, recent and upcoming graduates are positioning themselves to compete and thrive in a global marketplace.

Studying abroad for the sake of competitive market skills is a valuable asset. However, the desire for global proficiency is not the whole story.

Students are also seeking a space to better understand themselves, their connections to God, and their places in the world. Evidence of this can be seen in the burgeoning interest in spirituality among college students. In a 2004 national survey, more than seventy-five percent of new students reported an active search for meaning and purpose in life; while fifty percent suggested that they believed themselves to be on a spiritual quest and desired avenues to develop spiritually while in college. Many of these students reported that they expect their colleges to provide opportunities to pursue spiritual interests. Therefore, some of the best empirical data indicates that student interest and involvement in spirituality remains high.[11]

These broad trends may explain the increased interest in faith-based education. Enrollment in the 110 intentionally Christ-centered colleges of the Council for Christian Colleges and University has risen twenty-seven percent since 1997. That's more than three times as fast as the growth at all four-year schools.[12] Following a tradition of faith seeking understanding, Christian higher education offers "a liberal education that addresses the whole life."[13] The college years are considered to be among the most formative for spiritual development and a critical time to form identity, values, and beliefs. And it is during the undergraduate experience, perhaps more than at any other time that these essential qualities of mind and character are refined.[14] Many students report that the experiences of studying abroad or concentrated off-campus cultural immersion programs marked times of trials and triumph that led to their overall spiritual development.[15] Braskamp reflects, "some campus leaders refer to study abroad in terms of a *spiritual* experience. Living in a foreign culture provides a rich opportunity for students to better understand their own cultural backgrounds, values, and sense of self."[16]

What significance does this play? It means that students like Kate are not anomalies. More and more students are traveling beyond borders to get in touch with their world. The simultaneous rises in Christian education and international interest among students point to the growing imperative for those in education to better understand faith-based study abroad programs.

## Scholarship beyond Limits

Study abroad expands cognitive boundaries and provides a natural impetus for growth by removing students from their home environments and exposing them to diverse thinking. Study abroad and cultural immersion have been shown to increase scholarly engagement in students. It builds self-esteem, self-confidence, holistic learning, and respect for others.[17]

Qualitative and quantitative research has confirmed the improvement of cultural sensitivity, self-awareness, language proficiency, and career advantage.[18] The National Survey of Student Engagement reports that students who studied overseas engaged more frequently in educationally purposeful activities afterwards and reported gaining more from college. Students who lived with host nationals in home stays or dorms benefited even more in terms of integrative and reflective learning, and personal and social gains. The length of time spent overseas did not make a difference in the frequency with which students used deep learning approaches after returning to campus.[19]

Equally as important, these immersion experiences are an ideal venue to promote the type of cognitive dissonance that leads to spiritual reflection. UCLA's longitudinal study of higher education and spirituality in both secular and faith-based campuses confirms these findings and recommends study abroad as an activity to help students develop spiritually.[20] Similarly, a longitudinal examination at the University of Minnesota considering the effects of study abroad on civic engagement, provides strong empirical evidence that undergraduate students who study abroad during their college years become globally engaged in a variety of ways in subsequent years.[21]

A specialized curriculum that incorporates the practice of faith development, such as those included in the chapters that follow, seeks the important links among personal reflection, critical thinking, and spirituality in a global community context. Alumni of CCCU BestSemester Programs attribute spiritual and emotional growth to experiential learning factors such as their off-campus experience.[22] Parallel results can be seen in students attending Greenville College's Semester in Africa program, who demonstrated a significant gain in spiritual development between pre-test and post-test, as measured by the Faithful Change Questionnaire.[23]

These research reports are helpful in proving that cultural immersion pursues the mission of the liberal arts education in deep and meaningful ways. However, one only needs to speak with a student returning from off-campus study to realize that study abroad is a transformative experience. Kate, for instance, already displayed an impressive desire to become better attuned to social realities and act as an agent of change in the wider world; however, until she gained a better understanding of context, her works were futile. Effective faith-based study abroad and cultural immersion translates good intentions into responsible and thoughtful action, and well-intentioned students into globally conscious Christians.

Two important notes: first, authors have integrated student quotes and experiences to offer a firsthand view into the transformational experience. In all cases, the quotes remain anonymous or authors have gained permission for use on an individual basis. Second, this book does not distinguish between the experience of study abroad and cultural immersion. Study abroad refers to a scholarly experience outside of U.S. boundaries, while cultural immersion can be experienced in any location (including within U.S. borders). Cultural immersion can take place in any region or culture where the economy, language, or worldview is completely foreign. In either case, programs that expose students to the cultural other move them toward cognitive dissonance, and ultimately, spiritual transformation and global engagement. Contributors to this volume hail from a diverse array of international and domestic locations.

## Transformations at the Edge

The organization of our volume reflects the notion that students must grapple with personal identity and learn to deepen their social relationships if they are to be effective global actors. In this book, faculty and other study abroad practitioners document the processes by which students gain better awareness of their selves, discovering their roles in community and the intercommunal nature of human kind. They also learn the value of reaching across cultural lines to discover the value of solidarity and service to the global community.

In **Part I**, four practitioner-authors have highlighted the sorts of individual spiritual growth that can occur at the edge of the world. Exploring the personal aspect of spirituality and faith, contributors are concerned with helping students develop three primary components: the development of self-awareness; a sense of the interconnectedness between all things; and a relationship with a "higher power" or a "higher purpose."

The chapters that comprise this section suggest the vital need for student reflection—biblical, theological, anthropological, and psychological—on the nature of their lenses. Janine Paden Morgan invites educators and students to consider biblical narratives as they discern spiritual experiences along the journey. John Barbour juxtaposes two types of traveler, the tourist and the pilgrim, and suggests the value of self-recognition: "The kind of tourist we criticize asks only: 'Am I getting my money's worth? Is it worth it?' The pilgrim should ask: 'Am *I* worthy of an encounter with the holy, worthy to enter this church, mosque, or temple?' Many tourists judge the worth of the culture they visit and never examine what travel reveals about their own culture's values. The pilgrim, in contrast, should judge himself." Andrea Smith Shappell introduces pastoral theological reflection as a method of recognizing God's presence in relationships, and Lon Fendall emphasizes spiritual disorientation as an opportunity for growth. All of these writers invite careful reflection on individual spiritual formation. Their corporate contribution is a window into students' discovery of who they are and their place in the world.

In **Part II**, we are reminded that people are not only sacred but also social. For many people, the term spirituality is limited to exchanges within the self or between the self and the divine. Defined in this way, spirituality safely avoids the societal constructs of religion and remains intensely personal. This conceptualization, however, leaves a great chasm between the two terms and contrasts religion as institutional, even dogmatic, and spirituality as individual, subjective. Such polarization often obscures the personal elements of religious life and the corporate dimensions of spiritual life, portrays spirituality as positive and religion as negative and ignores the reality that many, if not most, spiritual experiences occur in an organized religious context.[24]

Christian spirituality, as we in this volume see it, encompasses the traditional definitions of spirituality, such as the search for meaning and purpose, but also grounds our explorations in the practices, heritage, and belief system of the Christian faith. William Teasdale justly incorporates these two concepts when he writes: "Being religious connotes belonging to and practicing a religious tradition. Being spiritual suggests a personal commitment to a process of inner development that engages us in our totality. Religion, of course, is one way many people are spiritual. Often, when authentic faith embodies an individual's spirituality, the religious and spiritual coincide."[25] Since the experiences of students during study abroad are realized in part by their relational understanding of one another within the group as well as other groups of people, we recognize the influence of religious practice to explore feelings, thoughts, and behaviors in searching for the sacred. This view takes into account the communal component of spirituality and recognizes that most students have spiritual experiences in the presence of a religious community.

Chapters within this section explore techniques to incorporate religious tradition while requiring students to take personal ownership of an alive, relational search for "the meaning and purpose we see in our lives—and our connectedness to each other and to the world around us."[26] The experience of living, studying, working, and praying together can offer great transformative potential. Students immersed in community recognize the impact of their choices on those in close proximity, which then extends to their responsibility to the larger Christian family. The essays by John Skillen and Don Briel focus on the opportunity to foster authentic community in study abroad settings, nurturing qualities of presence and engagement as essential virtues of globally engaged peoples.

Skillen's chapter demonstrates how the communal workshop can nurture the value of work and creativity as something more than personal self-expression or self-enrichment. He utilizes the Rule of Saint Benedict as an invitation for students to practice presence with one another and exercise responsibility toward the collective. In a complementary fashion, Briel's chapter brings students into close proximity with the heart of the Roman Catholic Communion. By exercising mind, heart, and hands together in residential community, these students discover a centuries-old faith tradition and a deep sense of spiritual belonging. Both authors offer hope that, as Darryl Tippens suggests in *The Soul of a Christian University*, students who discover spirituality in the rich context of community are likely to continue as an active member in it.[27]

**Part III** considers how program leaders can cultivate cultural bridge-building and empathy in students. As members of a global community, students must be prepared to reach across divides of cultural or political conflict to build bridges of peace and justice. We are our brothers' and sisters' keepers, wherever they may be. Loving our neighbors has global dimensions in a shrinking world."[28] Therefore, our students must be prepared to reach across ever-widening chasms of beliefs and cultures.

These four essays privilege the global dimension of our project by establishing bridges of commonality. Whether the goal is practicing simple disciplines of presence or walking beside those living in a cycle of poverty, the act of entering into relationship requires personal encounter. Essays by Laura Montgomery and Mary Docter, Ronald J. Morgan, David P. Holt, and Scott McClelland describe the transformative power of face-to-face experiences with the other. For Montgomery and Docter, cultivating world Christians is a cycle of learning that evolves slowly as students, "develop the capacity to encounter God in new contexts, to participate in the worldwide Christian church, to enjoy the rich diversity of God's creation." Similarly, Ron Morgan's essay assumes an active, rather than passive stance. He points out that praying in a French bomb crater or taking communion with fellow believers as they sing in French and German breathes life into otherwise abstract notions like loving one's neighbor or cultivating "catholic personality." In this section's third essay, Holt challenges students to overcome personal assumptions and political diplomacy and to relationally engage Muslim students in an Egyptian university. David P. Holt's essay describes the process of reaching across Muslim-Christian divides and instilling a sense of human community. As a result, students discover their place of privilege and work to understand how other cultures view the West and the role of U.S. policy in the Israeli-Palestinian conflict. Finally, this section would be remiss to silence the diverse cultural voice and ideological other encountered daily within U.S. boundaries. Scott McClelland's chapter guides the next generation of Christ-followers as they engage post-Christian urban communities in San Francisco, California. In the face of a pluralistic environment, students move from a position of power to vulnerability and discover that, "it is often through the basin and towel that the essence of Jesus comes through—and transforms lives."

In **Part IV**, we journey with students as they discover an active stance on solidarity and service. The Catholic Social Tradition teaches, "the basic moral test for a society is to look at how the most vulnerable members are faring. In a global society marred by deepening divisions between rich and poor, our Christian faith recalls the story of the Last Judgment (Mt. 25:31–46) and instructs us to put the needs of the poor and vulnerable first."[29] Love for our sisters and brothers demands that we promote peace and socioeconomic justice for all. This decrees the manner of our actions toward the environment and our global neighbors living in poverty. Therefore in cultivating empathy and solidarity in our students we are not proposing economic structures and political solutions, but focusing on the types of individuals who can live in and create this kind of world.

Travel for the purpose of service or study alongside the world's poorest communities is a growing phenomenon among American institutions, including short-term service-learning programs.[30] But such projects can be carried out with more or less sophistication and efficacy, with greater or lesser attention to communities among whom students will live, study, worship, and serve. Careful theorist-practitioners like Richard Slimbach urge Christian institutions to avoid paternalistic projects that can be more about meeting our needs than meeting those of poor communities. The three essays in Part IV, while concerned with structures and praxis, focus their attention to the attitudes with which Christians, and Christian institutions, approach communities in need. Richard Slimbach, Chris Elisara, and Thomas J. Meyers each urge the formation of programs that nurture humble, self-critical learners who are attentive to interconnectedness between communities and their natural environments, or between affluent Western lifestyles and the social realities that exist at the other end of our consumption. Their programs illustrate how Christian institutions can thoughtfully embody biblical theologies and historic denominational commitments in their engagement with populations in need.

## What We Work For

Kate's experiences on study abroad have shaped her choices and her understanding of global health concerns. As this book goes to print, Kate is enrolled in a master's program in public health. She retains her hope to "get in touch with others in the world," but now she has a better understanding of her call as an agent of change. And she is not alone. Her sojourner peers are becoming physicians, teachers, and business leaders. Some will return on trips with their churches, some will fundraise, some will work for change in environmental and consumer issues. One is working locally, at the grassroots level; another is going to Washington, D.C., to shape future policy decisions. The important lessons in consumerism, reaching out to others, solidarity, and communal faith that students gain on study abroad lead to a common outcome: communal reflection leads to individual praxis. Study abroad allows learning to become commitment to justice as students develop a disciplined sensibility to poverty and injustice. These students, like Kate, are on successful journeys into adulthood. Their experience at the edge transformed them into globally conscious and engaged Christians, concerned with their local community as well as the world far beyond their borders.

# PART I
# The Journey Inward

CYNTHIA TOMS SMEDLEY

*You made us for yourself, and our hearts are restless until they rest in you.*
—St. Augustine, *Confessions*

The restlessness of youth is not easily silenced. Questions of personal identity collide with the big questions of life: "Who am I? What do I believe? How can my small earthly life make an eternal difference?" Restless notions are not quenched with superficial words or Sunday school answers. In fact, spiritual hunger leads many young adults to press the boundaries of knowledge, to bump against authority, and to challenge the status quo.

We see this restless heart in the Samaritan woman at the well. She is a woman of little importance or distinction, save her ill reputation. Her private pain brought her to the well at midday, where Jesus was resting. Perhaps she did not want to be known. Perhaps she did not believe her life could prompt interest from anyone—especially not a Holy Teacher. But we have reason to believe that her heart was hopeful and restlessly awaiting authentic knowledge and love. Her encounter with Jesus resulted in a new understanding of her true identity and her relationship with her Creator. Her restlessness found rest in being known.

By unveiling the Samaritan's woman's true condition, Jesus expands the boundaries of self-awareness. Study abroad similarly compels students to face their queries, born in restlessness; the journey presents unique opportunities for self-examination and spiritual transformation. In this section of the book, authors aim to help students look inward and answer their restless questions with authenticity. Janine Paden Morgan examines scriptural examples of how

God can meet and change us on the road. Her chapter examines the inviting entryway to spiritual depth that the woman at the well found irresistible.

Moments of restlessness also provide a small window to the place of rest—where more authentic identity resides. The journey of spiritual transformation requires this inward focus. Andrea Smith Shappell examines the connection between theological context and personal experience to better understand these moments. Only in this place are we free to fully grasp ourselves in relation to the world. And just as the woman at the well discovered that God's work required movement beyond comfortable ethnic and cultural bounds, so we must learn to view the world in measured, personal, and faith-informed ways. For John Barbour, this means viewing our time of restlessness and exploration as a pilgrimage. By moving beyond roles as passive consumers, we become deeply aware of our personal connections to places and cultures. Thomas Merton, concerned with deep self-awareness, describes the purpose of education as teaching people to define themselves authentically and spontaneously in relation to the world—rather than imposing a prefabricated definition of the world, still less an arbitrary definition of the individual himself.[1] As study abroad leaders, we aim to help students look inward and answer their restless questions with authenticity. In this section's final chapter, Lon Fendall demonstrates how mentors can guide students through this authentic time of searching without dictating specific outcomes.

# CHAPTER ONE

# Doors to Transformation

## Janine Paden Morgan

*In this chapter, Janine Paden Morgan (Bible Instructor and Student Life Chaplain for Study Abroad, ACU in Oxford) employs insights from four influential social scientists and theologians who offer pertinent insights into the nature of spiritual transformation in liminal places. The anthropologist Victor Turner examines the place of "structure" and "anti-structure" in human social development.[1] Using the grammar of educational psychology, James Fowler classifies stages of faith development throughout a person's life, Stages 3 (Synthetic-Conventional faith) and 4 (Individuative-Reflective faith) being relevant to young adult spiritual development.[2] While Turner and Fowler give attention to life stages, two theologians are pertinent to the nature of spiritual growth and journey. Walter Brueggemann interprets the Psalms through a three-fold prism of Psalms of orientation, Psalms of disorientation, and Psalms of reorientation.[3] Miroslav Volf contributes to our understanding of what it means to encounter the "other," attesting that cultural distance from one's own tribe or ethnos is an essential component in the ability to embrace the other.[4]*

Walking the old city walls of Oxford around the medieval colleges that comprise the university, one might be struck by the myriad of doors. The doors are sometimes gothically ornate with intricate wrought-iron work, sometimes plain and simple. Doors are often massively large for ceremonial processions or occasionally laugh-out-loud tiny, forcing you to bend over double to enter. Often the doors are locked or are guarded by bowler-hatted porters, so that one can only catch quick glimpses of hidden gardens or of long, empty corridors. It is no wonder then that Oxford has inspired authors to write some of our most notable adventure stories, a place where hidden worlds could be behind the next door. Alice follows a waist-coated rabbit down a rabbit hole to a world full of doors. Bilbo, "bewildered and bewuthered," opens his door and accepts a wild invitation that sets in motion the battle for Middle Earth. Lucy flings open a wardrobe door full of fur coats to enter an enchanted land where there is always winter but never Christmas.

Like the protagonists of Oxford's famous fantasy literature, Christian students who choose to study abroad pass through doors to great adventure in strange new lands. And also like Alice and Bilbo, what they experience on the other side of the door is often filled with more than wonder: it may be challenging, confusing, even frightening. But in those places of discovery, if they are open to the possibility, the young Christ-followers may undergo transformations of character, perspective, and identity. For as Aslan reminds Lucy as she returns home to England through the wardrobe door, forever marked by her experience: "Once a queen in Narnia, always a queen in Narnia."

Deep transformation is not a given. Although travel does expand worldviews, it does not automatically transform someone from one state to another, magically conferring new, spiritually-improved lives. In this chapter, I explore how journey from home, in the opportunities and challenges it presents, can lead to transformation of the believer's sense of spiritual identity, to a clearer understanding of herself in relation to God and the world. To that end, I present a narrative reading of three biblical texts,[5] each of which offers insights to key dimensions of such identity transformation. The biblical narratives cannot be read as parallels fully applicable to our contemporary situation; rather they are suggestive of themes that are apropos to today's students traveling abroad: The story of Abraham's departure from his homeland demonstrates the necessity of cultural distance as a prerequisite to finding one's identity in God above all other allegiances. Jacob's journey narrative explores his identity in relationship with God, defined by a struggling recognition of God's abiding presence. Jonah's preaching to the Ninevites addresses themes of encounter with the other, one different from one's self, the stranger or even the despised enemy, and the cognitive dissonance that arises from such an encounter. Each of these journeys reflect an inner, personal voyage mirroring their external ones.

## Departure: Of Leaving Ur and Of Leeks

Brueggemann posits that Psalms of orientation (such as Psalms 1, 104, and 37) attest to the faithful goodness of God, characterized by the absence of tension, a "no surprise world . . . a world of no fear."[6] However, the move to deeper maturity often necessitates leaving behind safe places of orientation, creating space from known social structures. Such an imposed distance from normative life, which Victor Turner coined "anti-structure," creates a state of liminality, moments out of ordinary time and place, wherein rules about old structures and identities are broken in order to create new ways of looking at reality.[7] The biblical text is replete with stories of individuals who have left comfortable places, stepped through actual and metaphorical doors, who are forever shaped by their journeying into new places.

Such is the case of Abraham in the Genesis story. The text says simply, "So Abram left, as the Lord had told him" (Gen. 12:4). When Abraham received a clear imperative by God to "leave your country, your people and your father's household and go to the land I will show you," his willingness to leave his home would result in both promises and in purpose: "I will make you into a great nation and I will bless you . . . *so that* all peoples on earth will be blessed through you" (Gen. 12:1–2). For Kostenberger and O'Brien, the promises to Abraham are held in juxtaposition to the curses emanating out of Genesis 1–12.[8] Coming contextually on the heels of the disastrous Tower of Babel incident, where human-centered worship had replaced God-centrism, separation from his Chaldean culture was necessary for Abraham to become the father of all nations, something we infer would not have occurred if he had remained within his dominant culture. Throughout his journeying, Abraham comes in contact with a further range of cultures—Egyptian, Canaanite, and Perizzite, among others—but he continues to learn independence from these ethnic groups and learn dependence upon the God who is present in his life. In Hebrews 11, God commends Abraham not only for his faith in the promised heir, but also for his leaving and making his home in a foreign country. Abraham's allegiance to Yahweh was greater than his allegiance to his home culture; in moving away, he necessarily became a stranger to his own kin in order to strengthen his identity as God's person. Distance from Ur was necessary in order for Abraham to have a new belonging, to become a new nation.

Further, because Abraham obeyed and left his home, God was able to make of Abraham not just a great nation, but one with a much greater destiny, to be a universal blessing to *all* the families on earth. If Abraham had remained in Ur, his parochial point of view would never have been transformed. Only by separating himself from his native context was he able to become a blessing to all peoples. Only by aligning himself to Yahweh alone, "not knowing where he was going" (Heb. 11:8), does he become the father of all nations.

Leaving home often allows student sojourners to reflect upon and critically examine societal values and ideologies left behind. Fowler reflects: "Frequently the experience of 'leaving home'—emotionally or physically, or both—precipitates the kind of examination of self, background, and life-guiding values that gives rise to stage transition at this point."[9] Yet departure from home is insufficient in and of itself; it does not guarantee a transformative journey. Some students board an airplane without ever leaving home; others arrive in a new place but never engage, preferring instead to live as consumers, wandering about seeking the next self-affirming experience.

To counter these tendencies, those guiding students need to help them cultivate the positive attributes of presence and purposeful commitment to their new context. In our worship liturgies early in the semester at the ACU in Oxford program, we emphasize the importance of students' being present to their two new communities—their Oxford community and their new ACU study abroad community. We read Jeremiah 29:4–7, 11–13, where Yahweh tells the exiles to settle down in Babylon, seeking the success of that city, praying for its peace and prosperity. This week, as I prepare this chapter, ACU students are out and about loving Oxford; some have gone out to the Northmoor Trust clearing brush for habitat restoration, others are cooking and serving at St. Aldates' Alpha Course, others are involved in Oxfam, and one is even involved in a fair trade fashion show. Strategically, as a program, we moved away from having every Friday off for travel. Instead, we now give three or four longer travel breaks throughout the semester, which, incidentally is much appreciated by students. But in order to help students put down some roots in their Oxford community, Fridays are now devoted to our service-learning component. In addition to loving Oxford, ACU students commit to one another in what becomes a living, breathing experiment in what it means to negotiate true community, albeit community at a very incipient stage. Living in such tight quarters as we do at the ACU houses, we strive to be a "community of the towel," loving each other through service—never an easy task as we have five small kitchens that are shared by almost forty students. Another way to encourage student community-building is by allowing students space to organically engage one another about their shared experiences. In the C. S.

Lewis class I teach, I mentioned one day how Lewis was influenced for Christ by late night conversations with his friends, subsequently reminding them to "never underestimate the power of late night conversations in the kitchens," a phrase which showed up as a favorite quote on a student's Facebook later that day.

For contemporary travelers, two tendencies hinder growth: incomplete departures and purposeless wandering. By the term "incomplete departures" I do not mean to imply that efficacious "leaving home" requires complete severance from the home culture. As a concept, liminality itself suggests that one is straddling two worlds at once, neither fully leaving the one, yet not fully adopting the other. Unlike Abraham who never returns to Ur, in our case, there is no complete break from home. The liminality of study abroad requires students to negotiate the tension of two worlds, attempting to reconcile distance from and proximity to both the home culture and the new context. There is no exact formula for this; the tension itself creates the self-examination necessary for growth.

That being said, for some, attempts at proximity to their new context is limited by a constant looking back. John Skillen, in a later chapter of this volume, discusses the propensity of some to live in their virtual worlds back home, not learning how to be present in their current locales. For the Israelites, likewise, manna paled in comparison with onions: "We remember the fish we ate in Egypt at no cost—also the cucumbers, melons, leeks, onions and garlic" (Num. 1:5). Lot's wife is turned into a pillar of salt because she disobediently looks back at Sodom even as she is fleeing its destruction (Gen. 19:26). Both the Israelites wandering in the desert and Lot's wife represent those who block growth because they cannot successfully leave home. Anyone who has traveled at all can sympathize to some degree with the Israelites. (What American doesn't crave a bean burrito while traveling abroad?) Yet both the Israelites and Lot's wife stand judged for their complaints and long glances back. These are two important cautionary narratives to consider. It is easy to see how the Israelites' complaints are especially pertinent for consumer-oriented, choice-driven, comfort-seeking Westerners to hear. The idea of being fully present in the here and now is a call to experience and depend on God at every moment.

Second, growth is hindered by what I call the mark of Cain,[10] the curse of endlessly wandering about the earth (Gen. 4:13). While Tolkien wrote poetically in *The Lord of the Rings* that "not all who wander are lost," many in today's culture bear Cain's mark, demonstrated by an existential restlessness and

itchy feet. Where there is no sense of goal or destination, journeying becomes empty. Volf writes: "Departures without some sense of an origin and a goal are not departures; they are instead but incessant roaming."[11] Although the sense of adventure that invites exploration is good and natural, *restlessness* can be a symptom of a loss of meaning and direction, born out of being overfed and under-challenged. This restlessness is often reflected in one of the seven "deadly sins" known as *acedia*,[12] "sloth," or "indifference," a "been there, done that" attitude that is constantly on the look for the next thrill. The most apparent manifestation of this is that often, no sooner than students arrive at a new place, they cannot truly enjoy or be fully present to it because it is merely one in a long list of "must-see" places. Such consumer tourism diminishes the experience to an exercise in checking off tourist boxes.[13] Over a century ago G. K. Chesterton astutely observed that the sense of meaninglessness comes not from too much suffering but from too much pleasure, calling it a "harassed hedonism."[14] Hedonism centers on gratifying the self or in self-preservation at all costs, seen in student approaches to travel and sight-seeing wherein a Normandy foxhole or a Romanian orphanage has significance only if I am in the picture, my camera and me, gaining importance only as it relates to me and my story.

To find one's deepest identity in God, then, two movements are needed—presence and purpose. First, one must leave home efficaciously, practicing the quality of presence in new contexts, and, second, in purposeful movement toward something or Someone.

## Wrestling: Of Stones and Struggle

Jacob is not our classic hero; he is a grasping schemer out to manipulate situations in order to succeed in life. In his story, however, we glean three important themes pertinent to the spiritual growth of students traveling abroad: the first is the notion of God's presence in every circumstance; the second, how wrestling with God is not a thing to be feared but potentially spiritually transformative; and third, the need for memorials to mark significant events in our lives, both as individuals and as communities of faith.

On two occasions, Jacob meets Yahweh dramatically, both in places of liminality: one occurs at the threshold of a new country, the other on the threshold of his return to his homeland. Jacob first encounters God on his escape from Canaan toward Haran, where he dreams of angels ascending and descending a ladder from heaven. Fearful, alone, and far from home, Jacob is reassured by the Lord's renewed commitment to him: "I am with you and will keep you wherever you go, and will bring you back to this land" (Gen. 28:15). Here, Yahweh declares that he is not geographically bound to a given territory, a common misconception of Jacob's time, but rather binds himself to a covenant people. Jacob's second divine meeting happens much later, after he has spent years in exile with his uncle Laban's family. On the eve of his return to his native homeland, Jacob encounters an incarnation of God by a river ford, another liminal threshold, and physically wrestles with the Lord throughout the night (Gen. 32:22–32). At the end of the wrestling match, Yahweh changes his name from Jacob, "the deceiver," to *Israel*, "he who struggles with God," redefining not only Jacob's personal identity, but that of the covenant people of God that bears Israel's name. Brueggemann observes: "Conflict and struggle are evaluated positively in [Jacob's] story. They are understood to be essential for the emergence of Israel. Strife is valorized both within the human dimension and within the human-divine relationship."[15] This event marks the origin of one of Israel's basic cultural identities, a people who strive with God. Finally, upon his return home to Canaan, Jacob fulfills a promise to God by building an altar in Bethel, the very place where years before he had dreamed the ladder dream, acknowledging Yahweh, "who answered me in the day of my distress and who has been with me wherever I have gone" (35:3).

The first theme from Jacob's narrative immediately applicable to students in new contexts is the assured presence of God as Jacob leaves home and crosses new frontiers. After their first travel break, we ask students to reflect on moments during their break when they truly recognized God's presence in their travels, whether it be in the hospitality of a stranger, in the answer to a desperate prayer for help as the train with all their belongings leaves without them, or in the character of their fellow travelers. Articulating such a realization, like Jacob, helps them recognize those divine moments of encounter, moving them from a mere cognitive acknowledgement of God's care to a deeper *experienced* reality of it.

The second theme we garner from Jacob's story is the necessity for struggle with God for faith development. In the movie *Doubt* (2008), Father Brendan Flynn asks the congregation: "What do you do when you're not sure?" He speaks of the disorientation, despair, and isolation that occurs when someone is stricken either by private calamity or assailed by doubt, such as when a voyaging sailor can no longer see the stars by which he navigates his vessel.

Struggle with God can be a powerful bond, he suggests, an essential element for deeper growth.

In discussing Psalms of Disorientation, Brueggemann concurs, suggesting that struggle is a dismantling move, necessary for spiritual development, wherein:

> [We move] out of a settled orientation into a season of disorientation. This move . . . is much more a personal awareness and acknowledgment . . . [T]his may be an abrupt or a slowly dawning acknowledgement. It constitutes a dismantling of the old, known world and a relinquishment of safe, reliable confidence in God's good creation.[16]

Questions of disorientation as well as those of identity and belonging surface especially in liminal spaces, provoking reflective examination in ever-new contexts: "Am I a Christian simply by accident of birth?" "Where is God in my pain and loneliness?" or even "Do I believe in God anymore?" Brueggemann suggests that such questions are not acts of unfaith but acts of *bold* faith that lead to *transformed* faith. He observes: "The remarkable thing about Israel is that it did not banish or deny the darkness from its religious enterprise. It embraces the darkness as the very stuff of new life. Indeed, Israel seems to know that new life comes nowhere else."[17] For Fowler, the shift created by such a struggle in faith development, whether it be overseas in a cross-cultural setting or being away at university for the first time, is necessary for young adults to move from conventional parental faith into the enriched stage of owned faith.[18]

Finally, because we are enfleshed humans, there is something powerful about rituals, symbols, and memorials that help people move from cognitive knowledge into experienced knowledge. Reflecting back on his life, Jacob builds an altar in dedication to the Lord who aided him in times of trouble, remembering the presence of God throughout his journeys far from home. Most study abroad programs are strong in their requiring student journaling as an important ingredient for reflective learning; however, this is a private affair. Ritual, as one of the oldest forms of human activity, can help integrate and attune life in an increasingly complex world, especially life in community.[19]

At one of our first gatherings of the semester, we spend time meditating on the story of Jacob's ladder, a story of God's presence in distant lands. We ask those present to choose a word or phrase from the story, write it on a river stone, and keep the stone with them throughout the semester as a reminder of God's faithfulness. Phrases and words such as "I will watch over you," "I will not leave you," "stay," and "awe-filled place" recur. For our closing liturgy of the semester, we invite students to bring their stones to our gathering (always providing the week before extra stones for those who will invariably lose theirs). We read and meditate on the story of Jacob's return to Canaan, where he wrestles with God but ultimately builds an altar in remembrance of God's covenant with him. With our stones, we recount stories of God's faithfulness. Individuals share the phrases they chose and how those phrases played out throughout the semester, and we build a small community altar in the process. It is a marking experience.

Those who accompany students as professors or student life personnel would do well to help them build a memorial of some sort, especially at threshold times like the beginning and end of the semester, acknowledging such important transitional events. In so doing, like Jacob who takes his stone pillow as a foundation for an altar, we also declare, "Surely the Lord is in this place, and I was not aware of it" (Gen. 28:16).

## Encounter: Of Sailors and Enemies

"Who is my neighbor?" a lawyer asks Jesus, one of the key questions that must be dealt with in order to form *global* Christians. While movement away from one's own home culture allows personal identity to be shaped, that is only one part of the story. Real engagement with the social and cultural other—those of differing cultures, ethnicities, gender, sexuality, religious beliefs, nationality, worldviews, and any "ism" that divides—is necessary for us to be formed in the very image of God. What must be negotiated is the triad of self, God, and the other. First, it requires a willingness to see others as God does, being open to a God who works in alien peoples, acknowledging that the truths I know to be true of God for me and my group indeed applies to others as well. This concept interplays with a second critical point: that my understanding of the nature of God must be expanded, that the God I worship is infinitely greater than my personal and tribal concepts of who God is. This requires a personal adjustment as I align my life with the concerns of the God I worship. An examination of the story of Jonah explores these themes. Jonah struggles to come to terms with the nature of humanity in its particularity and universality, and thus must come to face the very nature of God.

As Jonah's story has become fodder for Sunday School, it is easy to overlook the radical dimension of this account as it relates to inter-tribal relations.

The book of Jonah develops in two parallel cycles: God's commissioning, Jonah's response, and conversation between the two. The first two chapters recount God's calling Jonah to preach to the Ninevites and of the consequence of Jonah's refusal to do so. Having been thrown overboard and swallowed by the great fish, Jonah breaks out into a psalm of thanksgiving to God for deliverance. The remainder of the story tells of God's recommissioning of Jonah to preach to the Ninevites. When his preaching is successful and they repent, Jonah is aggrieved, angry at Yahweh's compassion toward the hated enemy. In the account, we note that Jonah flees twice from engagement with the Ninevites—once on a ship sailing toward Tarshish in the opposite direction from Ninevah, and again when he goes outside Ninevah's walls after their repentance.

A first theme that is evident in Jonah's narrative is how God's commission to Jonah challenges his orthodox faith and national allegiance. In both of the narrative cycles, Jonah comes into contact with the "other." The pagan sailors in the first part (Jonah 1:14–16) and the Ninevites in the second (Jonah 3:5–10) are portrayed as responding appropriately in their interactions with Yahweh God. In contrast, Jonah remains bitterly ethnocentric, angry at the Ninevites' repentance and the consequent staying of God's divine judgment upon them (4:1–3; 9–11). Johannes Blauw maintains that the subtle message of the book is an argument for an anti-particularistic view of God's divine mercy, that God is at work among all the peoples of the earth.[20] Jonah is offered an opportunity to join God in his concern for those beyond the covenant people, "to be a light to the Gentiles, that you may bring my salvation to the ends of the earth" (Isaiah 49:6; cf. 42:5–7), an opportunity that Jonah has a difficult time accepting.

Further, when he finds himself in trouble, Jonah draws on rich Psalmic tradition in his beautiful, descriptive hymn of thanksgiving, praising God for his deliverance "out of the pit" (2:6); yet in the same breath, his narrow application of the Psalms makes him unable to extend God's merciful deliverance to those outside his own group: "Those who cling to worthless idols forfeit the grace that could be theirs" (2:8), an attitude further evidenced in his later complaint against God's mercy in light of historic Assyrian injustice (4:1–3). Jonah continually struggles to understand how God can show compassion to the idolatrous Assyrians who were not only Gentiles, but of all the nations, the despised enemies of state who had inflicted great violence and atrocities on the Israelites throughout centuries. God's feelings are clearly stated to Jonah in the closing pericope of the book: "You have been concerned about this vine, though you did not tend it or make it grow. . . . But Ninevah has more than a hundred and twenty thousand people who cannot tell their right hand from their left. . . . Should I not be concerned about that great city?" (4:10–11).

Even beyond encountering others different from himself, the challenge for Jonah is to align his character with that of the God he worships. From the very opening of the narrative, Jonah moves into a place of disorientation, a distress demonstrated in his fleeing to Tarshish. Typically, people feel disorientation when they perceive God as being unpredictable, undiscernable, or alienated from his people,[21] but in Jonah's case, it is God acting *in character* that places Jonah in a place of disequilibrium. He complains, "I knew that you are a gracious and compassionate God, slow to anger and abounding in love, a God who relents from sending calamity" (4:2). It is Jonah who is out of sync with God's character; his god is too small. Jonah fails to see God at work in other human groups and so misses out on expanding his understanding of God. For student sojourners, this is a critical point of growth. Engagement with those different than ourselves has the great potential to broaden our understanding of God beyond our cultural blind spots. It is "together with all the saints" that we have "power to grasp how wide and long and high and deep is the love of Christ" (Eph 3:18).

In the immediate years following 9/11, some of our ACU professors and students expressed misgivings about traveling to France because of that country's stance on the war in Iraq. Imagine their surprise when they saw that the American cemetery was filled with French and German visitors walking respectfully around the graves. A student called me over to see a tomb with a wreath on it bearing a simple message written across it in French: *Merci*. The students' views shifted; the world expanded. In today's tribalisms, the sacredness of one's neighbor in God's eyes, of God's solidarity with the *panta ta ethne* ("all the ethnic groups") of the earth, is an essential aspect of transformation.

The biblical text does not tell the end of the story. The book of Jonah simply ends with that provocative question to the Jonah in all of us: "Should I not be concerned about that great city?" God continually expands the limits of human understanding about his character, and that expansion often throws individuals into painful disorientation, necessitating not only a cognitive adjustment but also the alignment of their character with God's (cf. Rom. 12:2; Eph. 5:1), a God who continually expresses his desire that all peoples would know him. One of the great gifts of British churches in American students' lives is their concern for the world at large, manifested not just in social action, but in an abundance of prayers for contemporary issues and global concerns that are offered in a nonpartisan way and with no political agenda. Our students have been stunned and humbled by the numerous times American presidents or current global events have been prayed for publicly. They have been touched as the starving in Darfur are recalled even as they eat bread and drink wine at a communion service. Students comment that it is often through the prayers at church that they find out what is going on in the world. Such global awareness moves them out of parochial prayers for their own personal concerns for safety or for their personal friends and family, important as these may be, and into wider-reaching prayers.

At the conclusion of the Good Samaritan parable, Jesus challenges the lawyer with the question: "Which of these three do you think was the neighbor to the man who fell into the hands of robbers?" To which the lawyer replied, "The one who had mercy on him." Jesus concludes the interaction, saying to him as well as to us: "Go and do likewise." As the Father is, so are we to be.

## Conclusion

Examining the lives of our ancient progenitors in light of their travels provides insights for the quest to form "global Christians." Their lives track the movement of leaving home, of struggle with personal identity and God, and of deepening awareness of both self and the other—all necessary for spiritual growth. But although some biblical characters embarked on journeys with clear calls from God, while other more "accidental" journeyers had surprise encounters with the divine,[22] this variable alone does not determine whether their journeying ends felicitously (with appropriate spiritual outcomes) or infelicitously (with no measurable spiritual outcomes). Instead, formation seems to lie in the heart of the traveler, and in eyes that perceive who God is and how God is at work.

Abraham's iconic departure and his cleaving to Yahweh marks him as uniquely prototypical of those that must leave home in order to become the person God desires them to be. Jacob highlights how disequilibrium and disorientation in times of crisis allows for transformation of identities to occur. Jonah's story demonstrates the complex adjustments required to be able to encounter the other—a radical reshaping of concepts about God's universal concern for all peoples in order for understanding and empathy to flourish.

*Contra* narrow parochialisms in a world where a "clash of civilizations" is normative, God continually expresses universal concern for non-covenant peoples, opening up the possibility that "my enemy" may actually come to be "my neighbor."

When anthropologist Arnold van Gennep in 1906 first identified stages in the rites of passage, he used the metaphor of rooms separated by doorways: "The door is the boundary between the foreign and domestic worlds ... between the profane and sacred worlds. . . . Therefore to cross the threshold is to unite oneself with a new world."[23] As students open doors and cross cultural thresholds, they embark on potentially transformative journeying, uniting themselves to a new world, a new way of being, much as Abraham did thousands of years ago. Such a move may indeed transform people—as one student stated: "studying abroad was the first thing in my life that actually fulfilled the promise 'it will change your life.'" A final quote from Miroslav Volf is apropos:

> To be a child of Abraham and Sarah and to respond to the call of their God means to make an exodus, to start a voyage, become a stranger. . . . At the very core of Christian identity lies an all-encompassing change of loyalty, from a given culture with its gods to the God of all cultures. . . . The courage to break his cultural and familial ties and abandon the gods of his ancestors (Joshua 24:2) out of allegiance to a God of all cultures was the original Abrahamic revolution.[24]

Young people studying abroad have great potential to be a part of the Abrahamic revolution, finding their deepest identity in the generous character of Yahweh God.

# CHAPTER TWO

# Students Abroad as Tourists and Pilgrims

## JOHN D. BARBOUR

*John D. Barbour is Professor of Religion at St. Olaf College. In 2008–09 he led the College's Term in Asia program, which extends over the fall semester and the January interim. Students take four courses offered by East China Normal University in Shanghai, Chiang Mai University in Thailand, and CET Academic Programs in Vietnam. The instructors are local faculty; the class consists entirely of students from St. Olaf. A St. Olaf faculty member serves as field supervisor and teaches a fifth course that integrates the program. Students spend the longest period, eleven weeks, in Chiang Mai, where they have a home stay and study oral Thai language. This hybrid program thus combines elements of the typical "island" or self-contained program with opportunities for richer cross-cultural experience. In this chapter, Barbour reflects on how the ethics course he taught, and the entire Term in Asia program, challenged students to rethink their understandings of travel, including study abroad.*

Like pilgrimage, study abroad can transform a life. Recognizing this reality, Christian institutions of higher education should provide a distinctive approach to study abroad programs. Our educational mission more closely resembles the traditional meaning of pilgrimage than it does the typical tourist excursion. It would be misleading to say that a study abroad program is exactly the same as pilgrimage, for our primary purpose is educational, not religious. A religious dimension and motivation shapes our educational goals, priorities, and practices, while at the same time, many aspects of study abroad resemble the organized recreational travel of tourism. We need to see our study abroad programs as forms both of tourism and of pilgrimage. If we dismiss either analogy, we will lose sight of something significant.

Using the metaphors of tourist and pilgrim raises crucial ethical questions about students' experiences in off-campus programs. I want them to think about the benefits and risks of travel, what actions are right and wrong, and what virtues they should practice. I hope they will undergo attitudinal changes such as greater openness to other ways of life, deeper commitment to their values, and a desire to make their work express their faith or values. I hope that both the academic components and the experiential aspects of our program will affect students' understanding of their own lives and faith. Yet I am reluctant to be too predictive or controlling about exactly what outcome I expect from study abroad, for reasons I will explain later in this chapter.

The two extended study abroad programs I have led at St. Olaf College were each five months long and involved living and studying in several locations. On the Global Program, which I directed with my spouse in 2001–02, our group stayed for periods of about a month each at The American University in Cairo (where we were on 9/11); the Ecumenical Christian Center near Bangalore, India; Chinese University of Hong Kong; and Yonsei University in Seoul. We also made briefer visits to Switzerland, Thailand, and China. Students took courses from local instructors at each of the four bases, and I taught a course that ran through the whole program on "The Ethics of World Religions" that concluded with the challenges for Christians of encountering and living alongside people from other religious traditions. During my time with St. Olaf's Term in Asia program, which I led in 2008–09, our group stayed briefly in Japan, then studied environmental issues in China, Thai language and Thai Society at Chiang Mai University, and Vietnamese history in Ho Chi Minh City and Hanoi. I taught a course throughout the program on "The Ethics of Travel: Tourists and Pilgrims," which will be my focus here, with a concluding reflection on the Global Program. This ethics course was intended to help students understand their travels abroad as analogous in certain ways to tourism and to pilgrimage.

Both of the courses I taught counted for a St. Olaf general education requirement called "Ethical Issues and Normative Perspectives." This course introduces students to moral problems and forms of moral reasoning, including Christian examples. The course is not directly intended to shape students' character. My colleagues with the most expertise in ethics are frankly skeptical about whether academic courses have much effect on character. They say that an ethics course may simply give students greater ability to rationalize or to justify whatever they do, and that the students' characters are basically formed when they arrive at college. I don't completely share their skepticism, but it is probably wise to be modest about how much I can claim to have truly transformed student lives. My academic home is somewhat different from most of the educational institutions represented by the authors of essays in this book.[1] St. Olaf College is affiliated with the Evangelical Lutheran Church of America, and its mission statement affirms that we "provide an education committed to the liberal arts, rooted in the Christian Gospel, and incorporating a global perspective." The college tries to combine "academic excellence and theological literacy," and we argue in healthy ways about what that last phrase means. Although I am not a Lutheran, but rather a member of the United Church of Christ, I have come to deeply appreciate the Lutheran understanding of higher education. As I see it, St. Olaf's goal of being intentionally pluralistic is held in tension with the goals of understanding Christian tradition and affirming its value. Fostering a global perspective is also central to our mission, and studies abroad play a vital role in this goal. St. Olaf has an enormous investment in international and domestic off-campus studies, with 826 of our 3000 students studying off-campus in 2007–08. About seventy-six percent of our 2008 graduates had participated in an off-campus program.

St. Olaf is different from most colleges in the Council of Christian Colleges and Universities in that it is less intentional about forming students' whole lives. We don't call ourselves a "Christian college," but rather "a college of the church" or "a church-related college." Most of my faculty colleagues, I think, would say that influencing students to be better Christians is not one of their goals. We do not assume that students should come out in the same place in terms of faith positions or moral character. Personally, I am concerned that deliberate attempts to shape student character can become manipulative or over-controlling. At the same time, I hope our programs both on and off campus will deepen students' moral sensibilities, elicit their compassion, arouse their sense of injustice, sharpen their critical understanding of the world's problems, and motivate their idealistic attempts to do something practical about suffering and ignorance. Thus I am in the somewhat paradoxical position of hoping for transformation in the characters of my students while being reluctant to systematically program structures to shape students' whole lives, as some other Christian institutions try to do.

Probably the closest that St. Olaf comes to a deliberate effort at character formation is a January course at Holden Village, a Lutheran retreat center in the Cascade Mountains of Washington. Three times (in 1987, 1997, and 2007) I taught St. Olaf students an academic course for a month at this unique Christian community, where they participate in daily worship, chores, recreation, and village meetings and forums. At Holden Village, students integrated the formal study of theology with the life of faith. My ideal character-transformation program (where cost is not an issue) would take students to Holden Village, Iona Abbey in Scotland, and Taizé in France, to see how these Christian communities create innovative forms of worship and nurture cross-cultural fellowship. Students would visit a house church in China and a base community in Latin America or South Africa, to learn how these Christian groups struggle against social injustice in the light of their readings of the Bible. Since Christian character is formed in Christian community, I think students should learn how different understandings of the church influence the expression of belief and the practice of faith.

The Term in Asia program was rather different, though, than this imagined course in Christian communities. Participating in the 2008–09 program were two Hmong students whose religion was traditional ancestor worship and shamanism and an agnostic who was critical of most things related to Christianity. It was certainly not my purpose to convert them to Christianity, and the other students and I welcomed their very different perspectives on many topics. My approach to study abroad did not involve Christian devotional practices such as prayer, Bible reading, or common worship. Yet I hoped that my teaching and other interactions with students would help all of them on their spiritual journeys, giving them greater clarity and conviction about their theological beliefs and moral commitments and actions.

The course on "The Ethics of Travel: Pilgrims and Tourists" focused first on traditional Buddhist pilgrimages in Japan, China, and Thailand, comparing these journeys with Christian pilgrimage. The second half of the course explored modern tourism, analyzing its motives, practices, and consequences from various perspectives. Ethical issues related to tourism include economic justice, environmental impact, sustainability, and the character of interactions between tourists and local cultures.

One of my chief goals was to reflect on our own journey in the light of these resources. A helpful resource for this was anthropological studies of tourism.[2] These studies introduce such concepts as authenticity, culture as a performance, and the traveler's tale that tourists construct and share with others after the tour. Students realize that a study abroad experience is in most ways a typical tourist package. We book our accommodations before we leave, travel in escorted groups, see carefully selected fragments of a foreign culture, and want to know in advance exactly what will happen to us. While these arrangements are probably inevitable and necessary in educational travel, we should be aware of our study programs' similarities to the canned tourist junkets we often disdain.[3]

A paradox of contemporary travel is the phenomenon of anti-tourism. We are constantly trying to get away from all the other tourists, to "go native" in dress and eating habits, and to discover a genuine and "untouched" corner of the foreign culture. Anti-tourism can lead to a dubious and futile quest for a supposedly authentic foreign culture, and in Asia it usually reflects the assumption that the only genuine culture is a traditional or primitive one isolated from contact with the West and the modern world. So the hills of northern Thailand are crawling with Western backpackers looking for a pristine and idyllic hill tribe village. Anthropological studies force reflection on the mixture of cultures all over the world; they also help us realize that hosting tourism is a long-established practice in many traditional societies, and that cultures constantly evolve through creative adaptation to external influences and visitors.

Students read literary accounts of tourism, including parts of Alain de Botton's *The Art of Travel* and collections of "travelers' tales" in China and Thailand.[4] I asked students to write their own autobiographical travelers' tale that explores some ethical choice or dilemma that they each faced on Term in Asia. A student of Hmong background explored her conflicting desires to trust and to be cautious when meeting local Hmong people in Southeast Asia; her parents had warned her that local people would view her as a rich American to be exploited. Another student described her uncertainties during a home stay when she became friends with a young Thai woman who was the family's nanny, chauffeur, and essentially her servant. What kind of intercultural friendship is possible in these circumstances? One writer criticized the Thai practice of double-pricing whereby foreigners pay more for a taxi ride than local people. Another person examined her anxiety about doing the wrong thing during visits to Buddhist temples. And several students described as an eye-opening experience their hosting of American friends or relatives. After having lived with a Thai family for two months, they could see Americans from a distinctly different perspective. Autobiographical essays generate the self-reflection that is part of cross-cultural learning and transformation.

It was frequently important to turn class discussions from the readings to our own travel practices, blunders, and successes. One anonymous student evaluator appreciated this self-reflexive emphasis: [We understood] "that everything we were doing somehow had to do with this course." Another student said: "We learned how to be ethical travelers. How to watch what we were doing and what others did, to learn and be better people." A third comment: "We read about and visited tourist sites and temples and these gave us the opportunity to see and to be pilgrims and tourists."

The ethics of travel isn't just a matter of knowing what actions are right or wrong. It also encompasses reflection on the value of travel, the kinds of good it can bring, and what we should hope for and seek out. Toward this end, it is worth taking a self-critical look at student travel. George Gmelch describes the life of American students on European programs as mainly involving rushed touring of famous sites and partying with other Americans. He sees developmental growth in two areas: self-confidence and adaptability, or being able to cope with unfamiliar situations. Yet he admits, "most students do not learn much about European history and culture."[5] Most of these logistical interactions do not involve significant cultural knowledge. Nor, I suspect, are most students deeply affected by their travels. Learning to purchase a train ticket or order a restaurant meal hardly constitute transformation. Travel can be simply an exercise in self-aggrandizement, hedonistic indulgence, or building one's CV. What more should we hope for when we study abroad?

I try, in gentle ways, to raise the question of whether we truly want an encounter with another culture. I knew my students' answer to that question, because the Term in Asia program involved intensive Thai language instruction, a home stay, and an extended immersion in one culture; also, these students were exceptionally energetic, inquisitive, and adventurous. Yet still, to challenge myself as much as students, I wanted to ask self-critical questions about the purpose of our travel: Do we see other cultures as commodities to be purchased and consumed? By participating in this program, are we just buying an item for our resumes? Do we expect to maintain our comfortable American lifestyles without making adjustments? Are we willing to leave our safe "bubble" of American friends and genuinely encounter another culture on its terms? Do we expect to recreate our home culture abroad, or are we willing to experience the challenges and discomforts of another way of life? Do we want a program where everything is planned, structured, and predictable, or are we open to what is unknown and not foreseen? Do we think we are entitled to have all our desires and demands satisfied in our accustomed way? Do we want simply to gaze at exotic people from a safe balcony or bus, or do we want an engagement with another culture that teaches us how they perceive us?

These questions may help students and faculty recognize that we yearn for something more than ordinary tourism. Our anti-tourism reveals something significant about our hopes about travel: a latent religious dimension often inspires and motivates our journeys. We wish, like a pilgrim, to be transformed. We want to come back as different persons. We want our travel to influence the rest of our lives. We hunger for more meaning than can be provided by the tourist industry, even as it sells us spiritual tours of sacred places and so-called "authentic" cultural experiences where no other tourists are visible. Anti-tourism reveals our hunger for something more than canned experience, shopping for trinkets, and finding a predictable cup of Starbucks café latte.

The kind of tourist we criticize asks only: "Am I getting my money's worth? Is it worth it?" The pilgrim should ask: "Am *I* worthy of an encounter with the holy, worthy to enter this church, mosque, or temple?" Many tourists judge the worth of the culture they visit and never examine what travel reveals about their own culture's values. The pilgrim, in contrast, should judge himself. I think that students abroad should be like pilgrims in these ways.

My course on "The Ethics of Travel" introduced students to the Christian tradition's intellectual resources for thinking about pilgrimage. Students read a narrative by the fourth-century Spanish nun Egeria, Sir Walter Ralegh's poem "The Passionate Man's Pilgrimage," parts of John Bunyan's "The Pilgrim's Progress," Jonathan Edwards' sermon "The Christian Pilgrim," T. S. Eliot's "Journey of the Magi," a historical study of pilgrimage in the early Church, and an analysis of why Luther and Calvin criticized pilgrimage.[6] Students considered similarities and differences between these understandings of pilgrimage and our purposes in an academic study program.

Although we explored this rich tradition of Christian thinking about pilgrimage, I did not provide a theory or theology of how Christians ought to travel. The course was better at exploring the ethical challenges of travel than it was at formulating a Christian normative perspective. I did not find many contemporary texts that discuss tourism from a Christian point of view.[7] We discussed recent assessments of tourism by a Marxist, a follower of Foucault, and several environmentalists and proponents of ecotourism, but an adequate Christian ethic of travel and tourism remains undeveloped, so far as I know. I'm sure that my limitations as a teacher played a role in the course; I'm better at raising questions than proposing answers, and more interested in narratives about personal experience than in theories. I hope students took away from the course some insights that will shape their own thinking about the ethics of travel, including interpretive skills to discern moral issues and new ideas about the purpose and value of different kinds of travel.

Long after students have forgotten the details of my course, as well as the other academic components of Term in Asia, they will remember the individual people they got to know. Several students said that for them, the best part of the program was getting to know our Japanese guide Shinji, our Chinese guide Chris, and Tram, the Vietnamese student who accompanied us through her country. They will remember their Thai buddies and the families who hosted their home stays. St. Olaf students experienced common concerns and enjoyments and discovered a sense of shared humanity that reached across social, political, and religious boundaries. We cannot know exactly how these bonds of cross-cultural friendship will affect them in the long run, but I hope that these human relationships will indeed bear fruit. I think that students gained a more thoughtful and discerning understanding of the interconnections of American and Asian cultures, and of the ways that global challenges and individual decisions are related.

As I have indicated, I am ambivalent about the ideal of intentionality in influencing student character. On the one hand, structured programming may be the crucial step in implementing my hope that a study abroad experience will have a transformative moral effect as well as imparting cognitive knowledge. Yet many of the most significant effects of off-campus studies are not predictable or programmable. For instance, some Term in Asia students pursued further contacts with a particular lecturer who had an experimental farm, and one student even spent part of the autumn vacation harvesting rice on that farm. It is possible to over-structure our programs, when what we should be doing is encouraging our students' own initiative. On Term in Asia, students purchased toys and children's clothing for an orphanage in Hanoi and a Shan refugee camp near the Thai-Burmese border. They also volunteered to teach English several afternoons to Shan refugees in Chiang Mai. Students conceived of these service projects and carried them out pretty much on their own; I simply made the financial arrangements to support them.[8] Several students reported that for them these were among their most memorable and significant activities in Asia. "Intentionality" in designing courses and programs has to encompass our openness and receptivity to students' own ethical concerns, and our willingness to improvise on the spot to support their efforts.

One of the most significant transformations resulting from a study abroad experience is greater wisdom about when to judge and when not to judge. Judgments about what? Travelers encounter a different culture's attitudes to time, clothes, food, gender, religion, work, recreation and leisure, authority figures, and a hundred other things. In Vietnam, we were challenged by a 1969 video played for us at the Cu Chi tunnels that celebrated the Viet Cong's "American-killer heroes." We puzzled over whether and how to criticize our Chinese professor's opinions about the environment—for instance, his advocacy of China's continued heavy reliance on burning fossil fuels. It was difficult and upsetting for us to discuss Tibet with Chinese students or tour guides, when many of us were deeply concerned about what often seems a policy of cultural genocide. As a faculty member concerned about the academic rigor of our program, I struggled with judging and not judging as I questioned whether I should try to push for more student-friendly class discussions, more probing critical analysis, and familiar American assignments. Was this imposing an American standard on foreign lecturers with a rather different approach to education? If I wanted to simply recreate American classrooms abroad, what was the point of leaving home? Yet when some of our lecturers were (in my judgment!) boring, disorganized, or confusing, I struggled to decide whether, when, and how to intervene. Some of the differences one confronts in another culture are matters of etiquette, aesthetics, or convenience, but others can lead to serious moral reflection and to challenging the ways of a foreign culture.

Christians have fervent convictions about ethical matters that they need to articulate. They also need to learn how to suspend judgment, appreciate other understandings of morality, and tolerate other points of view, even about essential truths of their faith. I want students to gain not only intellectual understanding of other religious traditions and foreign cultures, but also attitudes of profound respect and imaginative empathy. On Term in Asia, we were instructed in and practiced Buddhist meditation at several points. We contemplated the Zen rock garden at Ryoan-Ji in Kyoto and sat in silent stillness at other temples. We climbed Tai Shan, a Chinese sacred mountain that has been a primary pilgrimage destination for Taoists, Buddhists, and Confucians. I am certain that foreign travel generally, although not always, increases open-mindedness. One student evaluation linked this change to learning not to judge: "We became more sensitive to our own quick interpretations because we were aware of tendencies to judge, and so were more open-minded and aware when we were interacting in different cultures." This student realized, I think, that we cannot avoid making judgments all the time, but we can learn to reflect on and revise them, and to make wise decisions about when to express them.

I continue to wrestle with how to move students beyond cultural relativism. An open mind is not an empty mind. Being aware of another culture's differing moral values does not mean that you do not have your own ethical convictions and sometimes need to articulate them or act on them. The question of when and how moral convictions should be expressed in another culture is sometimes pretty clear. Students will usually agree that nineteenth-century British colonialists were justified in stopping the practice of suttee, the ritual suicide of widows. They think that child abuse and sexual exploitation in any culture should be opposed by a Christian, and that economic justice and compassion can and should be expressed in every society. Exactly what form charity takes in contemporary China, or how to be a good neighbor when touring Vietnam, are questions that often require interpretation and cultural knowledge as much as strong convictions or courage. It is important to talk with students both about specific moral quandaries and the broader issue: When and how should we make moral judgments in a foreign land, and when should we refrain from judging, or at least not express our moral assessments until we have learned more?

There are intellectual resources for thinking about cultural relativism. Margaret Midgley, for instance, discusses the implications of the fact that we are usually more willing to praise than to blame another culture—although this, too reflects a moral evaluation.[9] Yet knowing when to judge or not judge does not come from a theory, but is rather a matter of practical wisdom earned by experience. The challenge of helping to guide students to wiser moral judgments arises in many unpredictable ways and is surely one of the most significant roles for faculty and support staff on study abroad programs.

Bernard Adeney argues that Christians living with people of other faiths need to have both epistemological humility and ontological conviction.[10] Liberal Christians are often perceived as being better at epistemological humility, while more conservative or traditional Christians are often perceived as more forthright or courageous about asserting their convictions. Students and faculty abroad need to balance virtues that are sometimes set at odds; we should combine prudence and modesty about our claims to knowledge with clear-sighted conviction about what we believe.

When assessing how much our programs really transform students, we should consider two things. First, transformation does not always mean dramatic outward change, but often involves what scholars of conversion call "intensification," that is, greater clarity and conviction about what one already believes. Transformation often means a deepening or more complex awareness, not radical alteration to a different worldview. Second, my experience with the Global Program in 2001–02 showed me that transformations are often not visible, even to students themselves, for many years. In most ways we participants in St. Olaf's Global Program never left our little American bubble, eating and talking mostly among ourselves and having very few experiences of genuine intercultural exchange. Yet many students were left yearning for a fuller immersion in another culture, and often with a vital desire to serve people in other cultures. This was expressed later by more than half of the twenty-seven students in the form of volunteering for the Peace Corps, the Lutheran or Jesuit Volunteer Corps, church service projects, teaching in another culture, or working with nonprofit groups serving abroad or within the United States. That lives were altered by this program was also evident in new plans and hopes first imagined in a sketchy form by twenty-year old returning students, and realized years later in vocational aspirations, studies undertaken, service activities, and friendships and interests actively pursued. Political and religious convictions were clarified and rethought; hearts and minds became more receptive to needs and opportunities for justice, mercy, and compassion far away and next door. I know, too, that study abroad experiences have a large impact on the kind of recreational travel that St. Olaf College alumni seek out in later years. Some effects may take a generation to be evident; I have seen how alumni of the college encourage their children to study and work overseas, sometimes in the very same study abroad programs in which they participated.

While it is important for us as educators to be intentional about our purposes, as Christians we also recognize that God transforms lives in many ways we cannot predict or control. For many Christians, being a pilgrim means viewing all of one's life as a journey that may involve transformative encounters with God. I may not fully understand the most significant effects of study abroad until long after I have returned, when memories and insights from my geographical travels illuminate or are illuminated by later parts of my life's journey.[11]

# CHAPTER THREE

# Reflection as a Means of Discovery

Where Is God in the Experience?

**ANDREA SMITH SHAPPELL**
(University of Notre Dame, Notre Dame, Indiana)

*Andrea Smith Shappell directs the Summer Service Learning Program (SSLP) at the Center for Social Concerns of the University of Notre Dame. She is an Associate Professional Specialist, Concurrent in Theology, with an M.A. in Theology from Notre Dame. Each year 210–250 students in the SSLP spend eight weeks in service with agencies or churches across the United States. Notre Dame Alumni Clubs sponsor the students by choosing the sites, providing room and board, and giving a scholarship to the students. When students return to campus, they meet in groups of eight with a graduate student facilitator for three discussion sessions, integrating their experience with the theological readings of this three-credit, pass/fail course. The SSLP is one of many programs and courses offered by the Center for Social Concerns, the community-based learning, research and service center of the University.'This chapter will explore the methods of theological reflection and social analysis which are introduced to students before the immersion experience and applied in their journal assignments during their eight weeks of service in cities across the United States.*

As a college student in the 1970s, I found a new dimension of my life opening up as opportunities to put my faith in action presented themselves: while visiting a woman in a nursing home each week, I recognized the value of conversation; during an Urban Plunge for forty-eight hours in the inner-city, I experienced ways in which churches were responding to poverty; from teaching a summer Bible school with a Catholic parish in Appalachia, I learned about a hidden people in my own country. These were enlightening experiences in and of themselves, but it was the reflection on the experiences, particularly pastoral theological reflection, that drew out the meaning of the encounters.

Building upon my early experiences and education, I have taught service-learning courses in theology for more than twenty-five years and have looked at a variety of methods to engage undergraduate students in pastoral theological reflection. I have looked for ways to adapt the ideas of the founders of the clinical pastoral education method for students who are not ministers but are interested in making connections between the challenges that arise from their experiences of encountering people in need and their own beliefs, motivations, and understanding of the world.

I currently direct the Summer Service Learning Program, a three-credit theology course that is grounded in an eight-week service experience in cities across the United States. Students apply for sites based on the type of service they would like to practice, often related to the discipline of their majors. The pre-med students are eager to serve at free health clinics; students interested in education opt for summer schools or Boys and Girls Clubs; other students work in homeless shelters, camps for people with disabilities, or homes for pregnant teenagers, among other sites. Notre Dame Alumni Clubs across the country determine the sites and are available to support the students during the eight weeks. The Alumni Clubs with the James F. Andrews Scholarship Fund provide a $2300 scholarship for each student at the completion of the program so that students do not forego summer income.

The academic dimension of the SSLP begins with two orientation sessions. The first session addresses causes of poverty and includes break-out sessions dealing with the specific population with whom the student will work. The second orientation session introduces the methods of pastoral theological reflection and social analysis as well as the major themes of the summer syllabus. In this chapter, I will provide an overview of pastoral theological reflection, discuss sources for theological reflection, and then give particular attention to a method of theological reflection and a method of social analysis that the students implement in the SSLP immersion experience. I will con-clude with comments about the living situations during the immersion and the unique dimension of Alumni Club involvement with the SSLP.

## Overview of Pastoral Theological Reflection

Pastoral theological reflection has its roots in the clinical pastoral educa-tion movement founded by Anton Boisen, a minister in the Congregational Church, in the 1940s. Boisen developed the concept of "living human docu-ments," pointing out people as the most forgotten source of doing theology. He writes, "Just as no historian worthy of the name is content to accept on authority the simplified statement of some other historian regarding the prob-lem under investigation, so I have sought to begin not with the ready-made formations contained in books, but with living human documents and with actual social condition in all their complexities."[2] This is a fruitful insight for students who engage in cross-cultural service-learning experiences. They may read about social injustice, but when they encounter relationships with people who are suffering from that injustice, new questions arise that challenge their understandings of their theology and their place in the world.

A second Protestant minister who was instrumental in the development of clinical pastoral education is Seward Hiltner, a Presbyterian minister and professor at the Princeton Theological Seminary from 1961–1980. Hiltner's focus was on the clinical pastoral method of theological reflection in ministe-rial training. Key to this method is the integration of psychology with theol-ogy in the analysis of ministerial encounters.[3] But it was Henri Nouwen, who greatly admired and studied Hiltner's work, who made this method known to a wider audience of "ministers," including undergraduate students. Nouwen was grounded in psychology and theology with advanced degrees in both dis-ciplines and had the gift of writing and speaking of the integration of the two disciplines in a way that appealed to many people.

As a student in undergraduate pastoral theology courses at Notre Dame in the 1970s, I was drawn into a process of reflecting on experience that was modeled on Nouwen's "Competence and Contemplation" in Creative Ministry (1971) and "Ministry to a Hopeless Individual" in The Wounded Healer (1972)[4]: writing what happened, analyzing the event or encounter, and link-ing the experience with insights from theologians. Don McNeill, CSC, a pro-fessor of mine (and also, importantly, a student of Hiltner's at Princeton, and a colleague of Nouwen's), designed undergraduate theology courses in which students were engaged in service relationships or social awareness immersions in conjunction with reading, writing, and discussion assignments. This three-stage process proved to be life-changing for me and many other students who came to better name our understanding of who God is and how we are called to put our faith in action. My hope in the SSLP is to continue to invite students into pastoral theological reflection, meeting current students in the places where they are open to integrating theology with their experiences.

## Sources for Theological Reflection

As a service-learning course at a university, we turn to traditional sources of studying theology: the writing and lectures of theologians, Scripture, and church documents. In addition to these sources, we want to draw special attention to the "living human documents" that the students encounter in the SSLP: the people with whom they interact and build relationships with during the eight weeks. For many students, theology becomes alive in a new way when they recognize God in their relationships or when they grapple with God's relationship to suffering in light of the neglected child they meet or the drug addict who is struggling to break addictions. In the second orientation session and in the guidelines for journal assignments, through our focus on methods of theological reflection, we invite students to cull through their experiences in relationships and begin to recognize insights and questions related to theology.

## Pastoral Theological Reflection Method

Patricia O'Connell Killen and John de Beer provide a helpful framework in explaining pastoral theological reflection to the SSLP students. They assert that theological reflection "nurtures growth in mature faith by bringing life experience into conversation with the wisdom of the Christian heritage. To practice theological reflection we must be able to pay attention to and inquire about the meaning of our individual experiences, our world and our religious heritage."[5] Thus, the reflection process facilitates the search for meaning.

The dichotomy that Killen and DeBeer set up between life experience and the Christian tradition makes the process more accessible to students. If one draws only on previous experiences, understanding will be limited. For example, as one student wrote, "It is easier to look at a situation and think that a person caused his own homelessness than to think about what role society, and one's own self, had in the situation. If a person is allowed to believe that poverty is a result of one's own faults and not society's, then it is easier to believe that it is okay to deny the homeless their rights, such as to healthcare." If we look only at the individual's role in social success or failure, we may ignore our Christian responsibilities for the well-being of our neighbors. On the other hand, we also find dangers in drawing only on our religious tradition. A student might hold, for instance, the belief that only people who believe in God go to heaven. What judgment will this student carry into service relationships with people who are atheists? Another might believe that economic security is a blessing from God, a view that becomes troubling when considering those who are economically poor. Will the student presume that poverty is God's judgment? Entering into relationships with people who are economically poor often challenges students' understanding of what it means to be blessed by God.

Theological reflection offers a place where tradition and experience intersect, a place where experience and religious tradition converse with each other. This place is also named the standpoint of exploration.[6] The intersection points out that our understanding is enhanced when we draw upon both tradition and experience, instead of just one. My goal is to guide students who are engaged in cross-cultural service-learning through this process of reflection and integration.

A further insight from Killen and DeBeer points to the theological understanding that undergirds this process. In the Christian tradition, the rich heritage that is a source of wisdom and guidance presumes "the profoundly incarnational (God present in human lives), providential (God caring for us), and revelatory (source of deepening knowledge of God and self) quality of human experience."[7] This understanding of God working in our lives and in our world leads to one way of describing theological reflection that students easily adopt, finding God in experience, then naming this experience with theological language.

In the SSLP Orientation, students view a video clip of a sermon that Henri Nouwen gave at the Crystal Cathedral in 1992, in which he reflects on the process of being chosen by God, blessed, broken, and given.[8] We view the segment on blessedness in which Nouwen describes an encounter with one of the core members in the L'Arche community in which he lived.[9] Janet came up to Henri after a prayer service and said she wanted a blessing. Henri responded as a Roman Catholic priest and blessed her "in the name of the Father and of the Son and of the Holy Spirit" while making the sign of the cross over her. Janet responded by saying, "Henri, that didn't work!" Henri was confused at first, but then, drawing on his experience of living in the L'Arche community and realizing what Janet needed, he embraced Janet and said a much more personal blessing, telling Janet that she was a beautiful woman and that even though she was hurting right now, that she was the beloved daughter of God and that God loved her. Janet affirmed that the second blessing worked.

When Henri drew only upon his formal, traditional ministerial training, he did not fully respond to Janet's needs. Yet by drawing upon the wisdom of the Christian tradition and connecting those insights with the knowledge he gained from the experience of living in the L'Arche community, Henri was able to respond to Janet's request in a meaningful way. From this example, we hope that students will find ways to make their own connections between experience and tradition.

The students in the Summer Service Learning Program write journal assignments twice each week using a method we adapted from Robert Kinast. He outlines an appropriate acronym for naming one's experience:

N—narrative
A—analysis
M—meaning
E—enactment[10]

Following this model, students describe an encounter or event (*narrative*), then reflect on that incident (*analysis*). To consider the incident's *meaning*, students link their experience and insights with those from the tradition they've studied, particularly the course readings, Scripture and related outside readings. Each journal exercise ends with ideas about moving from insight into further action.

This framework has proven helpful for students as they seek to understand the new situations they face in cross-cultural service situations. When students are struggling to make sense of encounters that bring them face-to-face with challenges to their beliefs or understanding of how the world works, this method of theological reflection assists them in processing and learning from the situation. In that process, students explore and discover new insights and questions.

When asked about belief in God or religious practices, students often express whether or not they regularly attend Church. For some students in the SSLP, however, liturgy has not been a meaningful place for them to grow and flourish in their faith lives. What I observe with a number of students in service-learning courses is that the service experience is a re-discovery of God. Students often find God incarnate revealed in what they thought would be the most unlikely places, in the woman who is homeless or the child who is severely disabled. Such discoveries often open students to look for ways of connecting their meaningful service relationships with liturgical and other religious practices.

As one student wrote, "I have never been a very religious person . . . I do not attend a church service every Sunday or pray regularly, and it's not out of laziness or a lack of respect for God, who I do fully believe and trust in. It is in fact disrespectful to pretend to be religious at this stage in my life and perform practices." While working with children at an inner-city neighborhood center, this student discovered God in the children and reflected,

> I view the children as the source of energy, or force that "jolted" me out of my tendency to trust only my experiences and use those occasions as my only justification for believing in God. The experiences (with the children) will always have a tremendous influence on the way my faith is shaped, but I hope to be able to take a more exploratory stand in terms of my religion by practicing more of the traditional aspects of Catholicism.

The immersion in the SSLP was a starting point for this student to return with new questions and insights to the religious practices and theological understandings of the faith he had grown up with but had not fully embraced.

Scripture is a source for many students that both brings insights but also gives rise to questions. Service experiences can bring new ways of looking at traditional beliefs and assess how God is continually revealed to us. In one particularly challenging relationship a student reflected,

> When I first arrived at (the hospice house) a volunteer told me that one woman was a bitter individual. From speaking with this patient I learned that she was in a failed marriage. She lost her sight in her mid 20's, and she now cursed God for once being able to see and then taking it from her. Now as she lay on her death bed she was even more upset with God, because she could not do for herself. . . . She was diagnosed with kidney failure, had massive general edema, which

was causing a great deal of pain and she always complained of her skin burning. I worried about her because she was on her death bed and she cursed God. She was not a Christian and she had no faith, so where would her soul end up eternally?

Trying to find insight into this troubling experience, the student's beliefs were challenged as he referred to Scripture:

> There is a passage in the bible where Jesus says, "No man can come to the Father except through me." How could I be at peace when I knew deep down in my heart, even if no one else admitted it, where her soul was going? I often asked myself could God actually send people to hell even if they are truly good people? . . . Everything that happened to her was not of her doing.

The student continued to reflect by reading theologian Michael Himes, who writes that the only criteria for the last judgment is described in Matthew 25 and that the criteria is how one treats the least of their brothers and sisters.[11] This understanding of the afterlife opened up new ways for this student to think about this woman's soul. In what ways was God revealed to this student through this challenging encounter? The student continued to struggle with how to make sense of his experience with this woman's goodness and his worry about her soul in eternity, finding conflict between tradition and experience while searching for a response to his struggle.

The readings in the course are carefully selected to address some of the questions and issues that often arise for students as they work in inner-cities and isolated rural areas with people who come from backgrounds very different than their own. Theological themes of displacement, compassion, and *agape*, as well as ethical issues related to poverty, race, and violence are included in the course readings. Displacement is one issue that resonates with nearly all students.

A student teaching ESL classes in a Latino community was particularly struck by her experience of being displaced and lonely. She wrote, "In these past weeks, I have been called out of my comfort zone. I do not know anyone who lives close to here. I feel isolated, almost cut off from the world. But then I read this: 'The paradox of voluntary displacement is that although it seems to separate us from the world—our father, mother, brothers, sisters, family, and friends—we actually find ourselves in deeper union with it. Voluntary displacement leads to compassionate living precisely because it moves us from positions of distinction to positions of sameness, from being in special places to being everywhere."[12] This passage, the student continued, "really showed that though I am feeling sorry for myself right now, if I am able to get out of my own head, and really experience what I am feeling, to more fully understand through experience what the people I am serving feel, I am in more solidarity with them. Though out of my personal comfort zone, I have entered into another, larger comfort zone: the comfort zone of solidarity, of knowing that I am not alone."

The idea of displacement, of moving out of our ordinary and proper place in order to meet others who are quite different from ourselves, challenges us to embrace being lonely and uncomfortable. Addressing our discomfort is not just about personal growth, but following the way of Jesus to build solidarity with those who are considered the least among us, a theme that is further developed in Part IV of this book. Students in the SSLP find the theme of solidarity expanded from a personal insight to a broader, global perspective in the writings of Catholic social thought—in particular, in John Paul II's understanding that "Solidarity is not a feeling of vague compassion or shallow distress at the misfortunes of so many people, both near and far. On the contrary, it is a firm and persevering determination to commit oneself to the common good; that is to say to the good of all and of each individual, because we are really responsible for all."[13] Students grapple with understanding God's providential care for all as well as the Christian responsibility to create a more just and humane world.

## Social Analysis

The second method of reflection that students apply during the immersion and in the required follow-up discussions is that of social analysis. Drawing upon the work of Peter Henriot, S. J., and Joe Holland in *Social Analysis: Linking Faith and Justice*,[14] we use an example to walk through the four stages: (1) Immersion: A student is teaching in a summer school in an impoverished neighborhood in Chicago, and she is stunned by the quality of education that kids in this neighborhood receive compared to the public high school she attended in a suburban school district. (2) Social analysis: Through multi-disciplinary research, listing the causes of the issue and following the question "why?" we come to further questions and further insights. Why is there such disparity in public education in the U.S.? We consider tax policies, parental involvement, quality of teachers, and more. (3) Theological reflection: In this model, theological reflection extends beyond Kinast's individual model as discussed above. Looking collectively at the issue raised, we ask, how are communities of faith called to respond to this issue? Students turn to Catholic social thought and explore principles such as the common good (the right and duty of all people to participate in society, seeking together the well-being of all, especially the poor and vulnerable) and human dignity (the understanding that every human being is created in the image of God and worthy of respect). Students can explore these principles further in Catholic social teaching documents and the writings of theologians that address specific social issues. (4) Pastoral Strategies: From this process of analysis and reflection, what new strategies do students propose to address this issue? Students research ideas such as charter schools or longer school days, as well as broader policy changes like equal funding for all schools.

For their final papers, students can choose to write a Theological Theme Essay or a Social Analysis paper. A student who worked on the border of Texas and Mexico applied social analysis to the immigration issues that she faced each day. In the theological reflection section of her paper, she explored the principle of solidarity, arguing that prayer alone is not enough: "(A priest) describes well that the way people at the border region have responded to the crisis of violence is in a pious way, with '1,000 rosaries for peace.' Yet, if we really were to act in accordance with Pope Benedict XVI's demand of societal compassion and suffering with, . . . [p]eople must act in organized and communal ways to put hope into action. People must understand the core of solidarity as 'human co-responsibility' as Jon Sobrino describes,[15] and actualize, although dangerous, this solidarity."

In the SSLP, we hope to find more placements in which students can see faith communities implementing social analysis, so that there is a wide variety of opportunities for students to see how people of faith are involved in the integration of prayer, direct service, and social action.

## Opportunities to Enhance Theological Reflection

Theological reflection often continues in the variety of conversations students have throughout the summer. Members of the Alumni Clubs arrange for room and board for the students, which could be at the sites or with alumni families;

in some cases students work in their hometowns and live with their own families. Fruitful discussion with on-going reflection can take place in any of these settings but can be especially poignant when students live in community. A student who taught in a parish summer school in a Latino neighborhood wrote, "Living with two Jesuit priests ended up being one of the highlights of the summer. I would work hard every day, but in the evenings I could chat with the priests and really build on my experiences. These dinners sometimes would end up lasting two hours as we discussed pressing social concerns, current events, and how the Catholic Church fits into it all."

Alumni Club members, either as host families or during occasional dinners with the students, also engage students in discussions about the readings and the service experience. One particular student was challenged in a unique way to defend her faith. She reflected,

> As part of our SSLP experience this summer, we have enjoyed the opportunity to speak with local Notre Dame alumni and Boys and Girls Club benefactors about the children. Not surprisingly, these dinner guests often ask us about the role our faith plays in the service we perform. During one spirited discussion about the importance of faith, a disillusioned Catholic turns to me and pointedly asks, ". . . I'm interested. What's so special about the Catholic faith? Is it really helping you that much this summer?" I look down at my plate and then raise my eyes to meet his. "Sir," I respond, "In a world run by the powerful and ambitious, the Catholic church is radical. It is radical for the simple fact that it is built on one principle: self-gift. What other philosophy preaches that to reach the highest state of perfection—namely relationship with God—you must descend to the lowest states? They say that love has no bounds, but that statement is true only because we do not allow our love to have boundaries. The paradox of Catholic love is that it is built on humility not pride or glory. I can speak for all of us—this summer has been an exercise in humility."

In a response after reading this reflection, the questioner added, "I am a Catholic who still sees evil and will always be vigilant. I see in your words and your spirit the goodness and kindness that serve as an antidote to an awful lot of the bad that I've experienced. You've scrubbed away some of the cynicism that I carry. Best of all, you have illustrated what the Church can and should be."

The opportunities for discussion with mentors and challengers have proven to be fertile ground for all parties to reflect more deeply on their service experience and their beliefs. The students carry insights and questions from these discussions into the theological reflection in their journal entries and final papers.

## Conclusion

The experience of being in service relationships with people who are marginalized in society is a fertile place for theological questions to arise and for one's faith to be challenged or confirmed, a point further discussed by Scott McClelland, Karen Andrews, and Brad Berky in Chapter Ten, among others in this volume. Theological reflection and social analysis have been used for decades by people of faith who are searching for meaning, and both have proven to be very effective in helping students work through their experiences and come to new insights. The processes are not necessarily completed during the summer immersion, though, and we require all students to take a follow-up discussion course during the semester of their return. Even beyond the course follow-up, the questions that arise during the SSLP may percolate with students for years, leading to more study, prayer, additional service experiences, and insights that come from maturity.

The SSLP students often go on to participate in other courses offered at the Center for Social Concerns, such as the International Summer Service Learning Program, which is a four-credit course centering on eight-week immersions in developing countries, or one-credit seminars built around one-week immersions on topics like children and poverty; border issues; and the environment and sustainability. We also encourage SSLP students to continue to explore issues and questions by taking related courses, writing a senior thesis, and by getting involved in the local community during their remaining semesters. To ground their academic pursuits, students also have many opportunities on campus to be involved with a community of reflection and prayer.

The methods of theological reflection and social analysis plant the seeds for students to bear fruit for a lifetime. Over ten percent of the student body commits to a year or two with a service program after graduation. Many more carry a sense of vocation into their careers, pursuing ways to serve the common good. One student thoughtfully commented at the end of the SSLP course, "Two insights that I will take with me from this summer are that I cannot serve without God by my side, and my being yearns to be in community with others, and the most satisfying way to do this is by serving. The readings have really given depth to my experience and made me realize how rewarding it is to serve." For students committed to lives of service, theological reflection and social analysis provide the tools to continually recognize God at their sides in both personal and communal ways. Integrating experience with insights from the Christian tradition bring students to critical questions, which can open up creative ways of living lives of commitment.

# Seizing the "God Appointments" When There Is Cultural Disorientation in a Study Abroad Program

LON FENDALL

*Lon Fendall (Ph.D. in U.S. diplomatic history, U. of Oregon) was Director of the Center for Global Studies at George Fox University (GFU) in Oregon until his retirement in 2010. GFU has operated the South American Studies Program (SASP) since 2006. The program is located in Santa Cruz, Bolivia.[1] Santa Cruz is situated in a tropical part of Bolivia with high temperatures, humidity, and rainfall, in sharp contrast to the conditions in the country's high-elevation capital, LaPaz. The program has elements of an "area studies" curriculum, with courses in Latin American history, Religions of South America, and Spanish language. It also has an immersion component, with home stays for most of the semester and service-learning two days a week. About two weeks of each semester are devoted to historical, geographic, and cultural travels. This chapter focuses on the students' spiritual and emotional growth that comes about during and after their cultural disorientation experiences in South America. It particularly emphasizes the interaction of the program's faculty and staff with the students in moving through disorientation to insight and growth.*

The directors had expressed the health cautions numerous times during the pre-departure orientations. So when the student got sick—really sick, not just homesick—she wasn't surprised. She took it as part of the adjustment her body was making to a new diet, a new climate, and a host of germs eagerly attacking a body with little immunity. Getting sick was not especially traumatic. But her host family's reaction to her illness troubled her. They didn't seem to understand that she was genuinely sick and might need medical attention or at least would need time to rest and recover. The message she was getting from them was she was making too much of her symptoms and should be able to get on with the routines of her life. In the midst of the seeming lack of understanding, she yearned for her "real Mom," who would give her plenty of tender loving care and maybe some tried and true family cures.

This student's encounter with the lack of understanding from her host family is an example of the disorientation felt by almost all people who spend sustained time in cultures other than their own. This chapter will explore some of the ways the staff members of Christian study abroad programs are able to help students maximize their spiritual growth and minimize their emotional trauma amid the inevitable disorientation they experience in a new culture. Using the South American Studies Program as a case study, I will argue that students should not be shielded from cultural disorientation in study abroad programs. Rather, the experiences should be welcomed as God's opportunities to teach important lessons to those who seek to follow him more faithfully.

As Cynthia Toms Smedley points out in this book's introduction, many students who participate in study abroad experiences are hoping to achieve greater self-understanding, greater insights into their relationship with God, and a keener sense of their present and future places in the world. Smedley discusses the connections between cognitive dissonance and spiritual growth. She sees spiritual growth as an important goal of students' global experiences, a perspective we at George Fox University embrace.

For the phenomenon Smedley calls "cognitive dissonance," I have chosen to use the terminology of Murray S. Decker, who is a professor of intercultural studies at Biola University. In a chapter of a book on short term missions, Decker summarizes the literature on the process of adjustment experienced by cross-cultural "sojourners" (those undergoing sustained immersion in another community and culture). He reserves the term "culture shock" for the extremely dysfunctional experiences some sojourners experience and labels ordinary cross-cultural stresses as "disorientation." His choice of words and his general frame of reference may be influenced by the thinking of Jack Mezirow, a theorist on adult education, who speaks about "disorienting dilemmas" as an important step on the pathway of adult learning. Hence, the dilemmas and frustrations associated with new ideas or new experiences ought to be welcomed as a means of gaining formative insights. Mezirow's work fits within the framework of thought called "transformation theory."[2]

The most helpful part of Decker's ideas as I have thought about the SASP at our university is that Decker sees cultural dissonance as a positive step toward cultural insight and spiritual growth. He insists that spiritual disorientation is not a horrible fate to be avoided, but a welcome opportunity for the Holy Spirit to lead the believing student from deep cultural stress to a new plateau of spiritual maturity. He has repeatedly heard students speak about feeling that God was distant in their times of frustration in unfamiliar cultures and that their prayers felt empty and ineffective. They seemed to be in a spiritually dry place, and they felt guilty and frustrated that praying about these feelings didn't seem to help them. Decker draws on the work of a number of scholars in his field of intercultural studies who have studied the transition from euphoria and excitement upon entering the new culture to a place where there is confusion, loneliness, and frustration, where nothing seems to be familiar. These scholars associate the most extreme form of personal disorientation, culture shock, with extreme fatigue and an inability to cope. People experiencing culture shock can barely function within the expectations of their daily schedule, which they once had anticipated with such joy. A person experiencing cultural disorientation may not be in as much distress as those with culture shock, yet they may still be on the threshold of serious trauma.[3]

Decker knows from hearing students' narratives that though the lessons from cultural disorientation are not learned automatically, there is the hope of not only recovery but spiritual and emotional growth. If properly prepared and guided, Decker explains, students can work through this cultural disorientation. Decker's insights can be summarized as follows:

1.  There is much to be gained by studying and discussing cross-cultural disorientation before and after global experiences.

2. God understands the sojourn through the spiritual desert place for believers, and can help them to understand their own inadequacy and trust in God's healing and strength.
3. The frustration and despair students experience are common to the spiritual journey of most if not all followers of Christ.
4. While there is much to be gained from the prayer, encouragement, and counsel of others, any student's experiences with disorientation may be quite different from those of other students.
5. Some of the intensity of students' cross-cultural struggles comes from the normal struggles of late adolescence.[4]

For Christian faculty involved with study abroad programs, there are rich passages of Scripture to use in teaching and counseling before, during, and after the disorientating experiences. There are the stories of Jonah, Elijah, Job, and other biblical figures who reached such depths of despair they asked God to end their lives. There is also a series of chapters in the middle section of the book of Psalms in which the writer is brutally honest about his distress: "My heart is in anguish within me; the terrors of death assail me. Fear and trembling have beset me; horror has overwhelmed me" (Ps. 55:4–5). Later in this passage, the psalmist emerges from despair to trust and rest in the arms of a loving God. "But I call to God," says the writer, "and the Lord saves me. Evening, morning, and noon I cry out in distress, and he hears my voice" (Ps. 55:17). These passages speak of distress and even despair, but also of recovery, healing, and restoration.

The SASP at our university is first of all an academic program. But the program supports the spiritual goals of its host university and thus expects that spiritual development will accompany intellectual growth. The last sentence of the program's mission statement expresses its spiritual goals: "Our mission is to train undergraduates to express a heart of love in Jesus' name, feet of service in self-giving, and a spirit of joy in God's diverse cultural creation."[5] Implicit in that statement is the joy to be found in the richness of God's cultural creation as one encounters parts of it that at first seem uncomfortable and alien. After all, why *do* these people insist on driving on the wrong side of the road?

A common frustration among those engaged in Christian higher education has been the lack of collaboration between student life staff members and the faculty in achieving the shared goals of spiritual, personal, and intellectual development. Critics speak of a "silo" mentality that persists in spite of frequent efforts to bring the academicians and the student life staff together in partnership to nurture student learning. In "Collaboration to Labor Together," Norris Friesen and Wendy Soderquist Togami bemoan this lack of interaction and mention travel experiences as a means of breaking down the unfortunate barriers between faculty and student life staff.[6] They could have looked more carefully at the collaboration to be found in study abroad programs.

One way that we, the faculty and leaders at George Fox, developed the SASP was in selecting a married couple to be our overseas leadership team. The objectives of the SASP reflect the previous cross-cultural experiences of its founding director and his spouse, Ron and Carolyn Stansell. The Stansells served as missionaries in Bolivia from 1967 to 1985, including four years on the faculty at Bolivia Evangelical University (BEU), the host institution for the SASP. Subsequent to the Stansells' years of missionary work, Ron joined the faculty of George Fox University. Carolyn gained experience by working in the administrative offices of George Fox University. We determined that it was important to take advantage of the experiences and skills of both the director as a seasoned faculty member and his spouse, also experienced in working with students. These assets have proven valuable, and the Stansell's marriage relationship has given them important opportunities to collaborate in helping students to learn and to deal with cultural pressures.

Before proceeding with the discussion of the program, it would be helpful to take note of students' first impressions upon their arrival in Santa Cruz. Of course there are the startling first impressions of leaving home as winter is setting in (ours is a spring semester program only) and stepping out of the plane in Santa Cruz with its tropical climate of alternating dry and rainy seasons, both of them hot. The students with enough Spanish to understand some of what is being said wonder if they will ever be able to understand people who speak the language so rapidly and with different accents than their professors at home. Then there are the varieties of indigenous languages that make no sense to any of the students. And compared with their quiet neighborhoods at home, the students notice the constant honking of horns on the streets and the loud music that seems to play all night. Their residence halls in the States were sometimes noisy, but nothing like this. All of these things and more were mentioned in their orientations—the pushy vendors on the streets, the mysterious smells of the food, the bright green of the vegetation. Nothing can completely prepare students for the sensory overload experienced in that first encounter with a place that will be their home for sixteen weeks.

Disorientation and subsequent personal and spiritual growth take place during many of the components of study abroad programs, including the classes, the learning trips, the field experiences, and the home stays. I am drawing on the students' reflections during and after their participation in the SASP to trace the disorientation they experienced and the growth they also experienced during and after their challenging encounters with the Bolivian culture.

Two of the courses offered in the SASP are similar in format and content to the international courses offered on the home campus—"History of Latin America" and "Religions of South America." But as Ron Stansell teaches the courses, Bolivia itself and the greater Andes region becomes the laboratory for cultural insight, not just as a backdrop for conventional reading and discussion. Students read about the incredibly rich Incan culture and then get to nose around such places as Cuzco and Machu Piccu. They read about the flowering of a transplanted Spanish culture in South America and then go to places like Sucre and Potosi, whose silver mines provided the wealth essential for the development of the local Spanish economy and the prosperity of the elite back home in Spain. They move on to consider the influence of other European cultures and then visit Buenos Aires, where German, Italian, and French people blended their respective cultures with the indigenous cultures and formed a mosaic. They discuss the concept of religious syncretism in class and then get to study some paintings done by Peruvian artists depicting the blend of pre-Christian and Christian images.

One student said in her program evaluation that being in places like Machu Picchu helped her not only to grasp the material she studied in class, but also to form a mental picture of the places she did not get to visit. And another student asked a question that became an ongoing opportunity for reflection during the "Religions of South America" course. The students had been exploring Cuzco, the Sacred Valley, and Machu Picchu with a Peruvian guide who had spoken favorably about the traditional religious beliefs and practices of the people who had lived in these locations. He had also spoken of Christianity as an alien and intrusive value system. The GFU student wondered aloud if the guide's perspective was not, in fact, appropriate, even while she realized this perspective did not fit with her own Christian upbringing. Professor Stansell affirmed the importance of the student's question, let the students talk about it a bit, then read a passage from the book of Romans about God's truth being known in ancient times and being fulfilled, not contradicted, through the good news of the gospel of Jesus. He assured the students that the question would continue to shape their discussions in the religions course throughout the semester.

The student's question about the apparent clash between animism and her own Christian value system was an example of Mezirow's thinking about the formation of more sophisticated "meaning structures" in such encounters, allowing students to form more inclusive, discriminating, and permeable intellectual models. He says that experiences like the encounters with the Andean culture become the incubators for more advanced ideas and that these become fully formed only through rational discourse.[7] Mezirow's point here is one of the main reasons Christian colleges and universities go to such lengths to develop and operate study abroad experiences.

Another part of the SASP curriculum that generates considerable stress and thus leads to cultural insights is the teaching and learning of the Spanish language. Students come to the program with a wide range of previous study and competence in Spanish, but even the more seasoned Spanish speakers in the group find it to be challenging and sometimes stressful to function in an environment where they only understand part of what they are hearing. Also, they sometimes are not accustomed to the teaching methods of their Bolvian professors of the Spanish language. While host home and field experience placements are based in part on language proficiency, even the advanced students in the language have to struggle to communicate in these settings. Invariably both the advanced students and the beginners point to the host home and internship experiences as the most helpful in improving their language skills. And they typically speak of the language barriers in the home and internship site as a source of their initial disconnectedness and later regaining their equilibrium.

At the end of the program one student who had very little previous knowledge of Spanish reflected on the difficulty she experienced with Spanish. She said, without using the exact words, that her struggle with the language brought about her descent into disorientation. She realized how far behind other students she was with the language and how little she first understood when she arrived in her host home. But she came out of the experience able to value this part of the program for so many of her cultural insights, and she even reached the point of some competency in conversing in Spanish. For her, the language challenge produced the greatest disorientation and hence the greatest opportunity to grow spiritually and intellectually.

The part of the curriculum that most directly addresses the objective of guiding the process of cultural adjustment is the course called "Cultures and Customs." As they begin the course, the students have finished their first week in their host home. Other than a few who began being reasonably fluent in Spanish, they have struggled to communicate about even the most basic aspects of family life. The students have also just begun their field experience placement and are still trying to find their place in this new setting, without the comfort of fellow students being nearby. Moreover, they have tried their best to master the public transportation system to get to and from their host homes and field experience sites, sometimes getting off at the wrong stops or becoming so disoriented they have had to resort to calling the program staff.

The Customs and Cultures course thus begins when students feel themselves slipping into discouragement or even despair about functioning in the strange environment. Accordingly, one of the principal functions of the course is to provide an avenue for cultural insight and adjustment. The classes include discussion of assigned readings, lectures, guest presenters, and reflections on cross-cultural frustrations and insights. As students read about the process of becoming frustrated and disoriented and come to understand that it is inevitable in one's early encounters with different cultures, they begin to grasp what Decker says about the process of disorientation leading to new levels of adjustment and insight. On a spiritual level, they can take much comfort from knowing that their frustrations are not necessarily associated with failing to love people of all cultures, but are in fact important first steps toward learning *how* to love those who are different.

The program directors ask students to keep journals and sometimes ask students' permission to place journal excerpts on the program's blog, so the other students and their friends and families at home can walk with them through both the hard times and the exhilarating experiences. One of the journal excerpts that appeared on the program blog was a classic statement of cultural and spiritual disorientation. The student wrote about a traumatic experience that made her want to withdraw from her host culture. She had been on a public bus that took a different route than she had expected, so she was the last passenger on the bus passing through a part of town that made her feel uncomfortable. Moreover, she became uneasy, thinking that the driver who was trying to help her was making unwelcome advances toward her. In her journal, the student said, "For me it is just too hard to deal with all the cultural differences. I have found myself only wanting to hang out with my friends from school." Then she began to listen to her own rejection of the culture in what she had written and to talk herself into a better place. "What a tragedy it would be if I always kept myself inside my 'American bubble.' Why come all this way and not learn anything about dealing with the culture? That would be such a waste of a wonderful opportunity God has given me." That movement into and out of cultural and spiritual despair is exactly the kind of thing the Cultures and Customs course and the whole SASP is designed to facilitate.

The place of the Customs and Cultures course in the SASP program is a crucial one. Admittedly, it falls short of the impressive three-semester sequence in cultural studies in the Westmont College program described by professors Montgomery and Doctor in this book. Nevertheless, the outcomes of greater integration, empathy, and acceptance these authors associate with Bennett's work are what we strive to achieve in the SASP, especially in the Customs and Cultures course.

Beyond the curricular part of the SASP, there are many additional opportunities to learn and grow. Embedded in these experiences are some that may lead to cultural and spiritual discorientation and some that help students address their discomfort. After concluding that the chapel services at the host university were not very meaningful for the SASP students, the directors began scheduling their own weekly worship times during the chapel period. Students began with the singing of worship songs in English or Spanish, and individual students talked about the cultural and spiritual experiences they were having in the program and the lessons they were learning. Not all students feel comfortable speaking in these worship times about their spiritual struggles and victories, but there are enough to make this a rewarding and helpful part of the program. Students often look back on these worship times as safe places to be honest when things weren't going well and to learn that their experiences were more similar than different. When it seems to be needed, the directors presented brief meditations that relate to student needs and concerns.

The weekend retreats also appeared to have helped students in the cultural and spiritual adjustment process as well. Students spoke of the timing of the retreats being helpful, after the rigors of the Spanish intensive class and after the first week with the host families. The retreats have been held in comfortable hotels or retreat centers where the students have felt the freedom to relax, to catch up on sleep, to "hang out" with their friends in the program, to have fun, and to share with one another about their spiritual struggles and insights.

As one would expect, the home stays also stand out in the memories of the students as one of the most valuable and sometimes the most frustrating aspects of the program. For some, it was the chance to improve their oral skills in Spanish in ways they had never been able to do in classes. For others, it helped them to understand the priority the typical Latino families place on their relationships with family and friends. One student said she felt uncomfortable at first just sitting with a member of the host family, sipping tea, conversing, and saying very little. Yet over time, this student learned the momentous lesson that life was not just about doing, but of *being* with those with whom you are forming new and important relationships.

Students have written frequently in their journals about their experiences in the host homes. For example, one student wrote about the cultural disorientation that came from comparing herself with her "sister" in her host family. She felt like she had been pushed back into her growing-up years because of not being able to figure things out and to do things as well as others in the home. She spoke of being "shoved back into childhood," with all the insecurity and humiliation that phrase suggests. Another student had a much more positive experience in her host home and said this about her host family: "They are the purest example of love, generosity, and servitude that I have ever seen displayed in all the places that I've lived and traveled. They are hard working, family-oriented, and God-fearing. In the short time that I've been here I've laughed with them, cried with them, had deep penetrating conversations with each one, and learned so much about myself in the process."

Students found that their field experiences abounded with opportunities to deal with their cultural disorientation. Students spend two full days a week at a service and ministry agency they and the directors select to match the students' majors, life goals, and personal goals. Some students found the SASP field experiences to be a source of disorientation because their assignments were not made very clear, at least not in the ways they would have expected at home. In time, they realized the lesson to be learned is that making a contribution may not consist of accomplishing concrete things as much as being with the people and learning from them.

Along with the more formal and structured parts of the SASP, many informal opportunities have arisen, never scheduled, but always important. As directors of SASP, the Stansells have learned to function as counselors, mentors, friends, surrogate parents, and sometimes authority figures. As a married couple, they have had abundant opportunities to discuss the students' needs with each other and the ways each of them might be helpful to the students. They have found that these informal opportunities to minister to the students' disorientation come in unpredictable ways but with predictable regularity. Often students express their needs in the weekly worship times, alerting the directors to the need for one-on-one time with the student. For example, there was a student who was trying to deal with her puzzlement and anger that her parents had chosen not to tell her that one of her grandparents had passed away while she was in the program. Her parents apparently wanted to spare her from the feeling of loss and of guilt that she would not be able to be present for the family's grieving processes.

Students have valued the directors' willingness to provide a listening ear and words of counsel at such moments, and in the low points of their adjustment processes. Both the Stansells agree with Murray Decker that God is waiting eagerly for each student to come to the end of his or her own capability and turn voluntarily to the Divine, while they as God's agents on the scene can make God's love and grace known.

One might wonder how the directors of SASP have dealt with their own disorienting experiences as they have moved into and out of South American cultures each year and walked beside the students through their many adjustments. In some ways, their most disorientating experiences happened long ago, since they had spent so many years living in Bolivia. Through those years they learned coping mechanisms that have continued to be important in their capacity as cultural and spiritual mentors and role models. They can anticipate and address student struggles even in practical matters like getting sufficient sleep, maintaining a healthy diet, and exercising regularly. They have also made a point of enlisting people from home to pray regularly for the needs they express through e-mail. The ultimate challenge for the directors was leading the program in 2009, when a State Department travel warning meant they had to move the program to Paraguay, a country they had barely visited and where they had none of the relationships and contacts they had in Bolivia. While the directors experienced times of cultural disorientation in the new setting, the students at the end said they scarcely noticed.

The title of this book includes the phrase "the edge of the world," suggesting in part the distant and exotic destinations of some study abroad students. Bolivia is certainly not at the edge of the world. But any study abroad destination, whether distant or close, is filled with cultural challenges that hold the hope of great gains in maturity and spiritual growth. Good study abroad programs carefully usher students to the edges of their comfort zone and allow them to experience the inevitable slide into disorientation and despair. The staff of faith-based programs know that God wants students to grow in the times of cultural fatigue and even culture shock. There is little else more important to the mission of Christian colleges and universities than to see students come through the experiences of wondering and discouragement and emerge as stronger Christians and human beings.

One of the SASP students said she had been very comfortable with her life and her future until God sent her to Bolivia. Eventually she was able to look back and say it had been an amazing and life-changing experience. That is exactly what so many of us involved in international education hope will happen. We want to see personal and spiritual transformation emerge from confusion and despair. And we regularly get to see the rewarding results of that transformation.

# PART II

# Inward Journey to Outward Living

## Community as Teacher

CYNTHIA TOMS SMEDLEY

One of the signs of passing youth is the birth of a sense of fellowship with other human beings as we take our place among them.

—Virginia Woolf

Fellowship with Christ is fellowship with our brothers and sisters. Only as we become deeply aware of ourselves, our relation to the world and its people, can we begin to grasp the community as resource and reconciler. As students mature from inward reflection to outward embrace, they learn to nurture qualities of presence and engagement. Spirituality nurtured in the rich context of community leads to healthy human interdependence.

The New Testament uses the word *koinonia* nineteen times to describe this rich and complex approach to our corporate ventures in the world. *Koinonia* embraces a strong commitment to *Kalos k'agathos*, meaning "good and good,"—an inner goodness toward virtue, and an outer goodness toward social relationships.[1] In individual societies, we are raised with the notion that "I think, therefore I am." However, for collectivist cultures, the mantra is: "I participate, therefore I am."[2] As North Americans, our individual reasoning leads us to meaning-making and self-awareness of our place. In many other parts of the world, the self is validated only as a member of community. God's reflective design is that we are not alone—we are relational as God is relational.

Therefore, transformation takes place in the meaning-making of both the individual and community. Henri Nouwen writes, "In community, we are no longer a mass of helpless individuals, but are transformed into one people of God . . . . In community, our lives become compassionate lives because in the way we live and work together, God's compassion becomes present in the midst of a broken world."[3] In response to suffering, community acts as a mediator between the individual and the world. In response to injustice, community acts as a voice to advocate for the voiceless. In reponse to faltering, community acts to carry our burdens. In response to disbelief, community acts as an Ebenezer, reminding us of our salvation.

The experience of living, studying, working, and praying together offers boundless transformative potential. Students can only grasp a fraction of their true selves without discovering the community of their spiritual heritage and their fellow believers. In this section, Dr. John Skillen discusses how students better mature through three circles of community. With the help of St. Benedict's Rule, his students learn to practice presence with one another, while exercising responsibility toward the collective. Then Dr. Don Briel shares how an introduction to church heritage teaches students the value of a global, multi-cultural communion of Christians. Encountering the big questions of the faith, they can stand on the shoulders of the spiritual mothers and fathers that have gone before them. Having experienced rich fellowship, students grasp a sense of personal value as active members of community. This skill leads to the formation and preservation of transformational communities once students depart their *alma mater*.

# CHAPTER FIVE

# New Monasticism Meets Renaissance Bottega

Gordon College's Semester Program in Orvieto, Italy

**JOHN SKILLEN**

*Dr. John Skillen directs the Gordon in Orvieto program and divides his time between the program in Italy and Gordon campus. The Gordon in Orvieto (Italy) semester program, while arts-oriented and themed to the medieval and Renaissance period, is open to students from any major, and to applicants of Christian faith from any college. Each semester faculty and a maximum of twenty-four students live together in a monastery in the small historic hill-town of Orvieto. Students take an integrative course during the first month, and then select one from pairs of courses offered during each of the final three months in the visual arts, creative writing, history, and literature. Instruction in Italian occurs mainly in tutorial-format throughout the semester. Courses are taught by members of the arts and humanities faculty from Gordon College and other Christian liberal arts colleges, and by professional artists selected for the relevance of their own art to the guiding themes of the program.*

The Gordon in Orvieto semester program, first piloted in 1998, was the result of a decade of conversations among several friends and colleagues in the arts and humanities. Our concern was about how we ought to be responding as teachers, as well as in our own lives and vocations, to the unraveling of the Western classical-Christian cultural tradition. Believing in the value of that tradition as one that should not be lost, we asked ourselves how we might go about reconnecting a generation of largely a-historical post-culture college students to the tradition, when its compositional network of allusions and imitations and adjustments are no longer operative in the cultural synapses, as it were, of mental, emotional, and spiritual processing and response.

We sought for our students a vibrant experience of revisiting elements of pre-modernity for their relevance to postmodernity. Our thematic points of reference—though not slavishly or dogmatically followed—were the early Italian Renaissance in the arts, early medieval monastic life for our in-house guide, and ancient patterns of liturgical life (shaped time, *kairos* not *chronos*) in corporate and civic life.

We still cite our original vision statement—admittedly a tad extravagant in its prose:

> The Gordon-in-Orvieto semester program takes an experimental approach to learning in the landscape of our contemporary post-culture. The intent of the program is to foster in our students an attitude of responsive looking and listening for signs of new life in the traditions inhabited by artists and poets, saints and mystics, of the past, especially those of pre-modern Europe in Italy. With a discerning eye neither nostalgic nor ironic, we wish to explore the disintegrated fragments of the classical-Christian civilization of the West, raiding the past in order to rebuild the present.

We knew that revivifying for our students (and for ourselves) this sacred conversation with tradition as something spiritually as well as artistically and intellectually formative—as something that gets under the skin into the habits and rhythms of daily living—could not really occur if it was experienced solely as a classroom academic exercise. These underlying hopes and intentions needed to inform both our life together in our own in-house community, and be experienced in the civic context of a 2500-year-old town where the interplay between old and new is everywhere present in a palimpsest of layers (whether as an *Intimissimi* underwear shop in a thirteenth-century storefront, or as the medieval town hall now renovated as a conference center).

Our original statement of the purposes of the program remains:

- To provide contemporary American students—whose lives are lived largely after or without tradition—a vivid experience of tradition in the arts, spirituality and worship, and civic life.
- To inspire young people of faith to re-connect with the artistic traditions of the past, neither in a mood of nostalgia nor in a mode of academic dispassion, but to foster a creative response to the past in order to shape a humane future in the arts.
- To establish a workshop environment that invites collaboration between teacher and student, integrating listening and writing with seeing and doing, and emphasizing an interdisciplinary approach to the study of art, history and theology.
- To give students an experience of rhythms of life slower and simpler than the forms of contemporary American life (with its speed and size, its barrage of visual images, and its pervading sense of impermanence) by dining together, encouraging sustained conversation, experiencing the traditional liturgies of religious life and civic celebrations, living more closely to the earth in the midst of vineyards and olive groves, and by trading the automobile for the foot.

We understood that the spiritual formation of our students (and of faculty and staff as well) would need to be woven into the fabric of all of the three overlapping circles of community that define our program: namely, as a community of makers; as a community within-the-walls of our monastery headquarters; and via the community of Orvieto without-the-walls.

## 1. *Bottega*: The Classroom as Community

As for the academic program, our intent was to recreate something on the order of the Renaissance *bottega*. We imagined a workshop environment that brought together skilled professionals in the arts and humanities to experiment with new ways of recuperating traditional texts, genres, media, and styles; in a pedagogical mode that brought younger artists into the *sacra conversazione* of the tradition; and in a manner answerable to the audiences that these activities were intended to serve.

We encourage our teachers—certainly in the studio courses—to organize their classes whenever possible around a central project over which the skilled professional instructor stands as *maestro*, and therefore as a participant. The young artists join the *maestro* in subordinating their own personal inclinations and submitting their individual contributions to the harmony and integrity of the whole work. The intent is to offer a counter to the pedagogical model often typical of modern instruction that isolates the student in homework projects disassociated with peers and of which the instructor exists as evaluator, not as herself answerable to a final joint work.

As the historical/theoretical backdrop, our students study a cultural epoch (the early Renaissance) when art was clearly and universally understood as serving the uses and needs of the communities that sponsored and commissioned it (rather than existing, in modern art-for-art's-sake fashion, for the dispassionate aesthetic gaze of the viewer).[1]

Over the years, the *in situ* products of a collaborative workshop have often meant that students cannot take their work home with them to the States. But they can receive a different sort of satisfaction in knowing, for example, that their collectively-made series of ceramic-relief plaques of the Fourteen Stations of the Cross are installed in the contemplative garden of monastery San Lodovico, where they are actually used every year during the Good Friday Way of the Cross liturgy to guide the gathered congregation's devotions.

The ceramic wall mural of Noah's ark and the tile backsplash for the fountain created by another class enlivens the playground of the nursery school run by the sisters at San Lodovico, offering occasion for scriptural catechism through the arts. A portion of the open-air courtyard along the cliff's edge behind our present location at monastery San Paolo is envisioned as a Saint Francis garden. Shelly Bradbury's sculpture class (spring 2008) got a start on a monumental arched gate into the garden, each stone block carved in relief with a scene from Francis' life. Marino Moretti's ceramic class (fall 2008) transformed one area of the garden into a flock of birds to whom St. Francis might preach, and a school of colorful and whimsical fish as the congregation of that other creature-sensitive golden-tongued Franciscan preacher, St. Anthony of Padova. About thirty ceramic panels wait to be mounted as a giant wall mural Bestiary.

Even our humanities courses include collaborative projects. Dr. Liesl Smith's History of Monasticism created a Rule relevant for our contemporary cultural setting. Dr. Hevelone-Harper's Theology of the Image students learn how to paint icons. The students in Dr. Agnes Howard's class on women's social and religious life in medieval and Renaissance Italy attend monastic hours and perform plays. Poetry classes work toward a single book and performance. In short, the academic pattern moves toward a common product produced as a community of artists and learners for an actual community to use.

A bold example of this bottega approach, with its integration of artistic formation and spiritual formation, occurred in a class taught in 2003 by Bruce Herman that launched an ambitious mural cycle about the life of the Virgin Mary. The unconventional character of the course shows up in the syllabus: "This course will acquaint the student with the working methods, imagery, and aesthetic philosophy of the teacher. Students will work alongside the professor as assistants on a common project, and will be given the privilege and responsibility of acting as collaborators learning and working in an apprenticeship atmosphere." The students, emphasized Herman, worked hard "for hours and days at a time, sometimes engaged in menial tasks associated with the common project, other times engaged at a deep, principled level with the substance of the project—a mural cycle about the life of Mary, the Mother of Jesus, the Theotokos, or God-bearer."

Although Herman gave his students particular tasks in keeping with their interests and skills, every student had to prepare

> a meditation on all the Marian texts in Scripture—with a view to connecting with these texts *personally* (trying to remember events and persons in your own lives that have correspondence with Mary's events and relationships—eg. Anna, Joachim, Gabriel, Joseph, the Visitation, Annunciation, Nativity, etc.). Can you find equivalents (if less than supernatural) in your own lives in terms of events and/or personal relationships? How might these memories affect the way we select and compose a scene from the life of the Virgin? How do you incorporate the tradition and "translate" it into the vernacular of our contemporary life?

Incidentally, the project took several years for Herman to bring to completion back in his studio in Massachusetts. (The paintings, which evolved over time into two enormous triptychs, are now installed back in the cloistered chapel in the monastery at San Paolo, where they can do their work amidst a living community of students, faculty, artists, and pilgrims.) But in the catalog prepared for the paintings, Herman acknowledges by name each of the students "who participated in the inception and initial work on the Mary mural bottega project in Orvieto."

Another recent example of the bottega approach can be seen in Professor Tanja Butler's spring 2008 Art & Liturgy course. In her class the final project was to "create a prayer station" for one of the "mysteries" of the *Via Lucis* (the

Way of Light), the fourteen stations of the Resurrection paralleling the stations of the *Via Crucis*. The task of each student was to "select a station from the *Via Lucis* with which you feel an affinity. Using *lectio divina*, prayerfully identify one to four ways in which you feel connected to this scene from the life of Christ. Identify these connection points as words or simple phrases, themes you'll be developing visually." Having developed the visual elements, students were to "select a location in monastery San Paolo that has an appropriate connection with the content of your station" and then to "create a liturgy for your prayer station." Then the class worked together to draw the individual stations into a single integrated liturgy enacted by the whole community of students and teachers and guests.

In sum, the approach of these teachers was not to leave to the chapel office or the Bible department the job of applying curricular "subject matter" to the work of spiritual formation. Rather, they represent an attitude expected from our teachers: to integrate a deep personal encounter of a particular mystery of the faith into the very process and product of the art-making, and to do this work corporately as a community.

## 2. In-house Community as a Means of Spiritual Formation

The program's theme of revisiting the pre-modern for direction amidst the fragments of the postmodern was intended not only to characterize the academic program but also to infiltrate our daily in-house community life. That is, just as we might hearken back to Giotto or Masaccio to learn how to frame a narrative that linked scriptural plots to contemporary life, so we might do well to revisit the Rule of Saint Benedict for simple-yet-sophisticated discernment regarding the poisons and blessings that erode or sustain a bunch of people thrown together in shared space.

Parallels between the workshop and the dormitory have gradually taken on sharper focus. The common threat to each is the self-absorption of an I-culture: individualism in the arts, and narcissism in community life.

As we state in the introduction to the program Handbook:

> *The Rule of San Paolo* takes as its model the earliest and most influential of the handbooks for monastic communities—the sixth-century *Rule of Saint Benedict*.

Benedict has been called not only the father of Western monasticism but the "first European," largely responsible for articulating the principles and putting into widespread practice a form of Christian community guided by mutual service and mutual accountability in the midst of the social disintegration of the "dark ages" of the crumbling Roman empire.

But many astute spiritual writers and theologians of our own time see Benedict as a figure with new relevance for a de-Christianized Europe, for a socially-fractured global society, and for the "emergent church" of postmodernity.

It's easy to see a new dark age in the murderous tribalism now destroying the love of neighbor in many parts of the world (and which may appear distant to us except when terrorist attacks bring barbarism and fanaticism closer to home). Harder to get a handle on, yet closer to home for us folk living in the developed economies of Western democracies, is an encroaching narcissistic individualism. Seduced willingly by the technological wizardry whose high-speed evolution silences any critical perspective, we are rapidly becoming a society of solipsistic "I"-pods. Shut off behind our personally-designed interior worlds of sound-scape and digital artifice, we imagine that cyber-communities and "virtual" social networking can offer a satisfying alternative to real bodies really listening in real time and in real space, taking real risks on one another's behalf.

A number of leading faith-based writers are suggesting that our best hope for recovering healthy, morally-grounded social life will come through a sort of "new monasticism" in which small communities whose members are answerable to one another can model alternatives to the ego-centric materialism that everywhere threatens neighborly love and authentic self-acceptance.[2]

Most of the topics and chapter titles in our own program Handbook are taken directly from the *Rule of Saint Benedict*, and quotations from Benedict illustrate each chapter (such as *Let no one in the monastery follow his own heart's fancy*). The key elements of "intentional community" include the following.

We follow a common daily schedule. Classes (both the single integrative course taken by all students during the first month and the pairs of courses offered sequentially and intensively for four weeks each) meet from nine o'clock in the morning to noon, Monday through Thursday. Students can begin the day on their own, socializing or not over a simple breakfast, heading out for an early morning jog or cappuccino, or attending to a time of personal devotion (or rolling out of bed shortly before class). But often some sort of corporate activity of morning prayer and praise is initiated by students themselves—and receives the leadership's blessing!

After the morning class, we generally hold "chapter meeting"—a mix of announcements, exhortation on matters of housekeeping and community behavior, brief prayer, singing, and formal devotion presented by a teacher, staff member, or student. Then we stroll over to the local family-run restaurant along the central pedestrian street in Orvieto where students and staff eat a substantial midday meal together, with no rushing allowed. Happily, leisurely conversation is almost always the norm. The group chemistry varies from semester to semester, and now and again one has to caution against exclusive little groupings, but mainly our students are happy to mix it up with each other.

Supper is again taken together, at a later European hour. But the main portion of the afternoon and evening hours are available for students' own design of homework and studio work, and for personal choices about sketching, journaling, reading, walking, and deepening friendships in-house and in town. As one student describes the effect of this rhythm:

> The simplicity of that life wasn't confining or restricting; rather it allowed me to explore my world in new ways that fed me artistically and spiritually. During my free time after lunch, I would explore the small town armed only with my sketchbook and camera, quietly documenting Orvieto with all of its textures, colors, patterns, structures and hidden passages. My senses were awakened and stimulated so that I could see God, beauty and community, from the bricks and the gnarly carved tufa walls to the beautiful structure of the Duomo and the fog that would roll in and out of the hills of Umbria.

Students are expected to have returned from evening activities by eleven o'clock, when we bolt the big door (midnight on weekends, or to accommodate worthwhile cultural activities in town). We urge quietness in the night and good sleeping habits. We have had to respond year by year to the rapid and exponential availability—ubiquity—of Internet-based options for communicating with friends and family back home (from simple e-mailing a few years ago, to Skype, Facebook, and other social-networking means of sending of photo albums only minutes after returning from an excursion, and so on). The program handbook makes a case for our intentional curtailment of internet time, and for our commitment to the importance of maintaining our own bodily presence with one another, but we try to keep the issues open for discussion.

We emphasize collective responsibility for tidiness and cleaning, and being good stewards of resources and utility consumption. The passage cited from Benedict's Rule goes as follows:

> Let him regard all the utensils of the monastery and its whole property as if they were the sacred vessels of the altar. Let him not think that he may neglect anything. He should be neither a miser nor a prodigal and squanderer of the monastery's substance, but should do all things with measure and in accordance with the Abbot's instructions.

I'm one who can easily be discouraged by the amount of time and energy spent patrolling and fussing over the little things: the pile of dishes remaining unwashed in the sink; the disorder in the *sala*; the dust-bunnies on the stairwells. "We are failing miserably!" I can moan in private despair. How do we exhort without nagging? How do we balance policing from the top with an expectation of mutual accountability generated from within the students themselves? I am grateful when, at chapter meeting, a student beats me to the punch by giving a lesson in washing and drying dishes. How does one get across with charitable patience the subtle spiritual/moral disconnect in the student who is quick to propose a time of evening prayer to defend our community from spiritual warfare, even as he or she is responsible for leaving the dirty dishes from his evening snack for someone else to wash in the morning—perhaps a stronger threat to community peace and concord than demons at the gate.

Indeed, we don't claim to have perfected a formula here. But the effort is confirmed when I discover that a student isn't sweeping her room or making her bed because she has never in her life been expected to do so, or that a student doesn't know how to use the rag mop because he has never mopped a floor in his life. How poignant it is when a student speaks with gratitude about the simple matter of sitting down at table twice a day with the same group of people, practicing the art of courteous conversation, because she has never had that experience before, perhaps growing up with a single parent, or trying bravely to juggle a frenetic schedule of studies, extracurricular activities, and part-time jobs, long accustomed to grabbing something on the run, passing siblings at the microwave.

I'm coming to see as one of the critical "formation" aspects of our program—having so apparently little to do with daily immersion in Renaissance fresco cycles—is learning to make one's bed in the morning, or even to recognize the lethargy that leads us to slouch from one thing to another, leaning against walls for support, leaving single footprints at knee-height along the white-plastered walls of the monastery.

"New-monasticism," of course, signifies more than housekeeping. At the heart of the rhythms of *Ora et Labora* is the importance for the community of a simple daily liturgy of the hours together. But here, too, we have found no formula. I as director claim no particular wisdom in balancing a forced rhythm of pauses for prayer enforced administratively from on high, with the value of letting the desire for and enactment of such punctuations emerge from the students themselves. But plenty of students testify to how much more readily possible such liturgical shaping becomes in our simple life in a convent than amidst the frenetic schedules of campus life or in church communities that encourage little between private morning devotions and Sunday services and a weekly youth group.

As one student describes the impact:

> I was paradoxically required to do two things: simplify and ritualize. In all areas of daily life, these seemingly opposing forces came into play by asking that I leave the constant "obligations" and immediacy of American life behind (email, cell phones, internet-meandering, incessant homework, etc.), and replace it with a more liturgical way of living that involved a deeper commitment to the life of the community (shared meals, assigned tasks, joint living space, particular classroom style, exposure to the traditions of the Catholic community). ... in Orvieto I discovered great freedom in living a life of chosen obligation. Even now, nearly three years later, I often remind myself to draw back to my "Orvieto self."

## 3. In-town Community

Our attention to in-house spiritual life and formation is influenced by our approach to the third zone in which spiritual development is the issue: the larger community of shared Christian faith in the local town and church setting of the program. We have chosen deliberately not to try to meet all the spiritual life needs of all our students in-house, not wishing to become a "community within ourselves" that sabotages the equally fundamental purpose of the program to give students an authentic cross-cultural experience.

Orvieto provides an amiable setting in which our mainly (but not entirely) Protestant-evangelical students can discover ancient traditions of worship and spirituality still actively at work among the Roman Catholic community. That is, just as we are countering "individualism" in the arts and "narcissism" in our daily life of community, we are countering "parochialism" in our students' experience of the church catholic. A thoughtful and reasoned commitment to a chosen tradition of faith is a good thing, but not an un-self-critical narrowness that universalizes one's own accustomed patterns of prayer, worship, or spiritual labeling as normative for all cultures at all times.

We fuss about this aspect of the program. We want students out in the town. As the handbook states:

> An intention of the program is for students to have a respectful, accurately informed, and non-combative experience of the Roman Catholic tradition that has so deeply informed Italian culture as a whole and the art and culture of the Renaissance in particular. We hope to foster an atmosphere of open yet courteous conversation about the historical varieties of Christian spiritual and doctrinal expression, while honoring each student in her chosen expressions of faith.

We encourage students to participate in the established religious life of the town, perhaps visiting several churches during the semester or settling in at one, and certainly witnessing the grand liturgical services at the local cathedral. A number of students over the years, for example, have joined the choir at the thousand-year-old parish church of San Giovenale, welcomed by the young guitar-playing choir master. A staff-initiated first visit to the chanted service of Evening Prayer at the convent of a contemplative order of Franciscan nuns—for the "cultural experience"—usually leads to regular attendance by a few students each semester. A larger handful each semester will gravitate towards the Wednesday evening service of prayer and praise held by the area's lively Catholic charismatic renewal community. There, the guitar- and drum-accompanied singing turns out to be, for many of our students, the surprising closest-equivalent to the worship gatherings they enjoy on campus in the U.S., and a corrective to some of the prejudices instilled in them by Catholic-suspicious churches back home. A provocative shock occurs for our students when they see some of the same people at both the charismatic prayer service and the Vespers at the Franciscan convent: fellow believers who feel no dissonance between highly formalized contemplative ancient chant and contemporary singing "in the spirit," hands waving, tongues declaring.[3]

But we acknowledge the potential void felt by some students when they are completely unmoored from the largely collegiate-evangelical frameworks of spiritual and devotional and worship life (in the English language) that they bring with them. And yet someone in our administrative discussions will always speak up on behalf of periods of apparent barrenness. To experience one's absence or loneliness while sitting awkwardly in a mass that one only partially follows, listening to prayers that are so obviously serving as containers for expression of faith for those around you, while feeling silence in oneself, can turn out to prompt a sort of *via negativa* that is deeply efficacious in the long run. After all, so many of our colleges' study abroad programs are defined by the value of getting out of one's "comfort zone," an estrangement that turns out to be expansive. Then why ought we try to cushion our students against every sad moment of homesickness or cultural disconnect, when such *u-catastrophe* is exactly what we are hoping to occasion?

As one student articulates the effect:

> Being introduced to ancient traditions of Christian spirituality such as the Daily Office, the liturgy and silence allowed me to find fellowship with God in a new, creative and humbling manner. Connecting with believers from a different culture (and generation, at times) affirmed that, indeed, our faith unites us ... igniting a passion for God that had been previously buried in a sea of "consumerism Christianity" found in so many of our (post)modern churches today.

This student's testimony of gaining some helpful distance from the "consumerism Christianity" of her American experience represents the sort of u-catastrophe that we expect our program to provide. More surprising to me, given our emphasis on community life and conversation, is how often I hear other versions of this student's "liturgy and silence" phrase. "Prior to Orvieto the idea of silence was negative for me," as one young woman writes:

It is what I was when I couldn't think fast enough, was feeling intimidated by something, or what I experienced when I was in a classroom setting. In Orvieto the idea of silence took on a new meaning for me. Being surrounded by men and woman who had devoted their lives to God by becoming nuns or monks was new to me. I saw the devotion they displayed through prayer and meditation. In Orvieto life was silent enough for me to think in a new way, a clear way, because the voices that had been clouding my mind were far away.

Another student writes similarly regarding "stillness":

My time in Orvieto was where I began to learn the idea of making space in life. In America, with our fast paced and ultra-efficient lifestyle, from pre-packaged processed food to hand-held computers, I often felt that life was an exercise in overlapping and fitting events into the puzzle of my calendar. The transition to a quieter and more contemplative lifestyle was a difficult one. But it began to transform my concept of how spirituality influences life. I learned not to be afraid of stillness. I learned that the spaces in life are as essential as the events, and allow time to appreciate and reflect.

At first glance, I may not see the connection between our program's stated intention of recovering the sacred conversation of the great tradition and the discovery many of our students make about the spaces of silence. But of course all true conversation involves silence: listening, digesting, so far from swapping opinions or from the contemporary rhetoric of mutual affirmation that leaves no one open to change, or from the rapid-fire repartee that marks the dialogue of all our favorite sitcoms.

In sum, I take heart that we are doing something right in our bottega-meets-monasticism program when I receive notes like this one from an alumna several years after her semester abroad, saying, "My time in Orvieto has always been a place in my mind I can return to when I can't seem to keep my priorities straight. I just remember to take a breath and make a space for the divine."

# CHAPTER SIX

# An Intentional Roman Catholic Community

Integrating Faith, Reason, and Service at the Heart of the Church

### DON BRIEL

*Don Briel (Doctorat en Théologie Catholique, Université de Strasbourg) is direc-tor of the Center for Catholic Studies at the University of St. Thomas (Minnesota). In that role, he directs the University's Catholic Studies/Angelicum Program in Rome, a study abroad program affiliated with the Dominican Pontificia Università S. Tommaso d'Aquino (or Angelicum). The sixteen-week semester program is open to St. Thomas students who are majors or minors in Catholic Studies; students from other universities have also participated when space has permitted. In addition to conversational Italian, students take four courses, one taught by the Catholic Studies faculty member-in-residence during the semester, the other three, including a course on art and architecture in Rome and elective courses in theology, philosophy, and classical languages, taught by Angelicum faculty on the University campus overlooking the Roman forum. In 1999 the University of St. Thomas acquired a building on the Tiber River to house their students. The Bernardi residence has provided a number of advantages including the foundation for an intentional residential community where faith, study, and community intersect, one of the primary strengths of the program. The program's central focus on the integration of faith and reason, on the complementarity of rigorous intellectual inquiry and the life of prayer, was inspired by Cardinal Newman's insistence that the work of the college focusing on the formation of student life and the university focusing on critical debate must be drawn into dialectical relation.*

Created in 1993, St. Thomas' Catholic Studies initiative was the first of its kind in the country. There are now more than sixty academic programs in the United States and many others in Europe, South America, Asia, and Africa.[1] They were developed in order to provide an integrated, interdisciplinary account of the complex intellectual and cultural traditions of Catholicism in a variety of historical periods and geographical contexts. St. Thomas' academic department is the largest in the world with three hundred undergraduate and eighty graduate students pursuing degrees in Catholic Studies. The vast majority of undergraduates are double majoring in another field of study, ranging from finance, education, biology, and engineering to art history and political science. In 1996, the University created the Center for Catholic Studies to coordinate the work of the academic department and to develop a series of new programs designed to encourage the exploration of the comprehensive tradition of Catholic thought and culture both on campus and internationally. The Center now coordinates the work of the John A. Ryan Institute for Catholic Social Thought, the Terrence J. Murphy Institute for Catholic Thought, Law and Public Policy, and the Joseph and Edith Habiger Institute for Catholic Leadership. In addition, the Center oversees a number of publications including the quarterly journal, *Logos: A Journal of Catholic Thought and Culture*, a variety of lecture series and faculty development initiatives including week-long faculty summer seminars focusing on topics related to the intersection of faith and culture.

From the beginning students themselves began to develop and organize a variety of extracurricular activities and programs to complement their academic study of Catholic thought and culture. Working with both the center and the department, they sponsored floors in residence halls, Eucharistic adoration, clubs and service projects, a student newsletter, social events, retreats, and men's and women's houses on campus. However, because St. Thomas is largely a commuter campus, it was not initially possible for us to develop fully that residential academic community, which Newman had described as arising from the integral relation of the college and the university. The study abroad program in Rome offered that possibility in a unique way. We sought to create a living community marked by shared faith and academic inquiry, one that would bring into relation a sense of exploration and a sense of pilgrimage. To do so would require that we expand the understanding of the roles of faculty, administrators, and chaplains in order to create something that was, in our experience, unique. What finally made this possible was the choice of Rome.

On a first visit to St. Peter's Square, students immediately recognize the remarkable diversity and multicultural character of the swelling crowds of pilgrims who travel to Rome each year. In addition, because the Church is universal not only in its global governing authority and pastoral concern but also in the international character of the Roman curia, the striking cultural diversity of the clergy, religious and laity working and studying in Roman ecclesiastical institutions, students quickly grasp the comprehensive character of Catholicism's claims. Catholicism is in so many fundamental ways a global religion, and it struck us as essential to provide opportunities for our students to have an encounter with the universal and multicultural reality of the Catholic Church. As a result, from the very beginning of our development of Catholic Studies at St. Thomas, we had in mind an academic program in Rome. We recognized that study abroad programs in general offer a number of benefits, among them the sense of dislocation students inevitably experience in being detached from the familiar routines and habits of American culture, at least opening them to a reconsideration of their basic presuppositions about the nature of the good, the true, and the beautiful. As well, they offer new opportunities to expand the imagination and so to rethink the basic assumptions about the necessary conditions for an authentic and fulfilled life. Because Rome is at the heart of Catholicism, it adds to these general opportunities the specific possibility of immersing oneself in the long tradition of Catholic history, thought, and culture disclosed in singular ways in the city. Students' initial encounter with Rome focuses on two primary experiences: the St. Peter's Scavi tour, in which they are led under the walls of the fourth century Constantinian basilica to the ancient necropolis in which Peter's tomb is located; and tours of the catacombs, where students experience the early life of the Church in Rome, a life marked both by worship and by persecution.

The program provides a unique opportunity for students to trace the entirety of the Christian tradition from the Apostolic era to the present. In their art history course, students explore the remarkable development of Church architecture from its origins in house churches to its dramatic expression in baroque Rome. At the same time, they have the opportunity to gain a larger sense of the Roman church's complex responses to the variety of cultural, intellectual, and political challenges it has faced in its two thousand year history. They visit the tombs not only of Peter and Paul but also of Leo and Gregory the Great, Dominic in Bologna, Francis in Assisi, Catherine of Siena in Rome (and Siena), Ignatius Loyola, and John Paul II. In addition, they have the opportunity to encounter some of the greatest artistic works of the Western tradition. Their study is not, however, merely scientific or antiquarian, for the context of their encounter is that of a dynamic, living religious tradition—one which, as the narrator Charles Ryder in Evelyn Waugh's *Brideshead Revisited* noted, expresses "a coherent philosophic system and intransigent historical claims."[2] As a result, students are invited not only to explore the historical expression and contemporary significance of this tradition but also to deepen their personal and communal participation in it.

In 1996, we began discussions with the Dominican pontifical university of St. Thomas Aquinas in Rome with the goal of creating an affiliated program. We knew that we did not need to create another American campus in Rome. There are already a number of such programs in Rome, many of them quite successful. We saw an opportunity to create a hybrid program that would introduce our students to a pontifical Roman university with a rich history and a distinguished intellectual and spiritual tradition, a program that would draw students from around the world. The Angelicum, named for the Angelic doctor, emerged from the medieval *studium generale* in which Aquinas himself once lived and taught. The Dominican motto, *contemplata aliis tradere*, contemplation for the sake of others, reflects a commitment to bring study and prayer, faith and reason, into integrated expression. Many Angelicum students are priests and seminarians, and in all cases, students are pursuing their courses within a context of vocational discernment.

Because all St. Thomas students in the Catholic Studies/Angelicum program are declared majors or minors in Catholic Studies and thus not only share a commitment to explore Catholic thought and culture in sustained ways but also have in common a set of foundational courses completed before their experience in Rome, there is in place a basis for a community of shared conviction and understanding that is rare in study abroad programs. The program has sought to provide in integrated ways both intellectual and spiritual formation, with an additional emphasis on service during the period of study in Rome. In fact, one might argue that the program incorporates a series of overlapping and interdependent communities animated in complementary ways by the Catholic faith. The first is the comprehensive community of the Catholic Church, now experienced in a deeply universal sense in Rome, overcoming the parochial tendencies to see Catholicism only through an American lens. The second is the academic community of the Angelicum, in which students encounter not only the Dominican tradition but also a different pedagogical style, characterized by a strong emphasis on the value of the lecture and on a concluding oral examination, and a variety of intellectual and cultural expressions of global Catholicism. Finally, there is the residential community at Bernardi, one in which strong friendships are formed and commitments deepened, expanded and challenged. The implications of these mutually interdependent communities of conviction are expressed in the reflections of one of the program alumni, now a priest:

> This visit to the Eternal City, at the end of the Jubilee Year 2000, was a major turning point in my life. The history of the many saints and martyrs, my volunteer work with the Missionaries of Charity, and the example of Pope John Paul II strengthened my willingness to follow the will of God wherever he might lead. However, Rome also made me more realistic. I saw for the first time that the good and the bad, beauty and ugliness, saints and sinners, can coexist and in fact are always mixed together in this world. I also learned to value different cultures and traditions, to enjoy the diversity they offer, and even for brief moments to see the world with other eyes. Most importantly, I learned to question my own culture and to doubt its fondest assumptions. I realized that the Gospel makes demands of nations and cultures, not only of individuals.

This observation, touching on the relations of the universal and the particular, corruption and holiness, in this man's experience of Catholicism and culture was, in large measure, made possible by the structure of the Rome program. The administrative responsibilities for the program are shared by the director of the Center for Catholic Studies, an academic director from the Angelicum, the director of the Bernardi residence, the chaplain, an American Jesuit priest on the faculty of the Gregorian University, and the Catholic Studies faculty member-in-residence each semester. The collaboration, although complex, has resulted in a formation program that is unusually integrated and that allows students fairly wide freedom to explore personally the variety of expressions of Catholicism in Rome.

This is in rather sharp contrast to current models of university education. Many faculty in or out of study abroad programs express significant reluctance to influence directly the character or religious convictions of the students accompanying them. In large measure, this reflects a genuine personal modesty and a clear recognition that a faculty member's principal task is intellectual rather than spiritual. As such, they have neither the training nor the competence to oversee the students' moral formation. Nonetheless, students themselves are increasingly seeking to explore the moral and spiritual implications of their study of the relations of faith and culture, and in particularly interesting ways a new generation of young Christians is doing so with unusual intensity. They seek to share in that *gaudium de veritate* that Pope John Paul II described as one of the chief marks of a university. But it is necessarily the case that such joy in truth requires the need "to unite existentially by intellectual effort two orders of reality that too frequently tend to be placed in opposition as though they were antithetical: the search for truth, and the certainty of already knowing the fount of truth."[3] For this reason, we established a complex process of academic and pastoral formation that draws upon a broad collaboration of faculty, priests, seminarians, and residence life and spiritual directors.

One student, who recently completed a doctorate in history at Penn State, spoke of the ways in which his initial coursework in Catholic Studies had forced him to a more mature encounter with a faith he had begun to question and to a subsequent recognition that "the realities of religion were far more complex than mere mathematical abstractions and logical syllogisms. Thus, understanding faith required far more subtle and profound thought than I had yet done." These words do not, however, demonstrate merely the recognition that the operations of reason are never simply mechanical. Rather, this student is articulating that a tradition must be approached not only as a set of texts or ideas but must, in fact, also be encountered in its living history, in its popular legends and fables, in the lives of its saints, in its art and architecture, in its devotions and in its liturgy. This understanding led to what he calls an intellectual conversion, made possible by the "necessary intellectual tools" provided by Catholic Studies in introducing him to authors such as Aristotle, Augustine, Thomas Aquinas, John Henry Newman, and Christopher Dawson. But then he turned to his experience of Rome and to another kind of conversion, not directly the product of his intellectual reflections but ultimately complementary to it:

By an intellectual conversion I mean to say that over the course of my studies, I had become convinced of certain truths; however, these truths had not taken hold of my life. The intellectual conversion might very possibly have amounted to nothing had it not been for my experience in Rome. In addition to the normal course of studies, the Rome experience brought me into a tightly knit community of students seriously dedicated to the Christian life. There, I underwent intense spiritual prayer, connected to the long history and traditions of Catholicism, formed more fully Christian relationships, and discovered the joy of service while working with the Missionaries of Charity. In brief, in Rome I stopped merely thinking like a Christian and took the first steps toward living like a Christian.

Another student also stressed the importance of what he called the "intentional faith community" he encountered in living in the Bernardi Residence, "not reserving our faith, he said, "as something we do in private but allowing it to shape our daily lives." The five-story Bernardi residence itself was acquired after a year of housing students in a variety of student residences around the city. It contains twenty thousand square feet of living space and includes men's and women's floors, a chapel, a dining room, lounges, a computer lab, a roof top terrace overlooking the dome of St. Peter's and a wide panorama of the city, and an enclosed garden. Bernardi itself would play a major role in creating the residential community essential to the program. Another central aspect of that intentional community is the role played by the faculty member-in-residence. Many faculty members' experience with students is limited to the formal setting of the classroom or to academic advising. As a result, their opportunities for personal exchanges about the relation of life and thought, faith, and reason, rarely occur. But when faculty, and equally importantly their families, live, study, teach, pray, and travel with students over a period of months, different patterns of conversation and relations occur. Their role becomes that of the college tutor rather than the university professor. The same student described this experience in terms of a living tradition that "in the full sense is something that is alive and breathing; the past is treated with honor, but it is handed on to the future critically and consciously, not blindly. A tradition must be full of conversation about what tradition is and means for it to be alive." He spoke of the rhythm of prayer in the house, marked by the liturgy of the hours, the morning Eucharistic adoration at six o'clock and Mass at seven o'clock required for seminarians in the program (but in which many other students participate regularly). Weekly Community night begins with a Holy Hour followed by Mass, a discussion on a current topic related to Catholicism and culture led by seminarians from the North American College, and a formal dinner, often involving a guest, perhaps a diplomat to the Holy See, or the head of a Vatican office, a visiting bishop or a journalist covering Vatican issues in Rome.

A seminarian described his experience as one in which for the first time he understood what it meant to live in a "Catholic community . . . tighter and more united than any I have ever experienced." And he added that "the experience of this community was for me very formative as well; because the community was focused on our Catholic faith, we were able to challenge and encourage one another openly." However, another student noted that "it was important to stress that the 'faith community' stuff in no way excludes normal human life; it is a resounding response to the excesses of our popular culture, but by being more appealing than it."

In the *Idea of a University* and in a variety of other works on education, Cardinal Newman insisted upon the importance of the relations of the University and the College, a relationship that he thought was threatened both by the emergence of the new model of the German research university in the nineteenth century and by the overemphasis on the residential college in the traditional English system. Newman emphasized, "The University is for theology, law, and medicine, for natural history, for physical science, and for the sciences generally and their promulgation. . . ." In contrast, the College "is for the formation of character, intellectual and moral, for the cultivation of the mind, for the improvement of the individual, for the study of literature, for the classics, and those rudimental sciences which strengthen and sharpen the intellect."[4] In other words, the University is committed to the exploration and disputation of various theories and thus embodies what Newman called "the element of advance," or progress, whereas the College, focused on the formation of mind and character of the student, promotes a certain "stability," thus situating students in a living tradition. In a sermon preached while rector of the Catholic University of Ireland in 1856, Newman stressed the university's need to "reunite things which were in the beginning joined together by God, and have been put asunder by man." Insisting that he did not seek to blur the necessary distinctions between one science and another, or between faith and reason, he argued nonetheless "they should be found in the same place, and exemplified in the same persons." It is one of the principal concerns of the university, he said, "to destroy that diversity of centres, which puts everything into confusion by creating a contrariety of influences." A university must be more than a *caravanserei* of ideas and so it is not enough "to have two independent systems, intellectual and religious going at once side by side, by a sort of division of labour, and only accidentally brought together.... It will not satisfy me, if religion is here, and science there, and young men converse with science all day, and lodge with religion in the evening. It is not touching the evil to which these remarks have been directed, if young men eat and drink and sleep in one place, and think in another. I want the same roof to contain both the intellectual and the moral discipline."[5]

In contrast, as Alasdair MacIntyre has noted, contemporary higher education shares the tendency to compartmentalization characteristic of modern culture as a whole and he insisted, with Newman, on the importance of integration not only of thought but also its relation to life. He argued, "In a Catholic university what matters most is the relationship between what is said and done in the classroom or laboratory and what happens at Mass and in the life of prayer."[6] But such integration is particularly difficult to achieve in the increasing specialization of disciplinary perspectives, in the pervasive dissociation of private religion and public secular discourse, in the compartmentalization of student's lives and experience. Here, too, faculty including Christian faculty, hesitate to address the relations between faith and reason or tend to do so only within a sociological or historical context. As a result, the possibility of a more integrated formation of life and thought is simply lost. Nonetheless, MacIntyre argued, universities have an obligation to confront this compartmentalization and to provide sustained opportunities for students to reflect on the choices that confront them. In a recent meeting with the academic community in Prague, Pope Benedict XVI reiterated the importance of this integration in affirming,

> From the time of Plato, education has been not merely the accumulation of knowledge or skills, but *paideia*, human formation in the treasures of an intellectual tradition directed to a virtuous life. While the great universities springing up throughout Europe during the middle ages aimed with confidence at the ideal of a synthesis of all knowledge, it was always in the service of an authentic *humanitas*, the perfection of the individual within the unity of a well ordered society.[7]

This is perhaps singularly difficult to achieve at a time in which those various aspects of university life—academic, spiritual, and residential—have themselves assumed discrete and autonomous areas of influence.

MacIntyre argued that:

> In the past a variety of institutions, both religious and secular, have provided milieus in which individuals and groups were able to stand back from their everyday lives and judge themselves critically by a standard of human goodness external to and independent of those of the various spheres of activity in which they were engaged. And it was one of the works of the Catholic faith, and more especially of Catholic education, to provide within just such milieus an integrative vision of the human and natural orders, as well as the supernatural order, one that could inform not only education, but the subsequent lives of the educated, by providing them with a standard for identifying and criticizing the inadequacies of the social orders that they inhabited.[8]

Such a philosophy of education would be difficult to achieve in complex comprehensive universities such as our own but we thought that it might be possible to develop this kind of integrative formation in a Rome program. In written evaluations, senior exit interviews, and letters, alumni of the program speak of the experience of integration and community as the primary mark of the semester or year in Rome. "It is so obvious here in Rome, if only one has eyes to see it," one student said. He continued:

> In the Vatican Museums you can see the greatest works of art our civilization has ever produced. At the Angelicum you can learn the most profound truths we have ever sought to express. With the Dominicans and Missionaries of Charity, you can witness a path to a life more filled with peace and love than any other. This is what the living tradition of the Church of Rome offers to the youth of the world. This is what I came to Rome to discover more fully.

But in the context of the program, how is this integration achieved? I mentioned the rhythm of prayer in the Bernardi chapel, but students also find their way to local parishes and to any of the hundreds of Roman churches for liturgy and private prayer. In addition, the major feasts of the liturgical year are celebrated with the universal church at St. Peter's and in the long tradition of the forty station churches in Lent. As well, many students join other Angelicum students for Mass at the university chapel. Spiritual direction is required for seminarians in the program as part of their larger formation, but specific though less structured programs of formation are also in place for other students. The chaplain and North American College seminarians arrange a silent retreat on Lake Albano near the papal summer residence, trips to various monastic and religious houses to share in the life of contemplative prayer and active ministry of many Catholic communities, and pilgrimages to Assisi and Siena to encounter the legacy of Francis and Catherine. In addition, they coordinate the service opportunities in Rome principally in one of three local contexts, each of which has significant international expressions: the Missionaries of Charity, founded by Mother Teresa in the slums of Calcutta and now serving the poor in every region of the world, where students serve the needs of the poor in a residence for the elderly near the Circus Maximus; the Little Sisters of the Lamb, a French mendicant community with a house near the Lateran, and the St. Egidio Community, founded by Roman university students to bring to bear Catholic social principles on contemporary political and economic issues, which serves the poor at a soup kitchen near Santa Maria in Trastevere.

The academic program is overseen by the Swiss rector of the Angelicum, Fr. Charles Morerod, O.P. In each semester, students encounter the rich tradition of Rome's art and architecture in a course that has numerous on-site components, including one major weekend trip, in the fall to Bologna and in the spring to Ravenna. The course is taught by Professor Liz Lev, a well-known art historian who is also trained in Catholic theology and serves as a consultant on a number of educational, cultural, and religious programs in Rome. Students are also introduced to the comprehensive tradition of Catholic spirituality in a course taught by the Irish theologian Fr. Paul Murray, O.P., and choose an elective in medieval or modern philosophy, or patristic or fundamental moral theology, the last course taught by the theologian of the papal household, Fr. Wojciech Giertych, O.P. In addition, they take a topics course on some aspect of Catholic thought and culture taught by the Catholic Studies faculty member-in-residence. Courses have included a survey of the development of Roman liturgy, a course on martyrdom, and a survey of modern Roman Catholic history. Students also have the opportunity to continue their study of Greek or Latin, and all students complete a course in conversational Italian.

In a certain sense, I find our study abroad program unusual perhaps principally in its emphasis on the living tradition of Catholic faith and its expression in thought and culture. As a result, the focus tends to be more on the common weight of that tradition than on the individual exploration of its claims. Of course, both aspects are essential and in one sense inseparable, but the modern emphasis on autonomous experience and individual religious searching often makes it difficult to identify the nature and implications of a comprehensive religious and intellectual tradition such as Catholicism. One student spoke of his love of the Catholic intellectual tradition, and his intellectual satisfaction with philosophy since his first encounter with the thought of Thomas Aquinas in high school. But as he noted,

> . . . it is not enough to think about philosophy; one has to live it. To be fully in love with something, one must know it intimately, not abstractly. And, as far as I know, Rome more than anywhere else on Earth not only contains our past but also retains its vibrancy: The Churches and artwork may be centuries old, but the liturgies which take place in them are often full of life. Rome is the Eternal City, and eternity does not mean one second after another for an infinitely long time. Rather, God's eternity is the possession of every moment all at once, unceasingly.
>
> Catching a glimpse of St. Peter's from our rooftop terrace, taking classes at the Angelicum from vibrant Dominican priests and nuns, living with dedicated but fun-loving seminarians—it is clear to me that the present contains the fruits of the past and the seeds of the future. This is a living tradition; this is what I want to be a part of.

At the dedication of the Bernardi Residence, Cardinal Pio Laghi emphasized that Rome itself would be the great teacher in the program, disclosing to students a rich and complex ecclesial history, a long tradition of artistic and architectural creativity, a continuous engagement with culture. Each morning, students begin a forty-minute walk through the center of Rome, crossing the Tiber and moving through Piazza del Popolo, then walking down Via del Babuino past Trinita dei Monti, the column of the Immaculate Conception, Propaganda Fide, the house of Bernini, numerous churches, the Trevi Fountain, the Quirinale, the Gregorian and Biblicum, Trajan's Market, and up the hill to the Angelicum. Each evening they return, either retracing their journey or finding another route through the principal sites of the historic city center.

Chesterton famously argued that it is one of the strengths of tradition to free us from the tyranny of the present by revealing the complexity of historical development and authority. Perhaps nowhere else than in Rome can one sense the full range, diversity and continuity of the Catholic tradition.

The program has had a singular impact on the lives of its students. Alumni of the program have entered major seminaries, religious communities, doctoral programs in a wide variety of fields, schools of medicine, law, business, counseling, and education, and with remarkable consistency, they have indicated that their experience of the program in Rome has shaped their sense of what it means to live and to work within a vibrant and living tradition of faith. Nonetheless, we think that the program does reflect the hope that Pope John Paul II emphasized for a "new flowering of Christian culture in the rich and varied context of our changing times, which certainly face serious challenges but which also bear so much promise under the action of the Spirit of truth and love."[9] The Catholic Studies/Angelicum Program in Rome has become the capstone experience of the Catholic Studies department at St. Thomas.

# PART III

## Coming Face to Face with the Social Other

### Bridging Intercommunal Divides

RONALD J. MORGAN

"There can be no true friends without true enemies. Unless we hate what we are not, we cannot love what we are. These are the old truths we are painfully rediscovering . . ."

—Venetian nationalist demagogue in Michael Dibdin's novel, *Dead Lagoon*

"Ye have heard that it was said, 'Love your neighbor and hate your enemy.' But I tell you: Love your enemies and pray for those who persecute you, that you may be sons of your Father in heaven."

—Matthew 5:43-44

The world Jesus experienced was not very different from our own. In his day, as in our own, segments of the human family often faced off against one another, dividing along lines of nationality, ethnicity, religious affiliation, or political outlook. And yet Jesus called his disciples, then and now, to love and empathize with the cultural other. In the gospels, the practice of intercommunal[1] solidarity is more than a strategic project aimed at making the world a more secure place; it is an imperative of Christian discipleship. For as Jesus himself made clear, it is by loving and forgiving those called "enemies" that we prove ourselves children of God.

On one occasion, a Jewish man asked Jesus to define more precisely the limits of the Second Commandment, "You shall love your neighbor as yourself" (cf. Matt. 5:22, Luke 10:18). In response, Jesus could have emphasized the man's legal and moral obligations to those who shared his bloodline, religious traditions, or patriotic sentiments. Instead, he gave imaginative narrative depth to a spiritual principle laid down in the Sermon on the Mount: "Love your enemies and pray for those who persecute you." In the Kingdom, Jesus reveals, human community transcends socially constructed boundaries. As a consequence, life in the Kingdom requires the formation of meek, pure-hearted, peacemaking agents who love and forgive their enemies as well as their friends.

The story of a Samaritan man acting as neighbor to a Jew is a wellspring of wisdom for twenty-first-century American Christians. It reminds us that the call to outward-looking, intercommunal solidarity is at the very center of Jesus' life and teachings. And as the chapters that follow make clear, intercommunal empathy requires fair-mindedness: one must evaluate or judge the other by the same criteria with which one judges one's home culture. On the one hand, this implies a willingness to give the benefit of the doubt to that which is alien; on the other, it requires honesty about the blind spots and narrow places in one's own cultural outlook.

While the four chapters in Part III differ in terms of the geographic and cultural settings they describe—Mexico, Western Europe, the Middle East, and urban America (San Francisco)—they share the assumption that followers of Christ are called to act as agents of intercommunal solidarity in the world. But as each chapter also makes clear, if graduates of faith-based and church-related universities are to reach across cultural or political divides to build bridges of peace, cooperation, and justice, they must first learn to acknowledge and receive the other. Building a broad, embracing community and nurturing sympathy across social divides is one of the greatest joys of true discipleship. Solidarity with our neighbors creates a more stable place. More importantly, it is something all people need and most people want, to feel safety and joy in the presence of others. We are our brothers' and sisters' keepers, whomever they may be.

# CHAPTER SEVEN

# "With Open Eyes"

Cultivating World Christians through Intercultural Awareness

## LAURA MONTGOMERY AND MARY DOCTER

*And the Word became flesh and
made his dwelling among us . . .*
*—John 1:14*

*Laura M. Montgomery (Ph.D. in Anthropology, Michigan State University) is
professor of anthropology at Westmont College, where she teaches courses on
cultural anthropology, peoples and cultures of Latin America, cross-cultural
communication, gender, and social research methods. Mary Docter (Ph.D. in
Hispanic Languages and Literatures, UCLA) is professor of Spanish at Westmont.
Her courses include Spanish language, Hispanic cultures, and Latin American
literature. Both women conducted their dissertation research in Mexico and
have lived in the country for extended periods of time. With the help of a grant
from the Irvine Foundation, Montgomery and Docter created the Westmont in
Mexico program in 2002, and each has led the program twice thus far.*

*Westmont in Mexico is a hybrid, general education semester-abroad pro-
gram open to all students who have completed at least one semester of college-
level Spanish. Each fall, approximately 12-16 students journey to Querétaro, a
charming colonial city and UNESCO World Heritage Site located three hours
northwest of Mexico City. There, students live with host families and take the
majority of their courses with Mexican professors at the Autonomous University*

of Querétaro. *The Westmont faculty member teaches one integrative seminar to help students process their experience abroad and make connections between their academic work and daily life. They also participate in multiple academic excursions exploring different aspects of Mexican history and culture.*

*Westmont in Mexico's most important feature, however, is its unique three-semester cycle: students take a required orientation course on campus the spring semester prior to departure, an integrative seminar while in Querétaro during the fall, and an optional reentry seminar the following spring, all taught by the Westmont faculty member leading the program. In this chapter, we describe how this "cycle of learning" helps students become interculturally competent world Christians. Basing the program theoretically on Milton Bennett's Developmental Model of Intercultural Sensitivity and theologically on the Incarnation of Christ, we illustrate—with examples from students' writings—the evolution of their growth as they develop the capacity to encounter God in new contexts, to participate in the worldwide Christian church, to enjoy the rich diversity of God's creation, and to share their faith graciously with peoples of other languages and cultures. Moreover, we show how students become increasingly committed to reach out to others with Christ-like humility, empathy, and love.*

## Introduction

The Westmont in Mexico (WIM) program is designed to cultivate "world Christians": individuals who are able to encounter God in new contexts, to participate in the worldwide Christian church, to enjoy the rich diversity of God's creation, and to share their faith graciously with peoples of other languages and cultures. A critical feature of this process is the development of the knowledge, skills, and attitudes necessary to build relationships of mutual respect across cultural boundaries. In particular, this requires training in how to gather information, to recognize the role of culture in human experience, and to cope constructively with the challenges of cultural adjustment. Without this set of skills, students would have limited ability to "incarnate" the Gospel or participate in the worldwide church from a position of discernment, openness, and understanding rather than one of prejudice, fear, and ignorance. As described below, however, this outcome results from a process of increasingly sophisticated conceptions of themselves, other cultures, the church, and their understanding and practice of the Christian faith in relationship to culture. To help students along this journey, we have developed a three-semester program cycle including orientation, in-country, and reentry seminars.

In this chapter we describe this cycle and illustrate some of the pedagogical tools used to facilitate students' growth. In doing so, we draw on examples from student work that highlight the *evolution* of their journeys through this process as they employ their cultural "tools" in ways that deepen their faith and also help them discover and develop their own gifts and virtues. The skills and understanding required for effective cross-cultural communication and adaptation are more than just a body of knowledge to be mastered and recapitulated; they must also be lived and applied in ways that foster ever-maturing competencies. Therefore, we build all of the seminars upon a pedagogy of active learning. This learning proceeds along a trajectory that is often nonlinear and requires a supportive environment where students can risk failure yet develop the necessary resilience to press on.

Theoretically, we have built the WIM program and much of its curriculum upon Milton J. Bennett's Developmental Model of Intercultural Sensitivity (DMIS). For Bennett, intercultural sensitivity refers to "the way people construe cultural difference"; moreover, he continues, "it is assumed that such sensitivity can be described in developmental terms better than as a collection of specific behaviors. In other words, *it is the construction of reality as increasingly capable of accommodating cultural difference that constitutes development.*"[1] An individual's capacity to communicate and function effectively in a cross-cultural setting, then, is a function of the level at which he or she conceptualizes and reacts to cultural difference. The model is comprised of six stages that move from ethnocentrism to ethnorelativism. At the most ethnorelative stage, integration, one is truly bicultural, possessing the ability to shift one's cognitive framework and behavioral patterns as required by the context without a fragmented or inauthentic sense of self. Fundamentally, intercultural sensitivity rests upon the capacity to be empathetic rather than sympathetic: as Bennett notes, sympathy is ego- and ethnocentric in that it only requires us to imagine what we would do if in the other's position, whereas empathy asks us to adopt the viewpoint of the other, to shift our frame of reference from our own to the other's.[2]

This leads to the theological framework that informs the program: the Incarnation of Christ. In particular, we emphasize Christ's model of humility, empathy, and reconciliation. We cultivate these characteristics as we teach students "how" to learn, live, and communicate cross-culturally. In imitation of Christ's humility, we stress the limited nature of our understanding and knowledge and assume the position of learner: listening before speaking. Throughout the program, when students confront uncomfortable situations, we ask them to suspend uninformed judgment, reminding them that while they do not have to accept or embrace a particular cultural practice, they *must* first understand it. Just as Jesus does not redeem us by imagining our human condition but by taking on our human form, we, too, encourage students to take on the perspective of the other and embody empathy. As we do so, more often than not we find ourselves humbled, which moves us away from simplistic notions of what it means to comprehend the other and raises awareness of the many ways in which our lives are not yet fully transformed. Moreover, we often are surprised at the gifts of new insight into our relationship with God and with others that the host culture bestows upon us.

## Orientation

To prepare for their semester abroad in Querétaro, all students must take a semester-long two-unit orientation course taught by the Westmont faculty program leader.[3] The overarching goal of the course is to help students maximize their study abroad experience by preparing them for it intellectually, culturally, emotionally, and spiritually. In particular, we equip them to become interculturally competent individuals: people with the ability to adapt constructively to an unfamiliar cultural environment, to communicate effectively cross-culturally, to build relationships of mutual respect across cultural boundaries, to engage in cultural learning without pre-judgment or use of stereotypes, and to undergo positive reentry and re-integration to the home environment. Ultimately, this course provides the first step toward cultivating world Christians.

To guide how we present course content, we first assess students' intercultural sensitivity using the Intercultural Development Inventory (IDI), based on Bennett's developmental model.[4] Introducing the material at an appropriate level becomes important as beginning too far ahead of the students may result in resistance to new ideas and/or cause them to regress to more ethnocentric stages. In the five years that we have led the program thus far, students have consistently placed in either defense or minimization at the start of the course. In "defense," individuals simplify and/or polarize cultural difference. They tend to see the world in terms of "we" and "they," where "we" are superior and differences are threatening.[5] In "minimization"—a transitional stage between ethnocentrism and ethnorelativism—individuals are no longer threatened by difference; rather they minimize it and emphasize similarity. In the process, however, they tend to assume people from other cultures are basically "like us," and thereby see and judge others in a manner that is heavily distorted by their own cultural assumptions.

To illustrate how these concepts manifest themselves in our students, we'll use time as an example. Students in defense tend to see Mexicans as perennially "late" and are frequently baffled and offended by this "rude" and "disrespectful" behavior. When they move to minimization, their defenses are lowered and they may come to accept and even be comfortable when Mexicans arrive at a later time than expected. Nevertheless, they continue to see Mexicans as "late" (and use that language), for they assume incorrectly that Mexicans and Americans share the same "clock"—where one culture values arriving "on time" and the other is not offended by "being late." In other words, they still judge Mexican behavior *through their own cultural lens*—a monochronic one that conceptualizes time in a linear fashion and as a limited resource, and that values punctuality, detailed schedules, and deadlines. The Mexican, on the other hand, comes from a polychronic culture that constructs time non-linearly, sees it as a more abundant resource, and values relationships over the clock. Students in minimization have yet to fully appreciate that Mexicans are only "late" relative to the American sense of time, not to some universally shared one.[6] Thus, this stage of intercultural sensitivity, though much less threatened by difference, is still self-referential.

While minimization might seem like an attractive position for Christians because it emphasizes our common humanity, it presents multiple pitfalls due to its incomplete grasp of another culture's reality. The assumption that all God's children are like us makes it difficult to communicate effectively with those who have a different worldview, including fellow Christians, and to participate authentically in the worldwide Christian church. Instead, our goal over the three-semester cycle is to move students toward the ethnorelative stages of *acceptance* (where they can recognize cultural difference and its importance in human interaction) and perhaps even *adaptation*, a further stage that involves the ability to use cultural differences and intercultural skills to maximize understanding and relationships with people from other cultures.[7] Returning to our earlier example with time, note how one student reflects upon her maturation and transition from ethnocentrism to a more ethnorelative stage at the end of the orientation:

The most surprising thing I learned about Mexican culture is how differently they manage their time, something I have grown to admire. I used to think that a "slower lifestyle" was unproductive and inefficient. However, I have now come to realize that the polychronic nature in which Mexicans view time is something that is quite wonderful, for it leaves so much more room for building relationships with one another and truly appreciating each moment as an opportunity to become more connected with the world.[8]

In the orientation, therefore, we spend a great deal of time specifically introducing students to the concept of culture and how it shapes human experience, including their own. Through a variety of activities such as readings, simulations, reflective essays, and participant observation assignments, they study and reflect upon the ways different cultures conceptualize the self, responsibility, time, and locus of control. Students also explore different cultural styles of communication, learn to recognize and cope constructively with culture shock, and develop techniques to gather information about the new cultural setting.[9] Of course, all of the specific objectives listed above are designed to help students become more culturally sensitive individuals, more aware and observant of their surroundings, of others, and of themselves. One student describes her increased awareness in this way:

I never knew how deeply one's culture permeated into the choices one makes and the lifestyle one lives, mainly because I was unaware of how many of my own decisions have been dictated by the world around me. . . . What saddens me is that I never thought of most of these things [e.g. my goals in school, family relations, friendships] as cultural because I assumed that, for the most part, this is how things were done all over the world.

The skills and knowledge this student has acquired in the orientation class will help her in any cross-cultural context, whether abroad or at home.

In the final part of the course, we introduce students to specific aspects of Mexican culture in an effort to help them deal with anticipated challenges abroad. For example, we explore such issues as family, social class, gender roles, Catholicism, and patterns of communication, among others. Although most of this work is conceptual and introduced through readings, we illustrate the concepts with examples from our own experiences of living and

working in Mexico and other parts of Latin America. We also link this information to the cultural tools and skills that the course has been developing
throughout the semester. We strategically avoid too great of an emphasis on
cultural details before the semester abroad, as this tends to foster in students
a "recipe" approach that focuses on what to do (or not do) in specific circumstances that they may or may not actually encounter abroad. Instead, we stress
mastering the *principles* of cultural grammar that they can then use to generate responses as appropriate to the free flow of human interaction in any cultural setting, and in Mexico in particular.

Unlike most orientation "programs" or Saturday workshops, we dedicate only a very small portion of the course to providing students with
practical and logistical information about planning their trip and specif-
ics about the WIM program, such as travel arrangements, packing, money
matters, health and safety issues, the academic program, home stays, and
the region itself. Students who have just returned from WIM—and who are
currently participating in the reentry seminar—are invited speakers for this
part of the course and also serve as informal mentors throughout the orientation semester, which provides the returnees an opportunity to model
their skills as world Christians. A final goal of the course is to build community and trust among the participants by providing a supportive environment for students to risk and grow both individually and as a group.
As leaders we attempt to model this by frequently sharing our own experiences of missteps and successes in living abroad. We also provide opportunities throughout the semester for all of us—students and professor—to lead
devotions and share opportunities for thanksgiving as well as requests for
prayer concerning both our lives at Westmont and our upcoming semester
in Querétaro. Additionally, students complete a formal month-long assignment that requires them to "reach out" to two other participants in order to
see the risen Christ in the other.[10]

We assess student growth in the orientation class through their portfo-
lios. Students write approximately twenty short essays, including initial and
final self-assessments. Periodically, we ask students to reread earlier work and
reflect upon their growth. Based upon student work and the IDI results, we
believe that the course goals are consistently met and that a good deal of the
program's success abroad is due to the extensive orientation received before
departure. This assessment is also confirmed by the Mexican on-site coordinator and the students' host families, who frequently comment upon how

smoothly students adjust to their homes, how well-prepared they are upon arrival, and how culturally sensitive they are during their time in Mexico.

Although some students initially complain about the required course—believing an entire semester of orientation to be unnecessary—by the end, they come to see its value. As one student states, "I came into this class thinking that I had learned all I could about culture from my previous trips to Mexico. As this class ends I know now that my understanding was very little and that I have been introduced into a new way of thinking about Mexican people and myself." A common theme in students' final essays involves great personal growth and the ability to see the world differently, with "newly opened eyes": "All I can say to summarize what I have learned this semester is that my eyes have been opened . . . to the culture of my Mexican neighbors, and my eyes have been opened to who the person God created me to be truly is." Many also come to recognize their own, earlier ethnocentrism, and appreciate their growing understanding:

> All the abstract labels and terms have come to life as I have begun to train myself to recognize these cultural differences for what they really are—simply different ways of doing things or thinking of things. There is always a reason behind them, and they are not necessarily better or worse than our methods. Before I often saw these differences as haphazard and sometimes even offensive. Now I can understand the logic behind them, though without always having to embrace them indiscriminately as my own.

As we have seen, by the end of this course students realize that their previous "myopic outlook on the world [was] stretched and broadened" and that the task of becoming a world Christian is complex and challenging.

## "Engaging Cultures": In-Country Seminar

As students travel to Querétaro, Mexico, we continue to build upon the orientation course through an integrative seminar, "Engaging Cultures." Here students are challenged to use their skills to become acquainted with and love "the other," to experience another Christian tradition that is theologically and culturally different from the one in which most of them have been reared, and to consider the ways in which being in this unfamiliar context can deepen their understanding and practice of their faith. We do this through selective readings, careful observations, structured interviews, discussions, journaling, and reflective and analytical essays, all designed to help students continue to ask questions, to delve deeper, and to ultimately find answers or, when this is not possible, to encounter peace amidst the ambiguity. As in the orientation, students compile a portfolio of their written work that we use to evaluate their growth.

It is here, in this seminar, where the program most focuses upon students' faith development in the context of cross-cultural living. For example, as our Protestant, Evangelical students confront different aspects of Mexican Catholicism, they at times struggle to see how God might be honored or even present in this unfamiliar context. During the program, this frequently occurs during the September events of the "Fiesta de la Cruz," in which *concheros—* men, women, and children emulating traditional Aztec dancers—celebrate for three straight days and nights in the downtown city streets and participate in several religious services and other acts of devotion in Querétaro's *Templo de la Santa Cruz,* the Church of the Holy Cross. A veritable cacophony of drum beats reverberate in the narrow, colonial streets lined with banners of the Virgin of Guadalupe, while "floods of Aztec dancers" adorned in elaborate feather headdresses move to their incessant rhythms. During these festivities, we ask students to use their cross-cultural skills—specifically observation and interviews—to understand the meaning of the event for the participants as well as to reflect upon their own, personal responses to the celebrations. One student begins an essay by describing her initial confusion:

> As I stood in the *Templo de la Santa Cruz* I began to feel trapped, as if there were no way out. Directly after my entry into the beautiful and ornate building a string of Aztec dancers followed that seemed to never end, completely blocking the entrance into the structure. For some reason I felt utterly awkward, completely out of my natural environment . . . . The words to the chant, which were uttered at the same moment from each of the dancer's mouths, were to the "Dios" of the Catholic Church, but that seemed to be in contrast with what my eyes were seeing. With the offerings of fruits and grains outside and the dancing that used to take place before sacrifices to the Aztec gods or at religious rituals hundreds of years ago, I felt that something didn't line up.[11]

Here, as the student describes her observations, she demonstrates her uncertainty about the meaning of the unfolding events, her self-awareness of her discomfort, and, as we shall see below, her willingness to suspend pre-judgment. Realizing her ignorance, she continues the assignment by moving from mere observation to data collection and seeks an informant to help her understand what initially "didn't line up":

> Once out of the overcrowded church I was able to find a woman to ask questions about what was going on. During my time with this woman I began to feel more at peace. She explained to me that the reason that she does this year after year is as an offering to God: "It is not an easy thing to dance like this for that long. It is a sacrifice." The reason for her being there was truly to honor the God that she loved in one of the best and most sacred ways that she knew how: through ancient dance.

By gathering more information, the student successfully shifts her frame of reference to one of empathy, wisely realizing that "what [her] eyes were seeing" *initially* was only part of the story, one clouded by her own cultural biases and assumptions. Furthermore, she recognizes in the unfamiliar another way of praising God, believing in the end that God was indeed "honored and glorified" through the actions of the dancers. Finally, she concludes by considering deeper questions of the relationship between faith and culture:

> Is this festival a mixing of cultures and of Gods? Or is it the using of gifts of dance that God has given his people in a way that honors him? I think the answer . . . is a matter of the heart. If the heart of the dancers is for the Lord, then let them dance with zeal in whatever way they feel called. . . . [I]f this makes me uncomfortable then I do not have to take part . . . , but it is not alright for me to stunt other people's worship. . . . The woman that I interviewed knew exactly why she was there, and it was not to honor ancient Aztec gods but the God of Abraham, Isaac and Jacob—the God of the *Templo de la Santa Cruz*.

While expressing a hesitancy to embrace the practice as her own, the student is willing to display humility and to acknowledge that God and the church extend beyond her own cultural practices. She has begun to develop a more profound capacity to be a world Christian.

During their time in Mexico, many students attend Catholic mass with their families, worship at an evangelical church, or participate in the university's Christian fellowship. Though they seek to witness Christ through the ways they live their lives, they become aware that communicating the Gospel effectively in another society requires a cultural and linguistic fluency they are only beginning to acquire. Religious discussions with their host families and Mexican friends also cause them to reexamine their own understandings of Christianity. One student reflects on this in her final week in Querétaro:

> I have also become more aware of the influence . . . of American culture upon the American church and its teachings. Even in something as simple as the emphasis placed upon individuals versus the church body, I can see a bit more clearly now how worldviews and mindsets play an important role in the life and development of the church. . . . I feel more so now than I did before coming to Mexico that I do not have as much of a right to impose my beliefs of right and wrong . . . upon others. That is not to say that I do not believe that there are times when I should and need to speak up, but I feel more strongly now that it's more my place to raise good questions and discuss, rather than argue or push.

In her paper, the student recognizes that culture informs some of our interpretations of basic doctrines. She does not abandon her beliefs but is willing to reconsider her understanding and to assume a more gracious posture when she shares them, another characteristic of the world Christian. Five months later, at the end of the reentry seminar, she writes how "the entire Westmont in Mexico program" was "crucial" in developing and shaping her goals and future plans: to do human rights work in Latin America. Her newfound passion to be "a part of a process that helps to foster greater understanding between Latin America and the United States" illustrates how her participation in the program helped her discover her call to be an agent of reconciliation.

As shown in the quotes above, the program's goal is not to produce uncritical cultural relativists but discerning witnesses who can recognize God's presence and work in other cultural realities, both Christian and not, whose differences can be profound and seemingly unfathomable. For us, an ethnorelative Christian is in a constant state of discernment and is acutely aware of the ways in which our understandings of the Gospel and the Christian life are culturally and historically shaped and limited. We encourage students to ask, "How will being in this new place with people who share different assumptions and behaviors help me comprehend more fully God's presence?" Students often find that this new culture reflects the diversity of the creation that God himself has made and this new understanding gives them much to celebrate, as we saw in the student who attended and took the time to critically investigate and reflect upon the events of the Fiesta de la Cruz. An incarnational Christian also asks, "In this particular cultural context, what does it mean to act Christianly—to be the most faithful witness?" Operating at this level of spiritual maturity usually presupposes the prior capacity to see another culture on its own terms. In the early stages of developing this capacity, students may take on what might be seen as a simplistic notion of "everything is relative." This, however, is part of the process toward a more complex, nuanced, and measured view of cultural relativism: the ethnorelative Christian can recognize multiple ethical systems, appreciates the strengths and weaknesses of them, and carefully considers what it means to act Christianly within the context of a given culture.

Occasionally, however, students do describe a more profound crisis of faith as they discover its cultural contingency. This crisis can be even more attenuated given the normal maturational issues of identity and faith experienced by this age group as they move from late adolescence to adulthood, from espousing their parents' beliefs to possessing their own values. As faculty leaders, we have found it helpful to normalize the process, to create a safe place where these questions can be asked, and to encourage students to embrace the opportunity to reconstruct or reaffirm an authentic, Christian faith.

## Reentry

Because the overseas experience does not end when one returns home—or as one student notes, "while I knew I would change as a person [in Mexico], I did not realize that I would still be in a state of process at the end of the trip"—the WIM sequence concludes with a reentry seminar on campus.[12] Here, through a variety of active learning strategies, students have an opportunity to continue processing the overseas experience, to explore unanswered questions, to deal with the challenges of reentry (including readjusting to the now foreign "familiar"), and to continue reexamining their faith, the church, and the meaning of "loving others" in light of their experience abroad.

Students often express concern that many of the skills or perspectives they gained while in Mexico will fade away; that it will all "seem like a dream," as one student put it. To counteract that fear, we have them develop a personalized "Learning Contract" with a list of academic, personal, and spiritual goals along with specific, dated tasks and activities to meet them. For example, most students desire to maintain their Spanish language skills and accomplish this by committing to read Scripture in Spanish as part of their daily devotions, attending a local Spanish-speaking church, or volunteering in a bilingual school. These activities, however, meet *multiple* goals: while honing their language skills, students also grow in their faith, experience God and Scripture in new ways, and serve the local Latino community.[13] Throughout the semester, students reflect upon their progress both orally and in written essays. Additionally, as part of the class, students prepare an all-campus event in which they formally share with the community what they have learned and how they have grown.

Given the highly stimulating learning environment abroad, the degree of maturation that often outpaces their on-campus peers, and the often painful realities of reverse culture shock, students returning from off-campus programs frequently want to withdraw rather than engage.[14] In the weekly class meetings, they have an opportunity to share openly their struggles with readjustment:

> . . . I realized that there were many relational nuances and not-so-subtle actions that now felt foreign to me: people were short and to the point, . . . were constantly worried about time, and were generally bad listeners. All of these once-natural ways of being were now bothering me, bringing into my conscious awareness the comprehensive scope of the foundational changes within me as a result of my experience abroad.

Note here that in reflecting upon the aspects of home that bother and seem foreign to her, the student actually becomes more aware of her tremendous growth.[15] One goal of WIM, however, is that students not only grow individually as world Christians, but also that they model this in ways that enrich the campus community.

We have seen students achieve this in a variety of ways. Returning students, for example, frequently take leadership roles in Westmont's large student-led ministry in Ensenada, Mexico, where they not only use their linguistic skills but also explain and translate the new cultural context for their peers. Moving beyond the "dos and don'ts," they point out the underlying cultural logic of practices that seem odd or annoying to those with little cross-cultural background and even help avert potentially negative misunderstandings.

Essentially they become cultural interpreters and ambassadors for their fellow students. One student put it this way:

> Loving a culture involves more than just enjoying it while you're there. It includes having a desire to share it, or possibly a burden to open the eyes of people who have not seen or do not understand other cultures. I know now that I have a desire, and a kind of an obligation, to help erase stereotypes and bring respect to Mexicans and their culture in the United States.

Additionally, because of their own challenges of adjustment and readjustment, students express a responsibility to reach out to the other on their own campus. In the process, they influence their peer culture about issues of diversity and cross-cultural sensitivity in subtle and often powerful ways. One of the most significant moments for one WIM group occurred as a result of a series of articles published in the student newspaper following a controversial chapel talk. When a Latino student wrote about the need for greater sensitivity around issues of diversity on campus, two majority students responded with their own highly charged letters, angrily criticizing all minorities for being so "thin skinned" and urging them to "stop victimizing [them]selves." As we read and discussed these letters in the reentry class, WIM students felt the need to get involved. Some decided to write private letters to the hurting Latino student; others wrote public letters to the paper, two of which were published. In one, the "grieved" student asks her peers to resist the temptation to ignore or silence the voices of hurting students and instead invites us all to see our actions empathetically through "the others' eyes." "We owe this to Christ if we claim to be His followers," she pleads, "for it was He, our Lord, who 'made himself nothing, taking the very nature of a servant, being made in *human likeness*. And being found in appearance as a man, he humbled himself' (Phil. 2:7–8)." In this way, she concludes, "Instead of demoralizing one another in our misunderstanding, we need to embrace each other when one of our own body feels disassociated, especially by our own hand."

Another responded with "A Prayer for Help":

> Dear Father, please help me to make sense of all that is going on. Help me to not pass judgment but instead find the root of why people are hurting. Lord, I pray I would not be tempted to follow a path of indifference. Instead I ask that I would be able to listen and interact with people out of love. . . .

> Father, may our eyes be opened so that we may all view each
> other in your light. . . . Lord, please use what has happened so that we
> may better glorify you through respect and love for your diverse cre-
> ation in its entirety. Amen.

Once again, the student asks that "our eyes be opened" to a new way of
seeing, and thereby a new way of acting, one rooted in love, empathy, and
understanding.

Other students in reentry begin to "see" for the first time those previously
"invisible" to them.[16] One semester, a student's Learning Contract included her
organizing a party in the Dining Commons to show appreciation for the staff,
most of whom are Latino. The event was a success: twenty employees joined
the students to speak Spanish, enjoy typical Mexican desserts (prepared by the
students), dance to Latin music, and perhaps most importantly, to share stories. Another student in the course described how she has begun to challenge
her friends—with graciousness and patience—when they make what she now
perceives as racist comments, comments that before her experience in Mexico
she had not recognized as problematic. Like her peers before her during the
chapel incident, she has learned that to wound another is to wound oneself
and, more significantly, Christ. Still another student, who described herself as
too intimidated even to order pizza on the phone prior to her semester abroad,
now actively and publicly lobbies against human trafficking both on campus
and in the larger community.

As we have seen, students come home "with open eyes"—more sensitive
and empathetic to those who are different and with a desire to reach out to the
marginalized with Christ-like love and compassion. As a result of their entire
experience, they return transformed, more mature in their faith and with a
deeper understanding and experience of what it means to be world Christians.
Moreover, they return equipped and committed to transform not only their
campus but also the world around them.

# CHAPTER EIGHT

# Who Is My Neighbor?

## Forming Kingdom People in a World of Conflict

### RONALD J. MORGAN

*Ronald J. Morgan (Ph.D. in Latin American History, UC-Santa Barbara) is Associate Professor of History at Abilene Christian University. Since 2003, he has served as resident director of ACU in Oxford, a program whose General Studies core curriculum was designed for sophomores. ACU in Oxford is an in-house or "island" program: thirty-six students per semester reside in two Victorian houses in North Oxford and take courses taught by resident or visiting ACU faculty members. Students engage with the wider Oxford community through Service Learning in local institutions and involvement in local churches. Each semester, Ron leads a group excursion to the continent, while periodic teaching recesses allow students to travel around Europe on their own.*

*This chapter highlights Morgan's efforts to imbue the program's required International Studies course with values of international and intercommunal solidarity by complementing the study of Europe's conflicted history with theological reflection and experiential learning. Exploring Miroslav Volf's concepts of "distance" and "approach," he analyzes the complementary relationship of theoretical discussions to lived experiences in sacred places like Verdun and Taizé. The chapter concludes with a few reflections on the importance of nurturing hope over cynicism and despair.*

In a dramatic scene from Erich Maria Remarque's famous World War I novel, *All Quiet on the Western Front,* the German soldier-narrator gradually discovers the humanity of the "enemy" soldier he has killed in hand-to-hand combat. Lying next to his victim in a shell-hole, and having felt the convulsions and heard the groans of life ebbing away, Remarque's narrator now addresses the lifeless figure:

> Comrade, I did not want to kill you. If you jumped in here again I would not do it. But you were only an idea to me before, an abstraction that lived in my mind. It was that abstraction I stabbed but now, for the first time, I see you are a man like me. I thought of your hand grenades, of your bayonet, of your rifle; now I see your wife and your face and our fellowship. Forgive me comrade. We always see it too late. Why do they never tell us that you are poor devils like us, that your mothers are just as anxious as ours, and that we have the same fear of death, and the same dying and the same agony—forgive me comrade; how could you be my enemy? If we threw away these rifles and this uniform, you could be my brother....[1]

Rather than a triumphant celebration of good over evil, the moment is one of human grief and regret, as the survivor mourns the loss of the brother he never knew.

---

In the spring semester of 2009, students in Abilene Christian University's ACU in Oxford program explored together what it might mean to live as Kingdom of God people in a world of chronic human conflict, with particular attention to causes of and responses to intercommunal strife.[2] The context for such reflection was my course on International Studies (hereafter INTS 240), a revamped academic course that concluded with a student essay entitled "Who is my neighbor?" The course centered on three elements, each constantly interwoven with the others: (1) readings and discussions on the nature of conflict in the world—national, socioeconomic, political, or religious/denominational—with attention to models for dialogue and mutual understanding; (2) learning-oriented group travel to London (Imperial War Museum) and France (Verdun, Strasbourg, and Taizé); and (3) theological reflection, aided by influential Christian activists and scholars, on topics related to conflict and solidarity in the Kingdom of God. This new departure reflected a deep desire on my part to continually transform INTS 240, as well as the general ethos of the ACU in Oxford program, from "the mere communication of knowledge" to "the cultivation of empathy for the world around us."[3]

It should go without saying that, almost a century after the events described in *All Quiet on the Western Front*, we still live in a world in which mutual distrust and conflict fuel one another, resulting in a vicious cycle of hatred, alienation, and destruction. Yet in going abroad for study and exploration, these students have elected, whether consciously or unconsciously, to consider other visions of the world, other alternatives to the eye-for-eye ethic. What many of them long for is hope. In such a climate, those of us who teach international or global studies in a study abroad setting should help students balance a realistic discernment of global challenges and conflicts with a hopeful, Christ-shaped outlook.

My growing personal convictions as an American Christian living in Europe helped me to completely remake INTS 240 for Spring 2009. For some years, I had become increasingly troubled by how American political and religious discourse seemed to predispose my students to the inevitability (and thus, the justice) of conflict rather than incline them toward efforts at dialogue, mutual comprehension, and intercommunal solidarity. An opportunity to rethink such a worldview arose in 2008 when two colleagues, David Dillman (Political Science) and Paul Morris (Physics and Philosophy), taught an honors colloquium on the ACU campus entitled "Peace." Aware that Dr. Morris would be the visiting professor for the ACU in Oxford program in Spring 2009, I decided the time was right to pursue a related project. The aim of the course was not anti-war, per se. Rather, my fundamental purposes were two-fold. In relation to global studies, my aim was to stimulate critical thinking about the nature of both intercommunal conflict and intercommunal approximation. But as a disciple of Christ intent on forming globally engaged Christians, my goal was to foster in students the sort of introspection and self-awareness that would enable them, both now and throughout their lives, to consciously approach matters of human difference and conflict as followers of Christ who seek to love their "enemies," and not just as Americans.

As the vignette that opened this chapter suggests, positive engagement across tribal lines is part of the humanizing process essential to bridge-building. Yet, as theologian Miroslav Volf discovered not long after his native

Croatia declared its political independence from the former Yugoslavia, "the new Croatia wanted all my love and loyalty; . . . I sensed an unexpressed expectation to explain [to fellow Croats] why as a Croat I still had friends in Serbia and did not talk with disgust about . . . their Byzantine-Orthodox culture."[4] Like Remarque's soldier-narrator, Volf found his freedom to empathize with persons on the other side of the tribal divide constrained by the requirements of ethnic-religious-national loyalties. In response to his dilemma, Volf began "*to place identity and otherness at the center of [his] theological reflection* on social realities."[5] Central to Volf's exploration is the concept of "distance":

> What [Christians] should turn away *from* seems clear: it is captivity to our own culture, coupled so often with blind self-righteousness. But what should we turn *to*? How should we live as Christian communities today faced with the "new tribalism" that is fracturing our societies, separating peoples and cultural groups, and fomenting vicious conflicts? What should be the relation of the churches to the cultures they inhabit? The answer lies, I propose, in cultivating the proper relation between distance from the culture and belonging to it.[6]

For Volf, "Christians take a distance from their own [national, ethnic, even denominational] culture," not out of a sense of cultural self-hate, but "because they give the ultimate allegiance to God and God's promised future." Such distance, he argues, "*creates space in us to receive the other.*"[7] The authors of Chapters 7–10 in this volume, each in our own way, are describing our efforts to awaken students to how carefully self-imposed distance from their native culture(s) can create space in them to receive the other, even when that "other" may belong to a group whom the native culture labels as "enemy."

In Luke 10, the Samaritan "neighbor" displayed such an openness to receive the other. Seeing an injured man, he took pity and "went to him." The narrative, which speaks of approximation, of seeing and of coming near, is a compelling one. But is his action believable? In the social world that Jesus inhabited and described, would a flesh and blood Samaritan have aided an injured Jewish man on a Judean road? After all, just prior to this account in Luke's gospel, a town in Samaria refuses service to Jesus and his disciples because of their ethnicity and religious orientation, a breach of social etiquette for which Jesus' disciples suggest a fiery retaliation (Luke 9:51–55).

What often goes unnoticed in sermons or discussions about the "good" Samaritan is the fact that he makes his inter-ethnic gesture of kindness while traveling at some distance from home, less constrained by the social expectations and tribal doctrines that would certainly have prohibited such goodness. Readers of this passage, which is so central to Jesus' ethic of life in the Kingdom of God, are left to ponder whether the Samaritan's spatial and psychic distance from home is a significant element of the story.

Of course, the experience of what Volf calls "distance" is not an automatic by-product of geographical space between the individual and his home tribe; it is a mindset that must be cultivated. And as David P. Holt will argue in Chapter 9, one virtue that must result from such cultivation is the sort of fair-mindedness that evaluates or judges the other by the same criteria with which one judges one's home culture. On the one hand, this implies a willingness to give the benefit of the doubt to that which is alien; on the other, it requires honesty about the blind spots and narrow places in one's own cultural outlook.

A reading of Lee C. Camp's *Mere Discipleship* challenged my students to confront the sort of cultural Christianity that has formed many of them, a religious culture that often separates the gospel from the real world and worship from ethics, blinded by what Camp calls "Constantinian cataracts."[8] An ethicist and theologian, Camp urges his readers (and my students) to consider how their social location as (mostly) white, middle-class Americans shapes not only their sense of spiritual identity, but also the questions they ask of Scripture. In response to that challenge, my students demonstrated a willingness to confront questions about how the gospel of Christ speaks to human divisions, solidarities, and ultimate allegiances. And because Camp uses narrative illustrations from the American South, as well as from a social and denominational "location" shared by most of my students, they were better able to grapple honestly and introspectively with the possibility that they themselves practice a cultural Christianity (see Holt's further discussion in Chapter 9).

One student acknowledged explicitly that a "perfect storm" resulted when geographic and social distance from home made possible a less inhibited exploration of the sort of deep questions posed by Camp and others:

> [My study abroad experience] has, no doubt, facilitated a new way of seeing the world .... Exposure to the diversity of cultures has [challenged my conceptions of "normative"]. As a Christian, this experience has led me to ask, 'Who am I in this world?" sparking a change in [my] fundamental identity .... Lee Camp led me to think critically about global issues and conflict, such [as] whether Americans think

of themselves as *American* Christians or American *Christians;* and I feel that too often I associate with the former.... Reflecting on Camp's points on citizenship [while] stepping out of my cultural structure and norms has created the perfect storm for radical change in my identity, ... which, in turn, helps me to discover and understand my role in this world.

As the student's reflections suggest, a study abroad pedagogy that approaches global studies through the lenses of Scripture and theological reflection can invite the Christian student to aspire to Volf's "ultimate allegiance to God and God's promised future" as the cornerstone of personal and collective identity.

—————

The cultivation of distance is only part of this process; openness to the other is also required. Such openness is much more attainable for those who develop what Volf calls a "catholic personality," one "enriched by otherness, a personality which is what it is only because multiple others have been reflected in it in a particular way."[9] Such catholic personality requires "catholic" or "ecumenical" community, a point to which I return below.

Yet the world familiar to many American evangelical students is one characterized by parochial rather than catholic personality: many have received very limited exposure to the breadth of the Christian tradition; they have often not listened very intently to political-ideological viewpoints that diverge from their own (or their families'); and many form their social (and virtual) networks around very local "communities" or particular tastes in popular culture. Thus, an important step in their development as globally aware actors entails learning to read and listen widely, practicing what might be termed "open discernment."

To that end, students read an essay by Martin Luther King, Jr., entitled "Pilgrimage to Nonviolence." There the great civil rights leader models Volf's "catholic spirit," describing how he read the work of influential thinkers like Karl Marx "from a dialectical point of view":

In so far as Marx posited a metaphysical materialism, an ethical relativism, and a strangulating totalitarianism, I responded with an unambiguous 'no'; but in so far as he pointed to weaknesses of traditional capitalism, contributed to the growth of a definite self-consciousness in the masses, and challenged the social conscience of the Christian churches, I responded with a definite 'yes.'

By modeling an attitude of "catholic personality," Dr. King helped my students hear voices that would otherwise have remained completely out of their earshot. That they began to read Marx with more open minds was important; that Marx challenged them to think more critically about their Christian notions of social solidarity was invaluable.[10]

As noted above, however, my primary focus for INTS 240 was not so much on socioeconomic analysis, but on alternatives to violent conflict. In that regard, a student who previously would have covered her ears in disgust at such a notion, instead allowed herself to hear new perspectives on military conflict:

> First, one should understand how I used to view war. Having grown up with [family members in the police and military] . . . , it is second nature for me to be pro-war regardless of the circumstances. I did not take into consideration what Jesus has ever said about violence and hate, nor have I thought about how other people see war. . . . I was living in a closed-minded bubble and did not care to understand, or listen to any other opinion that was opposed to mine.

In their written responses to a variety of perspective-stretching readings on nonviolence, war memorials, or U.S.-European relations, students frequently admitted that they would not have considered these new points-of-view had they not stepped outside their normal social location.

## Experiencing Conflict and Embrace

The European context of ACU in Oxford lends depth and realism to any exploration of the related themes of division and rapprochement. Europe's long and painful history of intercommunal conflict—manifested most recently and tragically in two World Wars—has resulted in important contemporary efforts at political and religious bridge building.

Our main group excursion for Spring 2009 took us first to northeast France, where we visited the World War I memorials near Verdun. Visiting war memorials, I hoped, would enrich student understanding of the realities of war, and, following Lee Camp's prompting in *Mere Discipleship*, challenge student assumptions. The ultimate goal was to cultivate in them a desire, as American Christians, to be peacemakers in the world.

The particular choice of Verdun, which was a departure from our past visits to the World War II American beaches sector of Normandy, was strategic as well. In the first place, the case of World War II presents much less ambiguity than does the earlier "Great War." Through film (*Saving Private Ryan*) and television (*Band of Brothers*), the events of Normandy and World War II have become familiar, instilling in American viewers a sense of national pride, and rightly so. But when ACU students confronted World War I, it was much easier to ask "Why?" and to see soldiers (and nations) as victims in an irrational tragedy. Secondly, Verdun was preferable to Normandy in that, in the former case, Americans did not ride in on white horses. Indeed, Verdun was neither an American nor a British experience. This longest battle engagement of World War I, in which around 800,000 died, was fought between the French and German armies. In my estimation, therefore, Verdun was especially worthy of our exploration *because* it was not part of our national narrative. By turning our attention to a Franco-German military tragedy, we could simultaneously care about other peoples' stories while avoiding the self-congratulation that often accompanies the American pilgrimage to Normandy.

Classroom preparation for Verdun included two lectures that highlighted trench warfare and soldier-poets, in addition to readings on military-related themes, violence and non-violence, and the nature of public war memorials. Based on student writings, several articles stand out as particularly provocative. From the point of view of human psychology, Alfie Kohn challenged a growing assumption within American society that human nature is inherently violent. A 1957 sermon by Martin Luther King, Jr., preached in the context of the growing Civil Rights movement, challenged students to reconsider, or maybe to consider for the first time, Christ's teaching about love for enemy. Students were particularly moved by King's call to victims of injustice to see the best in their persecutors. Articles on the French "town that defied the Holocaust," Le Chambon-sur-Lignon, offered students a model of heroic, self-sacrificing actions rooted in Christian faith. Finally, students developed a much more nuanced understanding of the complexity of public war memorials by reading an interview with historian Edward T. Linenthal about the National Air and Space Museum's "ill-fated" exhibit on the atomic bombing of Hiroshima and Nagasaki, an exhibit that featured the Enola Gay aircraft. Linenthal's explanation of tensions that arose between military and veterans groups on the one hand and academic historians on the other, or, as he put it, between the "commemorative" and "historical" voices, helped students recognize the possibility of asking critical questions about war while honoring soldiers who act selflessly and in good faith.[11]

Such preparation made our pre-excursion visit to London's Imperial War Museum especially valuable and soul-searching for students. As a follow-up assignment, students were required to describe three museum displays and reflect on how each affected their understanding of war. Commenting on her selection of video footage by Geoffrey Mullins ("Battle of the Somme)," one student reveals the commemorative-historical tension:

> What effects a person more than seeing men no older than 30 laughing and smiling at the camera right before they march off to die? . . . [T]his [exhibit] reminded me deeply and realistically of all the pain that must have hit all the families of those men. I am so honored to have spent two hours time in this exhibit, time that all the men, of all sides . . . deserve. It was a beautiful thing to experience, but a disturbing one that riles me to want to keep anything like this war from ever happening again.

A week after our visit to the Imperial War Museum, we flew to northeast France, where the war memorials at Verdun certainly merit an unrushed visit. Students walked around the concrete installations at Fort Douaumont, gazed into the Trench of the Bayonets, and viewed stacks of human skeletons at the Ossuaire de Douaumont. Outside the ossuary, they walked among rows of graves for the identified dead and read a 1984 pledge of friendship between Helmut Kohl and François Mitterand, with the sort of "never again" sentiments so often found at such memorials. A student describes her experience of Verdun as "soul-impressing":

> Here I gazed out at a multitude of crosses that marked the deaths of thousands of men who fought in World War I. In the ossuary under the monument were countless bones of unidentified soldiers. The countryside nearby was pockmarked with millions of craters created by shells. I stood outside and remembered all the horrifying statistics I had read in the Imperial War Museum. Everywhere I looked I saw the touch of war, death, and destruction.

But our richest experience at Verdun, at least collectively, occurred in a bomb crater near the destroyed village of Fleury avant Douaumont, one of the nine "disappeared villages" identified in the surrounding countryside. Ninety-odd years earlier, the scene would have been one of horror. Now, surrounded by images of death and rebirth, ACU students and faculty joined in a few moments of corporate worship that mixed lament, judgment, and hope. For the student who saw everywhere "the touch of war, death, and destruction," the implications of sharing the Body and Blood of Christ were obvious:

> Later that day, we all shared communion in what had once been a village before the war began. Ashen hued leaves lay scattered on the ground, and I felt as if the wind that blew the leaves through the air was the breath of a thousand dead men. While we shared communion and talked about our impression of the day, I realized that war has nothing to do with loving your neighbor. God never intended mankind to go to war against each other. God is the giver of peace and reconciliation.

Another student bore witness to how classroom explorations, enhanced by the experiential dimension of a study abroad setting, resulted in holistic, spiritually formative learning:

> Visiting war museums [and] war memorials ... made me realize that war is prevalent in our world today and to consider the repercussions of all of the conflicts.... [R]eading ... on peace and reconciliation has opened my eyes to the method of nonviolence and to the ideals of a country that does not resort to violence as a means of solving problems. Through this educating process, I have been able to consider my thoughts on world conflict through a Christian standpoint and relate it to God's calling.

Leaving Verdun, we drove to the Franco-German border city of Strasbourg, a city that has historically been handed back and forth as a spoil of war, but that now serves as a symbol of European unity. There we visited the headquarters of the Council of Europe, a partner organization of the European Union; students learned about contemporary European efforts to transcend their divided and violent past. The fact that U.S. President Obama was to attend the NATO summit in Strasbourg a few days after our departure impressed upon us all the importance of such international efforts at mutual understanding.

Eventually we arrived in the French region of Burgundy, where our visit to the religious community of Taizé provided a meaningful experience of empathy and solidarity across national, linguistic, and confessional lines. For most of the calendar year, the Taizé community opens its doors weekly to visitors who arrive in small groups or by the coach-load from across Europe.

Volunteers greet these new arrivals in their own language, give them a brief orientation to roles, expectations, and schedules, and show them to lodging that consists, in most cases, of simple bunk-bedded cabins or tents with cots. The day-to-day routine includes community-wide prayers, morning Bible studies led by the brothers, group discussions (by age and language affinity) of those biblical texts, shared meals of simple fare, and service activity, with a little free time sandwiched between.

The Taizé Community has described itself as "a church brought together in diversity,"[12] a phrase full of implications for the formation of empathetic, global-minded disciples of Christ. On the one hand, the phrase points to the hope of unity in diversity, a more-than-skin-deep unity that many American Christian students long to experience. For the brothers of Taizé, who take vows of simplicity, celibacy, and community, this unity is more than a slogan or stated goal; the brothers themselves come from the Greek Orthodox, Roman Catholic, and Protestant ecclesial traditions, as well as from a wide array of national and linguistic origins. Gatherings for shared prayer and worship allow visitors a multi-sensory glimpse of the undivided church. Simple sung prayers rotate among a number of European languages, with French, German, English, and Latin prominent (but Italian, Spanish, and Polish not far behind). The prayers focus on Christ's cross and resurrection, along with life in his Kingdom, values that Christians from all backgrounds are ready to embrace. No spotlight shines on any individual musical or oratory "star"; even the brothers and volunteers who sing the sublime descants are virtually anonymous, seated inconspicuously among the large crowd.

In the conversations and essays that followed our Taizé experience, several ACU students acknowledged the value of joining in worship that was in neither their "style" nor their language. The simplicity of repeated prayers and periods of silence was difficult for some who were more accustomed to activity and movement in their worship gatherings. Yet the sense that the church was gathering in unity transcended issues of style; multi-lingual song gave an immediate sense of blurred boundaries between "us" and "them." As an English-speaking, evangelical American minority group at Taizé, ACU students were able to recognize their outsider status, to acknowledge that the Taizé experience pushed them beyond self-centered preoccupation with their own perceived needs, and to scrutinize the experience from other points of view. And it did not take long for this last principle to take effect. One female student, reflecting on conversations with Parisian high-school girls in a small group setting, observed:

Taizé for me was a realization: I am overly saturated with church in America. Christian education, youth groups, and summer camps have lulled me into thinking the world goes about faith as I do. I was ignorant to the lack of Christian community found in Europe until I heard these girls talking of church back home. They loved Taizé simply because . . . it was a place for them to explore and grow. It was a 1,000-member youth group. I don't think I'll ever forget those conversations. I may forget those words, but I won't forget the significance.

Her face-to-face encounter with European youth, for whom such experiences of spiritual community were rare, reminded this student that she had not journeyed to Taizé in order to meet her own needs.

The "welcome" of open doors, while not a feature we normally associate with monastic communities, is for the brothers of Taizé an essential characteristic of "a church brought together in diversity." As the following student reflection suggests, the inclusive nature of "the undivided church" touches the deeper longings of American students for whom "church" is too often associated with sectarian, racial, or social division:

I . . . really like the concept of Taizé. They invite people from all denominations to join with them and are so connected to each other, accepting others who come to join in worship with them. We all want to feel a sense of belonging wherever we are, whether it is with our family, friends, school, or church. When [Brother] Clement is talking about the Taizé community he states . . . : "[M]any young people say that they 'feel at home' when they find themselves at Taizé. And I must say that I too feel at home in this community which is preparing and anticipating the undivided church." This is a feeling I, personally, want to feel with my church [back] home.

Such hope for Christian unity is particularly poignant for many of our ACU students whose religious heritage has its roots in the Stone-Campbell movement of the nineteenth century.[13] The impulse that first guided that movement—to end sectarian division and unite as Christians around core principles and values—gave way to fence-building that isolated Church of Christ members from the broader Christian landscape. And although that more dogmatic sectarianism is fading, its legacy remains. Until a new generation confronts that legacy head-on, exploring how it came to be while seeking to engage with and love the wider church, the spiritual descendents of Stone and Campbell will play no role in restoring the undivided church.[14] Yet allowed to see an alternative model up close, students begin to feel the dissonance between their aspirations and the practice they know back home, and this in turn allows them to dream of a better way forward.

The pursuit of the principles of diversity and welcome is not simply about becoming a "nicer" church; the goal is that we become a well-rounded, mature, and more Christ-like church. Again, Miroslav Volf's observations on "ecumenical community" are germaine:

> In the battle against evil, especially against the evil in one's own culture, evangelical personality needs *ecumenical community*. . . . The images of communal survival and flourishing our culture feeds us all too easily blur our vision of God's new creation. . . . In order to keep our allegiance to Jesus Christ pure, we need to nurture commitment to the multicultural community of Christian churches. We need to see ourselves and our own understanding of God's future with the eyes of Christians from other cultures, listen to voices of Christians from other cultures so as to make sure that the voice of our culture has not drowned out the voice of Jesus Christ, "the one Word of God."[15]

For ACU students, the visit to Taizé offered a living model in the practice of ecumenical community.

## Practicing Distance, Instilling Hope

Several essays in this collection discuss the need to help students challenge their own cultural assumptions, a process that Miroslav Volf has described as the proper cultivation of "distance." Of course, such an emphasis on discerning one's own cultural identity and distancing oneself from it can lead to a sort of reactionary cynicism, resulting in an uncritical and wholesale devaluing of home and hearth. Indeed, at several stages prior to and during the semester, I recognized that by urging my students "to develop an uneasy conscience and a critical self-consciousness about [their] practices,"[16] I was walking a fine line.

Those seeking to form globally engaged Christians must offset the potential slide into cynicism by offering students an education in hope, one that highlights Christ-like and constructive alternatives for dealing with intercommunal difference and conflict. It requires attention to Christian individuals or communities, past or present—like the Christian community in Le Chambon-sur-Lignon—whose lives render certain biblical doctrines believable for new generations. Such individuals, notes James McClendon, "are the vivifiers, the exemplars ... [whose] lives cry out to us."[17]

The firsthand experiences of tangible models of empathy and bridge-building, like those experienced in Strasbourg and Taizé, will contribute to an education in hope. Indeed, in their experience at Taizé, a number of my students encountered a life-affirming model that inspired them to hopefulness rather than despair. One student found at Taizé an incarnation of what she had always hoped was possible:

> As followers of Jesus Christ we serve a Prince of Peace. It is his teach-
> ing that tells us the best way to deal with injustices and the problems
> of this world: we must love our enemies, for they too are our neigh-
> bors. My visit to Taizé, a [monastic] community in France dedicated
> to peace and reconciliation, showed me how realistically the hope
> to love our enemies can be played out. For centuries religious wars
> have plagued the world, ... but at Taizé ... all are welcome. All hatred
> seemed to fade away while I sat silently inside the sanctuary; peace
> and reconciliation began to seem much more attainable. I had always
> hoped a place like this existed .... By seeking to understand rather
> than turn away [those of] differing religious backgrounds, Taizé has
> been able to build a community based on the teachings of Christ that
> attracts hoards of young people each year.

As another student noted, the experience of worshipping with peoples from every tribe and tongue awoke in her a deep realization of the joy that awaits those who will reach through the linguistic veil: "One must search out his neighbor to experience God as well as express him. God created all, loves all, and is with all. 'Mon voisin est tout, mon voisin est Christ.' 'Mein Nachbar ist alle, ist mein Nachbar Christus.' 'My neighbor is all, my neighbor is Christ.'"

Sadly, the soldier-narrator of *All Quiet on the Western Front* discovers too late that his enemy is "a man like me," a living, breathing, and relational human being. Too late, he recognizes the inadequate, hateful caricatures that nation-alistic propaganda had imposed upon his understanding. Too late, he realizes that by killing his "enemy" he has diminished his own life. For that protagonist, an education in global understanding came too late.

Happily for those seeking to form globally engaged Christians through holistic study abroad experiences, it is not too late to plant the seeds of intercommunal human solidarity. And the soil is fertile; many in this generation of young American Christians are longing to reap a harvest of peace.

# CHAPTER NINE

# Middle Eastern Mirrors for the Children of Empire

### David P. Holt

*Since 2002, David P. Holt has directed the Cairo-based Middle East Studies Program (MESP) for the Council of Christian Colleges and Universities in Washington, D.C. Students take four courses in Islam, Egyptian Arabic, the Arab-Israeli conflict, and the people and cultures of the Middle East. These are complimented by a one-week home stay, nine service project days, and cultural activities before a month-long travel component to places like Turkey, Syria, Lebanon, Jordan, Israel, and select Palestinian areas. In conjunction with site visits throughout Egypt during the semester, students listen to speakers—experts, diplomats, journalists, and religious leaders. More importantly, they engage their local Muslim, Eastern Christian, and Jewish peers in dialogue events that raise the importance of cross-cultural understanding in an increasingly global arena.*

Why care about the Muslim world today? Mainly because Muslims are fellow creatures bearing the same image of the same God, inhabiting the same planet, sharing the same life challenges. But people in the heavily Christian West and the predominantly Muslim Middle East are now at war both literally and culturally, risking a distortion of God's image with mutual suspicion and misunderstanding becoming perhaps two of the greatest casualties.

If Christian witness is something other than the politics of empire or nation, the Muslim world deserves our serious attention. Its people comprise nearly a fifth of the world's population and the second largest religion after Christianity. Geographically, culturally, and religiously diverse, the Muslim *Umma* represents interests, life conditions, and policy preferences that, if neglected or misman- aged, could result in continuous conflict with the West. In this sense, 9/11 is not unique but symptomatic.

Today, it is fair to say that most Westerners view the present conflict with the Muslim world as a result of cultural and religious difference, a default tem- plate allowing them to bundle their impressions of a hugely diverse Muslim world of peoples, states, traditions, beliefs, living conditions, and historical experiences into an oversimplified, undifferentiated mass called Islam. Of course, Muslims return the favor by indiscriminately lumping the Christian world together despite equally vast differences.[1]

The stakes of continued, mutual neglect are high. While misperception and misunderstanding may not be primary causes of conflict, they do obscure common attitudes, values, and interests that, if recognized, may help allevi- ate real sources of tension. For relations to improve in a world increasingly connected by globalizing trends in technology, political economy, and media networks, our mutual peoples need the time, opportunities, and resources to build trust with the help of people to people encounters. And trust only comes with repeated efforts aimed at abiding together. MESP is largely about prepar- ing the groundwork for abiding with our Middle Eastern neighbors as a jour- ney of self-discovery. Is it reasonable to assume that our Muslim friends, for example, can help us on this journey?

## Program Objectives

Allow me to begin with an important caveat that will hopefully clarify the atypical, sometimes confrontational tone that occasionally follows. My time as director of the program began with the American invasions of Iraq and Afghanistan. Rightly or wrongly, the consequences of these operations inflamed the whole region against the U.S. from the Levant to the Gulf and beyond, fueling instability and low-level conflict between Israel and her vari- ous neighbors, Syria, Lebanon, and the Palestinians. As a result, student expe- riences with the locals have never been isolated from the reaction of the Arab-Muslim street—riots, demonstrations, protests, official and unofficial accusations, aggressive diplomacy, violence, suspicion of American influence and presence, religiously inspired anti-American rhetoric, etc.— understandable responses that clearly cast a shadow on MESP encounters with the locals. Whether walking the overcrowded streets of Cairo, the labyrinth souks of Istanbul, Damascus, or Jerusalem, or the reconstructed beauty of downtown Beirut after fifteen years of civil war, MESP students have confronted local opinion expressing a range of opposition directed, not at them personally, but certainly at their religion and politics. Partly for this reason, MESP staff and students have labored patiently in defensive mode for several years, rebuilding trust with our Muslim friends in order to dampen the climate of suspicion caused by the onset of war in the region. And we could never have done this by arranging peer encounters that ignored the ongoing war of words and deeds at the root of Muslim relations with the West today.

Combined with personal influences like education, instinct, and temperament, these realities rightly or wrongly led me to ground the program in a focus on religion and politics. However controversial or confrontational the subject matter, I would seek to follow a middle path guiding our immersion activities with the locals bounded on both sides by several overarching principles that I hope promote more rather than less candor, deeper rather than more superficial relationships. In no particular order, I ask my students to be willing to:

- Acknowledge the problem—Our mutual peoples are at war both literally and culturally. No need to ignore the obvious. Begin with where people are and move forward as much as possible.[2]
- Learn to live in the grey zone—Endeavor to live out the implications of Paul's remark "now we see through a glass dimly." Find a middle path between dogmatism and skepticism that represents the humility necessary to deal with so much complexity.[3]
- Listen rather than talk—Instead of viewing this as an unfair gag rule violating the "equal time" principle, sacrifice it for another idea— namely, "I don't care what you know (or who you are) unless I know that you care"—that seems better suited to building trust necessary for more honest exchanges in the future.
- Avoid spiritualizing conflict—Do not rationalize the Christian use of violence, past or present, in a way that denies either the horrors of war or the complicity of Christian faith and follower in the carnage, however directly or indirectly. Think seriously about how

and why violence fits into God's moral economy, and be willing to confront the spiritual and practical implications of your ideas, avoiding "spectator" extremes like cheap grace talk of non-resistance on the one hand or fatalistic talk of the war as necessity on the other.[4]

- Value culture as a means of dignifying people—Don't over- or under-identify with the locals or the home front, since fixed commitments to a particular culture inevitably distort biblical admonitions calling you to remain travelers, literally or figuratively speaking, ever ready to distance yourself from unholy alliances and entanglements. Even so, the Good Samaritan model, calling you to fully engage the stranger in need, may test your ability to find a balance between over- and under-identification.[5]

- Compare with caution and empathy—Be wary of superficial comparisons that offer easy answers to complex questions. Be willing to acknowledge both difference and similarity. Avoid "denial strategies" like political correctness that embrace the other uncritically or willful denial and denigration that exclude them indiscriminately. Above all, first get your own story right.[6]

- Work out your own salvation with fear and trembling, leaving faith integration for the home front—Struggle with the "examined life" and its potential for disorientation and dissonance. Be willing to find a new equilibrium back at home without the need to tie up loose ends in Cairo.[7]

These principles are crucial in part because MESP is really not about the Middle East. While it facilitates and encourages students to cultivate local friendships, learn the local language, and appreciate much about the culture and people of the Middle East, the main objective of the program is to use the people and culture as a mirror allowing students to better reflect on their own culture, values, identities, and preferences. To be consistent, I hope to serve our Muslim hosts (or Eastern Christian hosts, or Israeli-Jewish hosts) in similar ways by creating a safe space for them to use our program as a mirror, and by providing opportunities for dialogue and relationship in which they also can identify and voice (self) critical reflection upon cultural, religious, and political values in ways that can only be enhanced by the sobering effects of contact with the alien, the stranger, even the enemy![8]

I am hardly original in proposing a thesis echoed by many essays in this collection that cross-cultural encounters provide one of the best ways to facilitate self-understanding, and that self-understanding in turn is a prerequisite for knowing the other. In part because self-understanding is obscured by culture, by a web of social and political obligations that shape our behavior and thinking from birth, cross-cultural encounters offer a kind of detour through and around the web.

These principles will become clearer as I discuss other program logos below, but they are all variations on the selected themes already mentioned. The "Program Notes" section describes the components of MESP. Intended for more than descriptive purposes, the discussion allows the reader to judge the compatibility of program objectives with program structure. The next section "Thyself and Other" covers important issues related to method or pedagogy, followed by "The Dialogue Encounter as Comparative Religion and Politics" section that attempts to link activities like dialogue events with the process of self-reflection. I conclude with some tentative remarks about the importance of MESP as an instrument of cross-cultural education.

## Program Notes

Students take four courses—*Islam, Egyptian Arabic, the Arab-Israeli Conflict and Change*, and the *Peoples and Culture of the Middle East*. While most Muslim women in Cairo wear the veil these days, I selected a non-veiled, Sufi oriented, female expert on Islamic art and architecture to teach the Islam course on site in Cairo for about nine weeks.[9] There are always tradeoffs and constraints when teaching another religion. While I like the fact that students experience learning from a local Muslim, their perspectives are still limited—by ideology, age, gender, experience, attitudes, and more— as they learn about a complex religious civilization. As a result, I ask students to withhold judgment about Islam while in the Middle East before doing much needed additional reading back in the U.S.[10] I try to remedy these limitations by using readings, speakers, films, or site visits on off-days that cover alternative perspectives and practices. One of the best remedies, of course, is student experience on the street witnessing gaps between the vastly different worlds of orthodox and popular Islam.

Cairo provides a rich language-learning lab for Arabic. Four days a week, local instructors teach students Egyptian dialect, which is understood by most

Arabic speakers in the region. While few students master enough of the language to communicate effectively with the locals, the language component achieves two main goals. The first is to show respect for the local culture and religion (How often do Cairo taxi drivers follow up questions about what I do for work with the question, "What do you think of Islam?"), while the second attempts to pique student interest as a means of promoting further study in the U.S. or the region after graduation.

As director, I also facilitate two other courses—*Peoples and Cultures of the Middle East* and *Conflict and Change* (the Arab-Israeli conflict). Speakers, readings, encounters with student groups, site visits, films, and country briefings all examine the maze of human complexity that make up the modern Middle East. Courses are supplemented by a one-week home stay; nine days of service project commitment; a cultural activities option[11]; and finally, numerous encounters with Muslim, Eastern Christian, and Jewish peers in Cairo and other countries. In part because of a busy MESP travel schedule, formal cohort spirituality usually means student-led devotionals four days a week, along with occasional meetings on the road, unless students have time to visit one of the many options in Cairo with local friends —Eastern Orthodox, Catholic, Anglican, Evangelical, even Muslim.

For MESP, home stays dovetail nicely with one of the region's cultural strengths, the ethic of hospitality. But unlike programs that use these as a primary means of housing, language, and cultural learning, MESP has had to calibrate its expectations for reasons somewhat self-imposed. For example, I sought out Muslim and Christian families that represent something closer to the more common profile of Egypt, religiously conservative and lower income from neighborhoods like Imbaba and Garbage City, a decision meant to avoid warehousing students with upper middle class, English speaking families very much like them.[12]

My decision makes arranging home stays more difficult. Media-generated local attitudes toward Western foreigners as immoral and immodest, views not altogether unjustified, lead more conservative Muslim families to hesitate before welcoming a student in the home overnight. The same families harbor a culturally embedded even if plausible suspicion of Christian interest in Islam as missionary in nature, a view reinforced by the political climate. Additional modesty barriers exist even after reassuring families of the strict MESP behavioral code. Young male guests are understandably unwelcome in many households that include veiled mothers and daughters, especially with males of the family working or absent during the day. Female guests face discretionary issues regarding how they conduct themselves in the presence of males in the family. And try as we might to match students with families that have at least one English-speaking peer, communication remains a central problem. These factors along with the usual difficulties matching personalities in a cross-cultural setting often results in a high turnover of families.

In sum, the success of home stays depends very much on a combination of luck, student initiative and flexibility, and generosity from a select number of Muslim friends of MESP who act as intermediaries in a culture otherwise well-defined by clearly marked boundaries separating Muslim and Christian. Despite the many rich friendships developed during this week and the opportunity for students to experience the culture, hospitality, and rhythm of daily life in Cairo, the home stay experience is one of the most uneven at MESP.

However, these shortcomings are offset by other opportunities. MESP begins the semester with a *Culture and Language Exchange*—for example, an opportunity for students to meet a Muslim or Coptic Christian individual willing to exchange emails and meet at least once per week for social activities or simple conversation with no boundaries other than mutual respect.[13]

The service-learning component is another way students connect with the locals. Presently the program offers English language teaching to Sudanese refugees and local Egyptians, a prison visitation ministry, elderly home care, a day care center, and an orphanage assignment in Garbage City involving baby care, the elderly, and the severely handicapped. If student experiences differ in quality and intensity, each location nonetheless provides them with access to people and parts of the city that help the immersion process. Using his experience at the *Sisters of Charity* Orphanage in Garbage City, one student returned after graduation to found his own NGO working with shelters and street children.

Service-learning offers a kind of on-site clinic in the study of human development. Observing so many resource and skill deficiencies faced by Egyptian care providers, for example, allows students to consider the weighty investment—educational, emotional, financial, linguistic, and cultural—necessary to effect change as a cultural outsider. One former student particularly gifted at language and cultural learning while on the program, for example, rejected offers to return to Egypt in order to work on development issues in favor of working to reduce the dropout rate of Hispanic youth in Texas. In her view, she had more personal and cultural resources to effect change at home.

While I always hope that program elements like service-learning will encourage students to return as alums, these kinds of teaching moments signal maturity worth celebrating.[14]

Despite all the intense activities mentioned above, students barely have time to absorb the lessons of interaction with the people, culture, language, and religion before departing the region. How then do we achieve our central aim of using the Middle East as a mirror of self-understanding?

## Thyself and Other

As the director of MESP, I encourage students to approach the people, culture, and the religion of the Middle East as a mirror into the sources of self as well as other. In an important sense already mentioned, the semester is not mainly about the Middle East, since many students will not remember most of the "stuff" we cram their heads with before leaving Cairo, nor will most return to the region any time soon. Instead, the local people and culture force them to examine themselves more closely. As a minority community in the midst of a dominant Muslim society that does not accept their worldviews and values without qualification, if at all, MESP students bear the burden of explanation and justification for ideas, beliefs, and practices they have seldom scrutinized as carefully.

I intentionally chose not to privilege student claims of Christian identity or the language of faith that flows so easily from a life of habit, indoctrination, and worship. Instead, I ask students to demonstrate their faith in relationship with both colleagues and local hosts. Because students come with widely differing ideas, experiences, and education in Christian faith, the burden of proving the substance of faith, especially in a cross-cultural setting, can be daunting. They may even be less encouraged after encounters with Muslim, Eastern Christian, and Israeli Jews who all seem content to remain in the community of their birth, another way of reminding students that if they were born in Egypt for example, they would likely be Muslim today.

This non-privileged approach can be disturbing. Hearing about the experience of a few returning students who struggled with faith issues, one student asked, "Is it true that when students come to MESP, they lose their faith?" Based on my fourteen semesters at MESP, I usually answer such questions by saying something like, "Yes, many do lose the faith they come with. But they typically realize that what they lost was not faith as much as some cultural substitute that they replaced with something better."

My instructional approach has its roots in reading political philosophy where I first saw the mirror of self and other reflected in a series of tensions between alternating elements like faith, reason, politics, civil religion, the foreigner, and competing moral visions of the good. From political philosophers, I learned that most individuals live in tension not only with the foreigner, but also with their own primary group—family, extended family, local community, city, state, nation, or empire—over how the good should be understood and shared.

When Aristotle describes man as a "political animal," for example, he captures a powerful truth about the human condition. As creatures of the herd, we are nested in a web of social and political obligations from birth that often predetermines our menu of preferences, values, and ways of thinking. This web of obligations naturally limits our capacity for [self] understanding, like the humans portrayed in Plato's analogy of the cave who, because they are in chains (presumably understood as obligations to the group), interpret the shadows accessible to them as reality. Plato's *Apology of Socrates,* recounting the execution of Socrates for corrupting youth with false teaching about the gods, models another human dilemma by reminding us that open talk about the sacred can be dangerous for citizens who publicly question official versions of truth about God. As director, I am constantly asking MESP students to examine the extent to which their own web of obligations shapes the most important ideas and values they cherish. Can they distinguish true Christian identity and obligation from other identities and commitments nested in the web?

Such questions beg comparative thinking in a disciplined manner. My own training in comparative politics taught me the difficulty of making fair, careful, cross-cultural comparisons in the realm of ideas, values, and material realities. The most careful scholars looking at the same data often disagree about the influence of culture on thinking and behavior, especially when compared to competing material influences of many kinds—economic, geographic, ecological, etc. If well-trained analysts have trouble determining the causes of values and social realities, can one expect students newly arrived in Cairo to make responsible street-level comparisons, for example, of causes for attitudes, religious beliefs, social conditions, and material realities?

Expressed differently, can they see how and why they are who they are and value what they value, and by extension, apply the same rules of analysis to their Muslim, Eastern Christian, and Jewish hosts in a fair manner? How can they claim superior values or spirituality to their Muslim peers if they are simply creatures determined by the cradle, so to speak? How can they know what "Christian" means if the term is not disentangled from other elements of culture, tradition, and history that have diluted, distorted, and polluted its core message over the centuries? Yet even if students cannot fully disentangle the "situated self" from the Christian believer, they are nonetheless obliged to explore what kind of selves they need to be in order to live in harmony with others.[15]

Students cannot do this by comparing apples and oranges. Hugh Goddard, one of few Westerners steeped in the historical nuances of Muslim-Christian relations, writes that Christians "are adept at comparing the wonderful ideals of the Christian faith with the painful realities of Islamic societies, and Muslims are equally expert at highlighting the obvious problems in societies influenced by the Christian faith while pointing to never-implemented Islamic ideals as the solution to these problems."[16]

The apple-orange fallacy, disseminating half-truths and propaganda in time of war, is especially relevant to Muslim relations with the West, since few issues resonate so strongly today as the charge that Islam promotes and endorses violence more than other religions.[17] It is a view reinforced by a constant barrage of violent media images as well as exegesis by Western critics using any number of Islamic sources in a selective, distorted manner wholly out of context. Precisely because students will continue to face such apple-orange comparisons on the home front for many years to come, I am compelled to unpack these same negative images and sources in a nuanced, careful manner. This usually means avoiding polar imposters like political correctness on the one hand that muzzle honest discussion about the harmful role that religion plays in mobilizing violence, and on the other hand, dogmatic allegiance that sees, hears, or speaks no evil about one's own religion.[18]

One way to avoid the apple-orange fallacy is by noticing commonalities of the human condition. Ideally, I want students to see Muslim counterparts as fellow creatures similarly nested in a web of obligations that both enables and constrains their respective life chances. I want them to see how the "comforts of home," like popular religion or patriotism, for example—otherwise important sources of stability in a world subject to turbulent change—may just as often reflect nothing more than conventional pieties and sacred histories intended to serve the interests of the state and organized religion. Conceived in this way, the comforts of home may not only inhibit direct encounters with other citizens (our Muslim hosts) located at the distant ramparts of a shrinking globe, but with a living God as well.

Deconstructing self and other is a comparative foundation for MESP encounters with the locals. It is right and responsible for students to consider, for example, that as guardians of the city and its morality, our fathers and mothers may be and often are wrong; that thinking and behavior are often a product of influences derived from country, culture, and context; that necessity and interest, however conceived, often drive individual and state behavior as much as or more than ideals or values; that religion, even if functionally therapeutic for individuals and societies, is mainly myth, often morally neutral, intellectually bland, and easily subject to political manipulation and mass mobilization; and further, that religion may be both a source of collective evil as well as the beautiful, the sublime, and the good. These are core even if banal truths that complicate access to a living God. And while God may surely transform whole lives in an instant, most of us, if we are fortunate, will only find true faith after purging in a refiner's fire that strips away, or at least exposes, the dross of worldly interest and ambition.

Ideally for MESP students, refining begins with at least two moral imperatives. First, they should try to understand how the human and material conditions of their lives influence, motivate, sustain, even threaten their personal identities, moral senses, and material interests. Second, using the empathic principle, they should apply the results of their reflections to their Muslim, Eastern Christian, and Jewish hosts, observing how similar processes might lead them to form alternative worldviews equally constricted by a nest of compelling obligations. For MESP, this is the beginning of a journey exploring self and other as a means of reconstructing genuine Christian faith otherwise obscured by competing obligations borne of necessity and the demands of the group.

Given the potential for conflict and controversy within the context of an intense semester, my role as a balanced facilitator must be intentional. I realize, for example, that students come to Cairo representing a spectrum of views that keep them engaged in debates, disagreements, and disputes. While I don't wish to fix this by imposing a false unity on the group, *I need devices that build common purpose, since most of the learning will occur as a result of interaction between members of the cohort rather than as a direct result of lectures.*

One important bonding agent and common denominator of purpose is the rules covenant. Much like any cross-cultural exercise, I use it to encourage a humble, adaptive posture vis-à-vis the local culture. For students and staff, it means compliance with more behavioral rules than exist for most study abroad programs—curfews, conservative dress, no dating, no exclusive cross-gender relationships, no public displays of affection, no smoking or drinking, to name a few. For reasons that will become evident below, I view the covenant as the price of entry to the semester, since any relationships or encounters between students and locals carry the MESP banner with it. If I am occasionally frustrated by local tendencies to negatively view individual student behaviors as collective American traits, I also recognize that the reverse also happens when students observe culturally sensitive norms that enhance the reputation of their nation, their families, and their religion. In the repeated words of our local Muslim grocer and his sons (referring especially to our female students), "Your students are very honorable, respectable people."

Aside from cultivating a respect for the people and culture, the rules covenant also acts as a thermometer of student attitudes toward moral relativism. Each semester MESP encounters a few rule-breakers, for example, who justify their non-compliance with reference to campus covenants that are apparently nothing more than "don't ask, don't tell" agreements, where each party agrees *de facto* to treat the contract as loosely binding if at all.

In an American context, such attitudes may signal an entirely legitimate change in moral reasoning among Evangelical Christian youth generally, reflecting a sincere desire for Christian faith less concerned with rules (law) and more with deeds (spirit). While such reasoning draws harsh criticism for its apparent imperviousness to shame not to mention its arguable, non-traditional theological hermeneutic, such criticism does not capture the ambivalence that characterizes student opinion. More often than not, students both (1) question traditional moral and behavioral expectations reflected in the rules covenant and (2) understand non-compliance as an ethical lapse threatening the integrity and short-term goals of the group, which include long-term access to individuals as well as institutions in the region. However incompatible these views may seem to some, they indicate a common-sense awareness on the part of students that like them, their Muslim peers (or Eastern Christian or Jewish) also live with the tension between willing spirits and weak flesh. Indeed, one of the commonalities our Muslim counterparts share with our students is a tendency to bend or break the rules not so much as an act of rebellion but as a protest against compliance for the sake of tradition. The real tension for some MESP students under covenant is to comply even while sensing a false standard imposed from both sides of the fence dividing cultures.

In the end, the point of difficulties with covenant compliance may not be to hammer students with a false standard of condemnation. Instead, such challenges should (1) signal the difficulties of compliance with moral boundaries in a cross-cultural setting, (2) serve as catalysts for exploring the degree to which covenant commitments on the home front reflect values arguably representative of true Christian faith, and perhaps most importantly, (3) prompt reflection on the tension between civil religious values like individualism and freedom, and *incarnational* values like personal sacrifice for the sake of others.[19]

Because disagreement, dissonance, and disorientation comprise so much of the MESP experience, I introduce students to a number of additional perspectives we seek to apply during our time in the region. In keeping with a concern for fairness, for example, I attempt to model this by *teaching left to the right and right to the left*. In practical terms, this means selectively pointing students in unexpected directions with alternative facts and perspectives that, even if arguable, serve as a check and balance against complacency, lucky guesses, or prejudice. Whether students defend or criticize Israel for its occupation of Palestinians; whether they blame Islam or the West for problems in the region; whether they advocate Just War theory or biblical nonresistance as models for dealing with violence as an instrument of statecraft; whether they support U.S. policies in the region or not; whether they have a big or small tent of inclusion regarding God's saving grace toward cultural others—in all these things, my main concern is to create opportunities for them to hear opposing views and alternative facts.

While students sometimes interpret this approach as waffling or moral indifference, I view it as a veritable summons to humility, a perfect match for the overwhelming complexity of the region and its subject matter—moral, political, and cultural. Clearly, answers to questions about salvation boundaries, attitudes toward Islam, or praise and blame in the Israeli-Palestinian conflict for example, require more time and depth of study than the program allows. The important thing in my view is that students use all available resources and experiences, especially a combination of cohort collegiality and tension in processing what they are learning, as a catalyst for whatever transformation occurs during and after the semester. All of these facilitate the goal of teaching students how to think, not what to think.

Cohort learning reinforces the principle of iron sharpening iron, one of the greatest acts of service students offer one another. Since they represent a spectrum of religious and political views, I ask them to jointly fly a MESP banner that reads, *empathy and understanding is not equal to agreement.* In order to reduce the risk of a costly, self-imposed gag rule that often results from student efforts to avoid controversy in favor of getting along, the principle instead authorizes a semester-long truce in a no-man's-land where doubt, uncertainty, and disagreement over religious and political truth are permitted even if momentarily, allowing students to engage both the locals and one another on safe ground. It quickly becomes apparent to students that the semester is less about arguing with the locals than with MESP colleagues about their own culture, identity, and faith.

In general, humility is an indispensable aid to cohort learning, particularly in the face of judgments about the other, whether Christian colleague or Middle Eastern host. If the self is a product of complex, numerous causes not easily understood in ideal terms of piety or rationality, students are obliged to respect both colleagues and locals as similar bundles of complexity. In part because humility acknowledges relative ignorance regarding so many comforts of home—namely, various truths about God, spirituality, and justice—it often serves to leaven the whole lump of learning during the semester. Even if only a temporary posture, humility is necessary if students wish to bridge what I describe as one of life's enduring chasms, namely, the discrepancy between the certainty, confidence, and boldness of faith many students bring to Cairo on the one hand, and their relative lack of knowledge and experience with faith on the other. If student judgments about things religious and political come partly through the lens of faith, the role of humility in sifting fact from fiction becomes central to the process of cohort learning.

## The Dialogue Encounter as Comparative Religion and Politics

As products of culture, MESP students naturally come to Cairo with a lot of baggage stuffed with the weight of obligation to faith, family, community, nation, and empire. From the time they hit the ground, they notice differences that beg explanation and justification, engaging in comparison by default. Since comparisons inevitably involve moral judgments, consciously or not, important warnings are issued against hasty assumptions and conclusions. Much of the semester is an ongoing exercise in alternately analyzing, judging, embracing, or rejecting both self and other, struggling to find a workable balance.

Perhaps the most effective way this happens is through peer encounters with the locals—Egyptian Muslims and Coptic Christians, Turkish Muslims, Muslim and Christian Palestinians, Lebanese Palestinians, and Israeli Jews. These encounters are often unequal and differently motivated. While predictable motives for cultural exchange and friendship often drive these events, the mere presence of American Christians in the present climate makes it hard for the locals not to harbor suspicions of American hegemony or missionary activity, especially in a global arena where American power already influences their daily lives in ways they cannot control. Fortunately, local skepticism eventually yields to other motives like the desire for showing hospitality, discovering commonalities, and finding friendship as an expression of faith—Muslim, Eastern Christian, or Jewish. When such encounters go as well as expected, students and their hosts may experience what I call a "diplomacy of tears," heartfelt expressions of mutual empathy, understanding, and emotional solidarity.

In order to enhance empathic sensibility among students, I begin the semester by using the phrase "children of empire" as a conceptual tool meant to help students appreciate the unequal nature of exchanges with the locals. While it appears to be a departure from my stated goal of neutrality, the phrase serves an important purpose by provoking students to see themselves within rather than above the maelstrom of conflict and controversy they so frequently discuss during the semester.

How does it accomplish this? First, the phrase is not intended to "kick America first," blaming the U.S. or great power status generally for everything bad in the world. Rather, it aims to sensitize MESP students to the fact that they come to the negotiating table safe and secure in their personal well-being and property in part due to the immense warfare, killing, displacement, ethnic cleansing, and territorial expansion previously achieved on their behalf by their forefathers, so to speak, deeds that inevitably accompany the emergence of all great civilizations, including America. Of course they are free riding on the foul fruits of empire rather than perpetrating its evils directly. But this is poor consolation in the face of evidence exposing their own role as active citizens discussing, debating, formulating, promoting, or abstaining from policies that may alternately assist or destroy whole communities.

For MESP students the message is clear—even as they decry peoples in the Middle East for using violence in defense of nation, religion, or even tribe, their own hands are not clean! In drawing attention to this reality, the phrase arguably does nothing more than evoke centuries of Christian commentary describing the struggle to live out Christian ideals in a world of competing attractions, commitments, and obligations derived from the group.[20] Even if students absorb the meaning of the phrase differently, the aim is to help them see themselves in the mirror when they point a critical finger at their Muslim, Eastern Christian, or Jewish counterparts for complicity in violence. More than anything, I want students to avoid cheap talk about peace and reconciliation before examining what this means in the lives of real people in context, including Middle Eastern Christians.[21] In my experience, this phrase has facilitated as much serious internal dissonance and debate among MESP colleagues as any thinking exercise they do.[22]

Given the nature of Muslim relations with the West these days, face-to-face encounters can differ widely in quality, depending on the people and planning involved. It usually takes several tries to get comfortable with a particular group or discussion format. In every case involving a local organization or institution, gaining the trust of gatekeepers is a must. If trust is lacking, gatekeepers can play the spoiler. More often than not in the case of Muslim-Christian events, they vacillate between trust and suspicion. It is a strategy often reflected these days in "dialogue of civilizations" rendevous where respective gatekeepers from each community make speeches about the importance of tolerance and mutual understanding while dismissing participants with a blessing more intended to signal the end rather than the beginning of mutual exchange.

Some of the timidity no doubt stems from a locally imposed gag rule governing Muslim-Christian relations in the Middle East. Supported by most ruling elites in the region, the rule is based on fear of opening old wounds or renewed conflict between Muslims and Christians that threaten members of both communities as well as regime stability. Less benignly, it also serves the interests of Muslim ruling elites desperate to preserve the myth of inter-religious solidarity for the sake of Western audiences, among other motives. Combined with other inhibitions to candid dialogue—the political climate and its offspring of suspicion, more conservative cohorts selected for dialogue, overzealous gatekeepers, and limited opportunities for repeated encounters—the chilling effect of authoritarian regimes muzzling free speech remains one of the most overarching obstacles to more honest exchanges, a consequence with much greater costs for our hosts than for us.

Despite these many barriers, students and their hosts find limited space to share important opinions on life, love, and hope for the future. Yet in order to respect and protect our hosts within this context of constraints, we encourage students *to listen and inquire rather than argue*. Even if distorted by what some might perceive as our own self-imposed gag rule as well as selection bias related to the need for English-speaking Muslims, MESP encounter events offer a rare opportunity for Christian Americans to actually hear at least a sampling of Muslim public opinion first-hand.

One result of course is that students hear a negative stream of critical commentary from the Muslim street. In the eyes of many Muslims, the U.S. trumpets values like democracy, human rights, justice, fairness, and the rule of law, but applies them in a selective manner more in line with American interest rather than principle. This is often expressed as routine U.S. support for authoritarian regimes in the region that are disdainful of human rights, democratic values, or public welfare. Any potential discussion of indigenous root causes for Islamic militancy, for example, is deflected by Muslim counterclaims blaming militant ideas and behavior on U.S. policies.[23] But even if our primary aim at MESP was to prepare students with debating points meant to counter such arguments, a brief review of US policies and activities in the regions' many trouble spots since 9/11—Iraq, Afghanistan, Iran, Lebanon, Syria, Turkey, Israel, Palestine, Saudi Arabia, or Egypt—is usually enough to humble the apologetic skills of the most ardent MESP patriot. Nonetheless, it is encouraging to hear from many US diplomats that the work we are doing in these 'unarmed' encounters is some of the best public diplomacy America can presently do in this part of the world.

One-sided as they often seem at first, critical encounters with Muslim youth can empower both sides if repeated with some of the same participants, a process allowing greater levels of familiarity and trust. The point is to get comfortable sharing common values and self-criticism. I view student encounters as somehow unsatisfying, for example, if after one or two initial meetings our Muslim friends are not comfortable enough to speak openly about shortcomings in the Arab world so many of them share privately among themselves or in cyberspace—namely a lack or deficiency of democracy, civil liberties, free speech, human rights, fiscal transparency, social welfare, health care, economic development, poverty reduction—unrelated to colonial legacies or Western hegemony. Likewise, I view it as some measure of success when MESP students acknowledge at least partial US responsibility for regional difficulties without jettisoning praiseworthy American values or interests vital to the safety and well-being of Americans as well as others around the globe. I especially appreciate when both sides begin to acknowledge how their respective societies use religion or ideology to help or hinder the good, however understood. Given the obstacles to honest exchange in the current climate, our practical aim with these encounters is to humanize the other by sharing a meal and discussing any number of subjects—a movie, dating attitudes and habits, questions of religious doctrine or popular belief, marriage and family issues, etc.—that help them see both similarity and difference. The challenge is to have all the participants emerge from these encounters with two arguably compatible goods in tact, namely, friendship and a critical sense.

But political debate often lacks the personal dimension necessary for real transformation. It is always easier to blame "the system" for moral, even spiritual shortcomings. This is harder to do when the discussion turns to ultimate categories like heaven and hell, salvation and damnation. In truth, we do not formally address these issues with our Muslim friends since the local gatekeepers unofficially discourage the comparison of religions. Yet MESP students and their Muslim friends handle these inhibitions in pragmatic ways. While both adhere to revealed, universal, missionary religions not easily reconciled in many particulars, for example, *most are able to put differences aside for the purpose of dining with the opposition* (or with friends). While driving to a soccer game in Cairo with a MESP friend, one of our Muslim hosts captured a rare yet timeless moment of human truth. "According to my religion," he said, "you are going to hell. According to your religion, I am going to hell. We might as well enjoy the game before judgment day surprises one or both of us."

If such reasoning seems uncommonly frank in a Middle Eastern context, relationship-building with Muslim, Eastern Christian, and Jewish youth only encourages greater openness by simply reducing the physical distance between human beings. As part of my desire to promote self-understanding, *I am intentional about using encounter experiences as a way to confront MESP students with the gravity of using revealed truth—for example, scripturally inspired doctrine—to make moral judgments about themselves and others that involve consequences both immediate and eternal.* If students typically confined judgments about salvation to the domain of the afterlife, for example, my concerns might not be as salient. But real-time judgments can raise the costs of interaction significantly. Ruling elites and peoples of many cultures, for example, commonly use salvation boundaries as moral markers to justify policies of exclusion or worse. My students often use propositional, doctrinal criteria in order to determine the boundaries of salvation and the cost of entry to heaven. For MESP purposes, my fear is that such criteria may become instruments of exclusion or separation from the very people we seek to embrace even if temporarily.

As a result of these concerns, I ask students to write an essay dealing directly with the subject of salvation boundaries. Because students come to Cairo with uneven experience with and aptitudes for apologetics, they usually benefit from the struggle to articulate, debate, and refine their more precise beliefs about who is or is not a member of the Kingdom. Even if Middle Eastern friends are the alleged targets of their concern, students quickly learn that other MESP students are the primary tribunal they face. While revealed Scripture may in fact mean what individual students say that it means, more often than not its meaning is contested by colleagues as well as others from the Eastern Christian, Muslim, and Jewish communities. Once again, a subject matter allegedly meant to judge the other turns on the importance of students first getting their own story straight.

This challenging assignment is complicated by at least two things. First, students lack the usual majority safeguards like families, campuses, and churches that typically mitigate the discomforting effects of doubt. Second, flesh and blood experience with Muslim peers offering friendship and hospitality make harsh judgments seem awkward, to say the least. Despite conventional indoctrination to the contrary, many students catch themselves saying things like, "I just cannot see God allowing Ahmad or Nahid to suffer eternal punishment in Hell." For many students, the process of discussing, debating, and articulating salvation boundaries is a disturbing time of personal reflection, dissonance, and doubt. Students summarize the effects of the assignment differently, making remarks like "it turned my world upside down," "I don't know where I stand now," or "it was really challenging, but it strengthened my faith." Even more conservative student voices affirming traditional salvation teaching rooted in Scripture often do so with greater circumspection and humility. Most often however, students affirm both tradition and ambivalence in the same essay. Whatever the results, I respond with a consistent admonition to continue the discussion with family, campus leaders, and pastors after returning to the US. If measured by abundant student testimonials over the years, few assignments yield as great a return as this one where students must engage one another and the locals about the character of God and divine expectations for the treatment of fellow creatures.[24]

## Some Final Thoughts

I began the story of our program by talking about a literal and culture war between the world of Islam and the West and the high stakes of neglect, particularly the continuing misperceptions, misunderstandings, and mistrust, that threaten everyone in a community of nations increasingly bound together by technology that can destroy the planet. I followed this by offering a localized, partial remedy with global potential, encouraging students to use their learning experiences in the region—formal coursework, group encounters, relationships, and travel—as an exercise in living the examined life. By subjecting their most cherished values, ideas, identities, and religious truths to the scrutiny of colleagues and locals, I hope students begin to articulate a spiritual maturity less nested in the cave of political life and more biblically rooted in relationships beyond borders. Whether in the process our local friends in the Middle East learn similar things about themselves or not, I am always grateful for the important role they play in the education of our young people.

Like so many instructors responsible for cross-cultural endeavors, I am agnostic as to whether students are really transformed by their experience or not. MESP takes many approaches designed to provoke student thinking accompanied by activities intended to build relationships against which ideas and ideals can be tested. By refusing to privilege the Christian faith in the midst of student encounters with colleagues and locals, we no doubt risk resistance at polar ends—some students reject evidence that should lead them to question tradition while others ignore facts that should encourage them to embrace it.

No doubt many students leave MESP torn between the demands of orthodox faith (as they know it) and the reality of change resulting from their experience in relationship with cohort members as well as local others, a tension not always reconcilable but nonetheless unavoidable. It is an emotional tug of war we hope is embedded enough to continue its disturbing effects back at home. Only students can decide how and when they process what they have learned. I am content if transformation happens in increments like new understandings of faith, civic responsibility, friendship beyond borders, or return visits seeking rediscovery, continued study, and vocational direction.

# CHAPTER TEN

# San Francisco Urban Program

## Encountering America's Future-Tense

SCOTT MCCLELLAND, KAREN ANDREWS, AND BRAD BERKY

SCOTT MCCLELLAND (B.A., M.A. Wheaton College, Th.M. Westminster Seminary and Ph.D. in New Testament from the University of Edinburgh, Scotland) has directed the San Francisco Urban Program of Westmont College since 2006, and teaches elective and independent study courses.

KAREN ANDREWS (B.A. Westmont College, M.A. and Ph.D. in English and American Literature from Claremont Graduate University), an SF Urban faculty member since 1997, teaches the urban studies course, English electives, and independent study courses.

BRAD BERKY (B.A. Gordon College; M.Div. Fuller Theological Seminary; four years doctoral level work completed at Graduate Theological Union in Berkeley, CA) is an SF Urban alum, professor with the program since 1990, and coordinator of vocationally oriented internships since 1996.

*These three colleagues join together to describe their contributions and reflections concerning their program, which originated in 1971. Housed in an elegant 1898 Victorian mansion on The Panhandle of Golden Gate Park, up to twenty-six Westmont and other Christian College Consortium students participate in a semester-long community living experience. Students serve in a vocationally oriented internship, engage in coursework exposing them to diversity and social justice issues in an urban context, and explore the integration of their faith through*

*service and church interactions within a unique post-Christian city. They offer
their reflections on why they feel it is vital for educators and students in the evangelical tradition to "Find Your San Francisco."*[1]

While it "looks like" and "feels like" America, it is unlike any America most
of these evangelical college students have ever encountered. Standing at
the Civic Center Plaza and awaiting the Inauguration of Barak Obama, the San
Francisco Urban Program (SF Urban) students stood among one of the most
diverse populations they had ever encountered.

Homeless men, interrupted from their morning slumber by the throngs of
people invading their space, noted the opportunity that "marks" were *coming
to them* for a change and panhandling would be easier today. An anti-war
protest was setting up next to a "Throw a Shoe at Bush" booth, where patrons
stood in line to mimic the actions of an Iraqi journalist by hurling footware at
a caricature of the outgoing president.

People from every tribe, nation, and tongue it seemed, biblical in scope
and filled with passion, were beginning to focus on the large screen that would
bring images from three thousand miles away, and across hundreds of years
of struggle. Our students experienced the crush of the crowd and the intensity
of the morning's emotion.

Then, a recognizable face on the screen, the Rev. Rick Warren, came to
the podium in the nation's capital to deliver the invocation. This was a person
the students had known of; they had read his celebrated book, and some even
attended his church. For most of them, this was a man who cherished values
they had been taught to cherish; for some, he stood as a hero to their churches
and parents. They were ill-prepared for the reaction of the crowd: jeering,
booing, catcalls, and epithets rained down upon the image. As their "hero"
prayed, the students were surrounded by Americans who had a very different view of who American heroes are. Less than two weeks in San Francisco,
these students were enmeshed in a foreign America, a world that they had only
heard about before—and in this America, their faith was not popular!

SF Urban's mission is to help students take their academic training and
connect it with an intensive internship wherein they can realize their passion
for vocational calling and service. Living in community in a restored 1898
Victorian, they work in a world-class environment and study urban issues
along with ways our Christian faith informs their vocational life. Yet, they do

all of this in a decidedly post-Christian context. That, with apologies to Robert Frost, makes all the difference.

As SF Urban staff, our challenge is to find ways in which we can move students from their pristine preparatory campuses (the program also involves students from several other schools beside Westmont), to a non-fatal impact with a world most have never encountered. We strive to help students not only experience their own future vocational lives, but to do so in a way that will prepare them for a changing culture that no longer sees traditional Christianity as a valuable aid to a civil society.

Spiritual transformation here is as much an un-learning as learning activity. We face the overriding question, "How can a person in this pluralistic environment, having its own stereotypical and negative views about Christianity, live as a follower of Jesus?" In a real sense, our students devour their sacred texts and discuss these issues as Jesus-followers had in the first century, from a position not of power, but of vulnerability. No longer dependent simply on apologetic defenses, these students soon learn it is often through the basin and towel that the essence of Jesus comes through—and transforms lives.

In this chapter, my faculty colleagues and I at SF Urban will provide a look at this post-Christian domestic landscape through the Bay windows of our 1898 Victorian facility that serves as the home for our twenty-six students and the program.

The City of San Francisco is a well-known, and admired, tourist destination. Yet its uniqueness in political and social views often provokes polarized responses. Even local journalists have tried hard to describe a place that has been both celebrated and demonized under the term "San Francisco Values."[2] *San Francisco Chronicle* writer Carl Nolte observed, "What are San Francisco values? . . . San Francisco always has been a bit schizophrenic. It is the city where the Republicans nominated Barry Goldwater; three years later came the Summer of Love. . . . It is a city where the Sisters of Perpetual Indulgence are town characters, and public bashing of religion is not the least unusual."[3]

The Beat Generation, Hippies, "free love," marijuana use, gay-rights, and LGBTQ inclusion into mainstream society are all part of those values.[4] Each trend seems to migrate outwardly, from The City into the American cultural milieu. Our students, in a sense, gain insight into their future, the context of their life and work as independent adults, since much of it is already available here. As one eclectic San Francisco writer put it regarding the detractors of San Francisco values, "They're the dinosaurs, and we're the meteor."[5]

Most of our students come from classic evangelical institutions holding to the primary authority of Scripture and dedicated to the integration of faith, learning, and living. The culture these students face here is not only unfamiliar to them, it can be antithetical to values with which they have been raised and educated. What could be considered a real-world experience, here, is an other-world experience for many.

As Christian educators, we at SF Urban believe it is important to guide our students' preparation in these present experiences of future challenges. Commentators representing a diversity of traditions have noted that an upheaval of immense proportions is shaking the foundations of what many of these students have had passed down to them.[6]

In Phyllis Tickle's important book, *The Great Emergence,* she notes, ". . . about every five hundred years the Church feels compelled to hold a giant rummage sale."[7] Along with Tickle, leaders such as Brian McLaren, Shane Claiborne, Doug Pagitt, Frank Viola, George Barna, and locally, Mark Scandrette, have all pointed out the paradigm shift that challenges Christians to reassess the ways we practice our obedience to Christ.[8] Such musings come out of a hearts-desire to display the "way of Jesus" over against the traditional presentation of propositional truth which feels foreign to most and offensive to many in this post-Christian environment.[9]

On average, churches are smaller here, and many of those supporting an evangelical style and/or doctrinal position have left the city for more favorable climates in the surrounding suburbs. In addition, San Francisco, as a center for those advocating gay rights, has most decidedly sided with the LGBTQ community whenever it appears the church and those communities are at odds.[10]

Thus we encourage students to describe themselves, when appropriate, as "Followers of Jesus" and not necessarily as "Christians." The former designation leads to open conversations here, while the latter reinforces negative stereotypes. This is new and uncertain ground for most.

Spiritual transformation, then, becomes an exercise in receiving as much as giving, a ministry of presence more than proclamation, extending the loving embrace of Jesus to many who have been wounded in his name. A city like San Francisco can best be served when others "catch our hope," and our students best reinforce their own hope when they provide it for others—a classic, and effective, spiritual transformation feedback loop.[11]

Our program provides opportunities for students to be in an active learning mode encountering the diverse communities that make up this urban environment. Unpacking stereotypes and offering a context for cross-cultural relationships, our Urban Studies course, internships (Urban Practicum), and electives give both the theoretical and experiential opportunities for students to interpret these encounters through their established evangelical reference points. These encounters provide a rich environment for conversation, growth, and the creation of new commitments.

All students participate in our Urban Studies course, a four-unit seminar-style offering that emphasizes active, student-centered learning. Spiritual transformation in this context often takes place as students begin asking authentic questions about God and their own place within this unfamiliar urban context. We find such questioning indicative of encountering a culture they have not otherwise experienced and one in which they wish to reconcile worldviews they brought to the city.

One of our recent guest speakers, Dr. Marilyn McEntyre, often says of vocation that we need to know our own stories—our starting places—as we discover the particular story we are called to inhabit.[12] We are also called to weave across cross-cultural boundaries. At SF Urban, we believe that self-understanding is critical to the learning process, so our students are encouraged to recognize their own home culture and social location. As Mary Docter and Laura Montgomery have discovered through their extended program of preparation for Westmont in Mexico (see their own chapter in this volume), we also see that students are better able to cultivate a posture of hospitality and generosity toward other people and viewpoints when they better understand and embrace their own stories.

Through challenging readings, weekly reflection papers on local church visits and other city encounters, large and small group discussions, group research and service projects, and oral presentations, students are encouraged to clarify their own beliefs and values in such diverse cross-cultural encounters. Trying to put "names and faces" to contemporary issues, we invite guest speakers from various sectors of city life to present important and challenging perspectives on relevant issues. Students hear from persons involved in opposing human trafficking (a large Bay Area problem) and from the LGBTQ community (both celibate and non-celibate gay Christians); they also travel to the Tenderloin and Bay View-Hunters Point (economically challenged areas in this expensive city) to hear from those being exploited as well as those bringing hope. As an off-campus program, we need them to "hear the language of San Francisco" even as they would, were they living in Italy, "hear Italian."

As Cynthia Toms Smedley reminds us in her introduction to this volume, study abroad programs "provide a natural impetus for growth by removing students from their home environments and exposing them to diverse thinking." So coming on SF Urban affords our students a chance to suffer dislocation—often in surprising ways. Some students actually feel like exiles—what many Christian theologians would call a central and necessary part of what it is to be a "chosen people"—living like exiles and aliens even in their home country.[13] This experience of displacement offers them an opportunity to relate more compassionately to the "exiles and aliens" who live and work among us in our cities, many of whom have come to this marketplace of ideas to re-invent themselves apart from the dominant values found in other parts of the country and world.

Students are often energized by the people and church communities who are working sacrificially to provide appealing and sustainable alternatives to the street culture. Such well-informed activism inspired one of our students to acknowledge that she, for the first time, "saw poverty, identified her privilege, and formed relationships with those whose social conditions are in complete juxtaposition to her own."[14]

Even commuting on Muni buses and the BART trains provide abundant (and otherwise rare) opportunities for encountering others, engaging with difference, and, particularly in our city, coming into contact with issues of sustainability and conservation that so invigorate residents here. One student reflected: "I am so grateful for the opportunity to live within a city and commute with its residents so that I can meet people where they are every day. Doing so has opened my eyes to things otherwise hidden by the privacy of driving a car and living in the suburbs."[15] She committed to continue her learning in her hometown by taking public transportation where available and not falling back into her car-centered culture. Similarly, another student highlighted public transportation as a window into urban culture, illuminating San Francisco's distinctiveness: "I think the public transportation system is just another way that this City has this 'we're all in this together' feeling: like how everyone agrees to leave their stuff on the sidewalk to share. It's quite incredible how in (these 49) square miles you can find yourself in another world. It seems like the community relationships are . . . strong for such an urban area."[16]

In all of the themes of the Urban Studies course—privilege and power, racism and poverty, sexual orientation and human trafficking—theological reflection plays a central role in our efforts to understand the city. As faculty, we encourage students to wrestle with the issues, taking time to reflect and not feel rushed to come to conclusions while they process these difficult and controversial topics. As we allow for complexity, students learn to honor the questions. This type of practice can be refreshing (and somewhat unique to some), and they long to continue this process well after the semester is over: "I hope that this kind of discussion and wrestling maintains a priority in my thought-life. Though it is easy to go with the easy answer, I hope this semester has entrenched the value of struggling through unpopular ideas and questions. . . . I have come to know that most issues are more complex than they might originally seem."[17]

Indeed, students crave to know how to live in the tension, the in-between places, while seeking answers to difficult questions.[18] One student responded to some new and more nuanced perspectives on several topics by noting: "I leave with more questions than I had when I came because people are harder to put in a box, tie with a bow and label 'truth' or 'morally correct.' I would not have it any differently. I would rather walk down the street, knowing there is nuance and diversity."[19]

This process involves something of a letting go of many of our preconceived notions about certain applications of Christian faith, urban life, and culture.[20] We hope and trust that this transformative process, while potentially uncomfortable, leads the students (and us) back to the center; to Jesus who "reconciled all things in himself."[21]

We believe that these encounters and assignments help our students work on strengthening their own centers—in Christ—while softening their edges in their various urban encounters. We hope to point our students to the truth found in such places as Mark 9:38–40 where, perhaps, we do not need to restrict partnerships or too closely guard who it is that influences us.[22] We are following a person, rather than a set of standards or rules; we can thus try to visualize others with Christ's eyes.[23] Through the Urban Studies course, and indeed all facets of the SF Urban Program, students learn to focus on Jesus Christ who we are following even in the midst of new complexities and contexts they have not encountered before. Each student is faced with discerning how, in this experience, following Jesus can be more relevant for them than ever before. No longer relying on the safety of culturally endorsed and enforced structures, but journeying boldly through risky places in this new America, they form a faithful dependency on a living God amidst many options.

Our students also anticipate a major challenge of reentry into their home cultures: "Going back to the conservative Midwest will be interesting, and I am eager to dispel all the negative apprehension so many have about the big, liberal city of San Francisco. . . . I am preparing myself for a very hard transition."[24] The Midwest isn't the only place skeptical of San Francisco's culture. A student from Orange County (which has a quite different social and political environment than the Bay Area) emphasized the negative perception of San Francisco held by her home community in a creative reflection she directly addressed to the city: "I'm scared to go home. People there don't like you; they have already told me. They call you a heathen harlot or Sodom, and one that corrupts. Some will be surprised that I am still a Christian; others will probably question whether or not I still am. I am scared because I know I am not the same person, but I am going back to that same place where people expect the 'same person.'"[25]

As they move from mere awareness on these issues to an informed activism,[26] our hope is they will bring an incarnated presence of Jesus to these contemporary issues. We believe they will find that Jesus is fit for this journey, and ministering God's presence in their lives may be the most effective way they can reveal him.

Our other major program piece is the Urban Practicum (Internship), a required eight-unit, twenty-four-hour per week involvement that engages students in a highly structured internship experience aimed at cultivating new vocational, cross-cultural, and critical-reflective skills. Somewhat unique is the breadth of the opportunities. Students are engaged in significant work experiences in whichever environment is most conducive to their educational goals. From the Financial District to the General Hospital and all in-between, students put into practice the knowledge and heart they learned in their classrooms. Internships offer students the opportunity to explore future career interests, as well as significant life questions. Students are challenged and inspired to navigate the unfamiliar—personally, relationally, and spiritually.

This is not merely job preparation (though such is a valued outcome), but rather these experiences help foster a holistic vision of Christian vocation and service—one that seeks to uncover the lived-intersections between "one's deep gladness and the world's deep hunger" in experientially rooted and theologically reflective ways.[27]

Believing that experience alone is not sufficient for transformative growth, the course has built into it numerous reading, writing, and mentoring components aimed at fostering the connections between theory and praxis, faith and world. Students develop, along with their supervisors, a clearly focused learning contract outlining specific personal, professional, and in certain cases, faith goals. Incorporating the submission of a weekly journal, two reading-response papers, and a semester-end portfolio, the course also requires participation in regular faculty-facilitated site visits as well as a weekly companion seminar on "Faith, Ethics and Vocational Formation."[28]

Students almost always come away with a heightened awareness of themselves as capable agents in the world, as well as a deeper awareness for the many complexities surrounding a host of socio-political, spiritual, and cross-cultural issues.[29]

Given the diverse, often-demanding contexts in which the students are placed, the challenges they typically come up against can be at once disorienting and rewarding. They are called upon to function effectively in largely unfamiliar workplace settings and in close relationships with those previously seen as the other, both colleagues and supervisors. Often for the first time, they experience what "minority status" feels like when it comes to conventional evangelical faith, lifestyle, and worldview assumptions.

The encounter with those who may have previously been seen as "outsiders" within mainstream evangelical circles can contribute to a season of doubt and confusion at any number of levels. We know, though, these often-difficult times are also a crucial development to moving toward a more mature, grounded faith and worldview stance. They experience "commitment amidst ambiguity" in relation to even the most perplexing of questions and competing truth claims they encounter.[30]

An example of this movement is what typically happens for students interning in an interfaith hospital chaplaincy program with which we've been affiliated for the past twenty-five years. Interns work with chaplain trainers/ colleagues and a patient population representing a wide range of faith and non-faith viewpoints. The primary aim is to incarnate a "non-judgmental ministry of presence" that is fully and equally respectful of all spiritual/meaning-making practices. Though many initially struggle with how this requirement will impact their own faith, what eventually occurs is rather surprising. Most discover that being open and present to the differences encountered (within a uniquely supportive and affirming environment) actually has a way of stretching and strengthening their prior Christian faith commitments. One female student gave voice to this saying: "my internship with the chaplaincy . .

. has taught me that while not everyone may share my beliefs, I can still be an agent of God's grace in a broken world simply by actively listening to others and living out the St. Francis commission to 'preach the Gospel always, using words only if necessary.'"[31]

These concrete experiences fit well with many faith development theorists influential within Christian higher education circles.[32] Students must be allowed to encounter a season described metaphorically as "shipwreck" marked by "threat, bewilderment, confusion, frustration, fear and loss."[33] Our contribution is to help them gain a confidence that the threats they encounter can be something faith-strengthening rather than faith undoing in any ultimate sense.

A recent female student expressed how she emerged from that "shipwreck" to a place of increased, and maturing, commitment: "as a result of my internship I've learned that my own way of being in the world is not the *only* way, but realizing this has helped me see I have a lot of work to do in relating my faith to people and issues outside the Christian bubble."[34]

While student experiences vary somewhat, at least three "givens" are discovered by each as they complete their internship:

**First**, they gain a clear increase in self-confidence—especially around how to better negotiate a range of professional and cross-cultural dynamics. For some, it is an unexpected surprise to discover that past life and classroom experiences have indeed prepared them well to meet the many challenges they encounter. In this regard, one student wrote, "As a result of my internship, I have discovered where my passions lie and how better to give voice to them at lots of new vocational levels."[35]

Transformation here comes in the form of supervisor affirmation as well: "One of the things we value about Urban interns is the energy and enthusiasm they have for learning and contributing to our work. They are exceptionally conscientious, kind and receptive to constructive feedback ... The preparation and guidance they receive from the Urban staff is something we also value, for this added structure is helpful in making for a richer collaborative experience at every level."[36] For many of these students, it is transformative to see how well their education on campus relates to their vocational needs through acquired skill sets, and also to the spiritual needs of others through a lived-out faith.

**Second**, they acquire sensitivity to ethical, diversity, and social justice matters—Given the faith-based vocational focus of the course, most students come away from their internship experiences possessing a greater sense for the tensions, joys and opportunities that faithful, Kingdom-based steward-ship involves. This is nothing less than a strategic advantage for their future vocational lives, and is attributable to their experiences in a world-class *and* post-Christian context.

**Third,** they have a heightened sense that conventional, proposition-based modes of evangelical faith witness are limited within contexts no longer persuaded by universal truth claims. While unsettling to many, this aware-ness is one that is unavoidable for those living and working in a city like San Francisco. In many cases, we find our students are already on a similar journey and so can better relate to the context they find here. As one student put it: "I have enjoyed meeting God in surprising places and diverse peoples—immi-grants I work for and with, hippies, on the bus, and on the street. So I thought: this must be what it means for God to be omnipresent."[37]

As for the role we as faculty play in facilitating the kind of transforma-tive growth hoped for, it might be fair to say that we are primarily "pastoral educators"—that is, ones invested in mentoring students both spiritually as well as intellectually, all within a living-learning faith community aimed at "creating safe places where obedience to truth can be practiced."[38] This pasto-ral role helps students to gain a greater appreciation for the value of being in a uniquely global/local, cross-cultural context in which confirmation and con-tradiction are intentionally fostered, critically-engaged, and celebrated.

All these encounters allow spiritual transformation to be a natural occur-rence, one that has an enduring value to our students particularly because it appears not to be forced. It also has the advantage of being formed in an envi-ronment most like that in which most students will exercise leadership skills at work and church through the remainder of their active lives.

At times, we have wrestled with trying additional forms of intentional programming to encourage the "spiritual integrative piece" of our program. Recent incarnations have focused on small group encounters with a design to have students share their present spiritual and/or personal journeys. Weekly opportunities also exist for students to lead corporate worship times using structures and themes from their backgrounds, or experimenting with less familiar forms that have their origins in other Christian faith traditions (such as prayer walks, foot-washing, and labyrinth meditation). Sometimes we, as staff, will just let them know where we can be found, attending an early morn-ing mass or sitting at a local coffee house, with the invitation that integrative conversation is available. In addition, we have "Duo" times when each staff member focuses on a group of students through regular one-on-one meetings to allow spiritual journeying to come up in conversation as a natural part of student reflections.

Yet for most students, it has often been in the "unintentional" allowance to grow at their own pace, having unregulated spiritual activities with real time for reflection, that have created an environment for greatest maturity. We show and say that we trust them to make some right decisions at this stage of their lives and as they encounter these challenges, rather than trying to ensure they can do no wrong. When needed, they know where to find friends for the journey home.

A Spring 2009 semester survey revealed a satisfaction with this level of intentionality: "I really appreciate the freedom of the program," wrote one student. "It makes the religious activities I choose to participate in that much more valuable and meaningful to me." Another student found a metaphor in bike riding: "It is time to lose the Westmont (or Christian liberal-arts-college) training wheels and see if a student falls or keeps on rolling along. It is a time to check yourself and realize what your spiritual life will be like after graduation, after friends leave, after theologically stimulating conversations are much harder to come by."[39]

The context of San Francisco was cited as a significant contributor to student spiritual growth. One student responded that she found new hope for the place of the church in her life, saying, "San Francisco gave me a redeeming viewpoint on the Church.... My perspective of the Church was quite negative, as it often felt too exclusive, and a contributor to issues of patriarchy, racial segregation, and greed. By attending churches in San Francisco, however, I was able to see how some congregations were actively involved in Kingdom work—they let the homeless sleep on their pews, they let everyone walk into their doors, and they weren't afraid to confront the issues people wanted to talk about."[40]

Perhaps a final story from our last semester will suffice. A male student from the Midwest sought an internship with a program focusing on HIV/AIDS prevention. Commenting after the semester was over, the supervisor admitted he was initially skeptical of the Christian college student's ability to understand the depth of this disease's impact on the LGBTQ community and to "fit in" with a department entirely populated by members of that affected community. But the student surprised him, representing his concern as one to rid this disease from "our community," confronting HIV/AIDS as a shared threat to us all. He was hired, and performed with excellence. Most memorable, though, was the site visit attended by two of our staff, where the student made his final presentation. We met in a packed conference room, filled with his colleagues in that department, who professed their newfound admiration for him and a program with such service-minded students. Spiritual transformation was a collective experience that day.

In reflecting upon his experience, the student wrote from the perspective of being a perceived enemy to co-workers: "As the only straight male Christian at _____, I learned what it means to be a minority and some of the issues/challenges others have with people like me. Through this I gained a deeper appreciation for those I worked with, and why Christians still have a lot to do in being more sensitive to how we come across to outsiders . . . I was so impressed with how accepted I was despite my "enemy status" at first and came to love everyone there by the end of the semester."[41]

Significantly, his supervisor saw the same dynamic at work:

> When I interviewed _____ and learned he attended an evangelical Christian college, I was doubtful someone like this would be a fit within our AIDS/HIV service agency. Over the course of the interview, however, I was won over by his self-awareness and empathy around the issues we deal with and hired him. This proved to be one of our best moves as we experienced one who was not only a valued colleague, but one who changed many of the negative stereotypes we had about Christians. As a result, I've come to see that those I previously considered as adversaries are closer allies than I imagined and I am thankful for this."[42]

A footnote to this—the supervisor asked to come back to hire another SF Urban student as an intern.

For the staff of SF Urban, it would be far easier if we tried to control the process, over-program, and convince ourselves that we have done all that is possible to get them through this semester with minimal scarring. But we find it is not our job to help them survive this experience intact, but to motivate them to seize the experiences and take in the moments and places where they meet Jesus in this city, and to keep walking with him in the unusual places he has now prepared for them. In this is Christ manifest to the world; the bearers of his image at SF Urban are released into a world and future for which they are now prepared, because they have now *been there.*

Character and commitment are formed in the crucible of engagement. It is what we can prayerfully offer as we guide our fellow travelers in this unique place: hope to those that need it. And we all need it.

# PART IV

# The Year of the Lord's Good Favor

## Cultivating Solidarity with the Global Poor

RONALD J. MORGAN

"The Spirit of the Lord is on me, because he has anointed me
to preach good news to the poor.
He has sent me to proclaim freedom for the prisoners
and recovery of sight for the blind,
to release the oppressed,
to proclaim the year of the Lord's favor."

—Luke 4:18-19

In Luke's Gospel, the Incarnation of Jesus occasions enthusiastic outbursts of joyful praise at every turn. From Mary's "Magnificat" to Simeon's temple exclamation—"Lord, now I can die in peace!"—Luke's witnesses express wonder at seeing God come near. These exuberant protagonists in the Incarnation drama anticipate real transformations in the world, from "salvation through forgiveness of sins" (1:77) to the righting of social injustices, as Mary herself sings: "[The Mighty One] has scattered those who are proud in their inmost thoughts. He has brought down rulers from their thrones but has lifted up the humble. He has filled the hungry with good things but has sent the rich away empty" (1:51–53).

But the One whom God "has anointed . . . to preach good news to the poor" also brings glad tidings of liberation to the "rich," indeed to all those who exercise some type of social power over others. The good news proclaimed in Luke 4 extends to the greedy one who builds bigger and bigger barns (Luke 12); it extends to a Pharisee whom Jesus invites to learn from the woman whose social position is much less esteemed than his own (Luke 7); it invites repentance of the "Rich Man" who lives in splendor behind protective walls while a beggar dies at his gate (Luke 16). Through these narratives and parables, Luke turns the notion of liberation on its head, acknowledging that *all* human beings, particularly the happily comfortable, should rejoice in the year of the Lord's favor.

The three essayists whose chapters comprise Part IV of this volume describe study abroad programs that bring U.S. students face-to-face with some of the world's poorest people in both rural and urban settings. They explore some of the ethical, theological, and pedagogical principles that provide shape to those encounters, and describe efforts to ensure that their programs truly benefit the poor. But Slimbach, Elisara, and Meyers avoid the paternalistic assumption that the American student goes among the poor as a rescuer. Instead, building on the work of Nicholas Woltersdorff and others, they advocate the multi-dimensional education for *shalom*, a peace that is only complete when we have "delight and joy" in our relationships with God, others, creation, and self.

# CHAPTER ELEVEN

# Learning from Slums

Study and Service in Solidarity with the World's Urban Poor

## RICHARD SLIMBACH

*Richard Slimbach is professor of global studies and coordinator of the Global Studies Program at Azusa Pacific University. He founded Azusa's Los Angeles Term and Global Learning Term programs, and has extensive experience living and working in poor communities. He holds a Ph.D. in comparative and international education and continues to participate in the design of cross-cultural programs based in the developing world. One of these, the Master of Arts in Transformational Urban Leadership (MATUL), seeks to catalyze movements for spiritual and social transformation within the slum communities of Chennai (India), Manila (Philippines), and Port-au-Prince (Haiti), among other cities. The program is embedded within a broader movement to link a new generation of Christian internationalists from the global North with those from the South in vocations dedicated to advancing God's shalom among the world's urban poor.*

Educational travelers now traverse a world where massive demographic, economic, and environmental changes are dramatically re-shaping the quality of life for literally billions of people. While a growing number of global problems defy resolution—including rapid population growth, failed states, disappearing species, and shrinking forests—there are two, in particular, that pose immediate and critical threats to the stability of the planet. One is the world's growing poverty and inequality: "a billion people living in dire poverty alongside a billion in widening splendor on a planet growing ever smaller and more integrated," according to historian Eric Hobsbawm.[1] The other is the accelerating impoverishment of the natural environment brought about by unsustainable levels of resource extraction and the rich world's insatiable appetite for stuff.

What we know as "the modern way of life" signifies an ambiguous global reality. On the one hand, the globalization of fossil fuel-based industrialization and consumerism has contributed to the planet's warming, releasing an estimated nine *billion* tons of carbon dioxide into the atmosphere every year.[2] On the other hand, that same industrialization process has enabled millions of people to climb out of extreme poverty. Families that once went to bed hungry and sick now have decent jobs, adequate food, and accessible health services. Their children, and the generations that follow them, will enter the world far removed from the extreme want that afflicted their ancestors. In fact, the world is no longer, as it used to be, one-sixth rich and five-sixths poor. Thanks to various "convergence" factors—like the diffusion of new technologies and the explosive economic growth in Asia over the last thirty years—the world will soon look quite different: more like one-sixth rich, three-sixths O.K., one-sixth barely making it, and another sixth desperately poor.[3]

But this doesn't tell the whole story. Over 1.4 billion people live at a poverty line of $1.25 a day—a life condition that is only aggravated by the recent food crisis, economic collapse, and rising cost of energy. Of these, over eight hundred million people (three hundred million of them children) still go to bed hungry every night. Nine hundred million cannot read, two-thirds of them women. An estimated forty million people live each day with HIV/AIDS. Every year 11 million children die, most before the age of five and only because they lack proper immunizations, safe drinking water, and adequate sanitation. Of those that manage to survive, eight million will endure years of slavery to pay off a family debt. Another ten million will prostitute themselves. And if they reside in sub-Saharan Africa, and make it to adulthood, they can expect to live, on average, only forty-one years—*half* the life expectancy of the U.S. and Japan.[4]

A "globalized" education has traditionally offered opportunities for well-off collegians to rub up against these wider, and oftentimes contradictory, world realities. The hope was that enriched understandings acquired abroad would lead to more ethically responsive lifestyles back home. But right living assumes right understandings, and students abroad increasingly encounter raw realities that resist simple explanations, much less easy solutions. This is because the causes are either not known, not well understood, or are so paradoxical and contradictory—so hopelessly intertwined with other issues—that they require a different type of global learning process.

The Irish political writer William Lecky saw only two ways to improve the world. The first was to learn how to capture the urgency of others' deprivation and desperation by actually *seeing* and *feeling* it firsthand. Beyond mere intellectual assent, this would require that one grant to others in far away and forgotten places the same basic humanity they presumed for themselves. This, according to Lecky, was the basis for finding creative ways to interact with "strangers" across the real differences. Direct involvement in the lives of diverse others would set the stage for the second means of world changing: finding ways to understand how *others'* interests are, in fact, connected to *our* interests.

This chapter attempts to illustrate a global learning process that meets these two criteria: *interacting firsthand* with a complex and oftentimes unsettling global reality as the necessary basis for *narrowing the distance*—both physical and moral—between "us" and "them," thus encouraging a more connected and responsive humanity. Our discussion begins with reflections on the astonishing growth of slums within third world cities.[5] This is a backdrop for considering the growing commitment among evangelical twenty-somethings to be agents of healing within a broken world. By forming communities of solidarity and service within forgotten places, an emergent generation of Christian cosmopolitans is seeking to build relational bridges between the world of privilege and the world of poverty, allowing *others'* experience to become *their* experience. What insights might the extraordinary conditions of informal settlements hold out for this new generation as it struggles to see, feel, and comprehend the global future they already inhabit? International study and service programs (like the one profiled later in this chapter) often serve as vehicles for student involvement in other social worlds. How might the leaders of these programs best help participants to enter into study and service relationships marked by solidarity with the common people? And how might these solidarity relationships reveal the essence of God's cause in the world, and our calling as Christian global educators?

## The New Squatopolises

Images of human deprivation are typically associated with remote villages in the developing world. But one of the most profound effects of an integrated global economy has been how it has rendered rural livelihoods increasingly obsolete. Under the pressure of drought, deforestation, and national policies that encourage industrial agricultural, family farms struggle to produce a surplus to sell in the market. Village life itself is perceived as a dull and dead-end existence compared with the opportunity-laden and upwardly mobile life of cities. The result is that poor people across the globe are packing their meager belongings, abandoning their ancestral lands, and moving to the cities—over 70 million people every year, 1.5 million people per week, 130 people every minute.

Few, however, expect to find uniform glamour and easy money. Indeed, evicted from an exhausted hinterland, most exchange rural poverty masked by bucolic landscapes and intact families for urban destitution built on reclaimed rubbish heaps, unstable hillsides, and desert fringes. They enter the city in sorrowful resignation, knowing all too well that they must improvise a precarious existence out of discarded land and industrial debris, turning themselves into street vendors, wage laborers, garment workers—anything to ensure their immediate survival. Their risky wager with the global urban-industrial culture is this: that some semblance of "the good life" will one day be realized, if not by them then by their children, by forsaking the farms, moving into shantytowns, working in factories, and exporting stuff to the rest of the world.

Their logic, at least statistically, appears indisputable. In 1950, eighteen percent of people in developing countries lived in cities. This rose to twenty-seven percent in 1975 and to forty percent in 2000, and projections are that fifty-six percent of the developing world will be urban by 2030. By that time, the global countryside will have peaked at 3.2 billion and begun to shrink. But there will be a further two billion more people on earth, ninety-five percent of them being absorbed within the poorest regions of the world, and overwhelmingly in poor cities like Karachi, Port-au-Prince, and Cairo. Already one billion persons—one out of every six—live in squatter communities. That figure is expected to mushroom to two billion by 2030, making one out of every four people on the planet a slum dweller.[6]

There was a time when urbanists envisioned the city of tomorrow as paradises of bourgeois prosperity, with ethnic tensions quelled and the environment mastered with concrete, steel, and glass. But for urban theorist Mike Davis, "Instead of cities of light soaring towards heaven, much of the twenty-first-century urban world squats in squalor, surrounded by pollution, excrement, and decay."[7] Indeed, a surplus humanity of epic proportions now finds itself carving out subsistence niches in what journalist Robert Neuwirth has dubbed "squatopolises"—urban spaces doomed by a lack of secure land to live on, clean water to drink, and jobs with any kind of future.

## The New Cosmopolitans

The impressive variety of field learning programs represented in this volume testifies to the hunger felt by many in this generation for a world made right. They know intuitively what Jesus taught centuries ago through word and life: that there is no escape or immunity from the struggles, heartache, and misery of the world. College students are confronted, day after day, with images of ethnic violence and environmental destruction, homeless children and exploited women, the AIDS epidemic and the moral decay in popular culture. They know it's there, just outside the gate of their subdivision or campus. It falls to them to figure out what to do about it.

Many choose to investigate these gritty realities firsthand, moving away from the fantasy worlds created by videogames, pop music, and Hollywood celebrities, and toward a capricious world. They often carry along a number of defining questions: Where can I find something to dedicate myself to and fall in love with? Should the focus of my learning be exclusively on my own development or should it also have a larger public purpose? If my learning isn't just about me, and involves a commitment to the world, won't it inevitably engage me with real problems endured by real people in that world? Finally, what hope and goal is big enough to enable me to serve in the midst of the world's pain without dwelling in fear and cynicism?

Among American Christians, excursions across cultural and geographic borders continue to multiply year by year. Actual participation figures are imprecise, but Princeton sociologist Robert Wuthnow estimates that upwards of 1.5 million U.S. church members participate in short-term missions trips annually.[8] Though brief and oftentimes lacking significant levels of engagement, they nevertheless reveal a generation eager to connect with a wider world. Curiously, the rise in faith-based world concern documented by Wuthnow coincides with what other religiosity researchers have decried as the seeping *loss* of faith and social engagement among young adults raised in evangelical families.[9] Evidence is marshaled that points to the demise of religious faith in the U.S., at least among Euro-Americans, and the rise of aggressively anti-religious feeling in the popular culture. In the past, if you were a self-declared atheist, agnostic, or secular humanist, you would have been a timid minority, on the defensive and routinely derided. Today, impassioned denunciations of both God's existence and organized religion have succeeded in making respect for belief in God more socially *un*acceptable than ever before.[10] The result is that the number of out-of-the-closet "unbelievers" has increased about fourfold over the last two decades, from 1 million in 1990 to 3.6 million 2009.[11]

As disturbing as these figures are, the large-scale disaffection of millennials from faith may have less to do with fallout from the contemporary culture war than with a perceived lack of relevance. "A major reason people are leaving the church, losing their faith, and staying away in the first place," contends missiologist Ralph Winter, "is because the church has not adequately stepped up to bat along with civil forces to beat down the corruption, disease, and poverty of at least a billion hopeless people."[12] In Winter's view, the problem isn't that those raised in the church are uninterested in world realities; they simply have not been sufficiently involved in them.

This is beginning to change. Nearly two centuries after the social reforms associated with the likes of John Wesley, William Carey, Catherine and William Booth, David Livingstone, Charles Finney, and William Wilberforce, we witness a growing segment of young Christ-followers stepping up to again right society's wrongs. Various labels attach to this insurgent and highly networked movement: "emergent church," "new monastics," "new friars," "new conspirators," and "ordinary radicals."[13] They represent a new generation of "posties"—post-denominational, post-partisan, post-modern, post-material, post-national, and post-evangelical*ism*. Most are impatient with old-school disputes over biblical inerrancy, original sin, or whether devout Buddhists are going to heaven or hell. Their concern is much more basic—for a vital Christian spirituality embodied in everyday acts for social justice shorn of evangelical dogma and spectacle. Their faith finds root in Jesus' historic messages, especially what is found in the Sermon on the Mount (Matt. 5–7) and the Nazareth Manifesto (Luke 4:18–19). In both sermons, Jesus announces a new world order that, in terms to the fractures of the world today, is "being fulfilled" in the proclamation of good news to at-risk children, exploited women, the landless, and those stricken with infectious disease. Society is no longer viewed as a sinking ship awaiting rescue by an immanent "rapture." What matters is repairing the ship in small, slow, and intensely local ways. And with a priority concern for the most distressed corners of the planet.

## Learning from Slums

In the public imagination, there is perhaps no place more miserable than the third world slum. Since it first appeared in the 1820s, the word "slum" has been used to identify the concentration of grossly inadequate housing, acute over-crowding, chronic health hazards, and an assortment of unwholesome activities. Today, it designates the fastest growing, and most unprecedented, global social class on earth, one that is radically and permanently disconnected from the formal world economy. A variety of vernacular names attach to them, all of them virtually interchangeable: *bustees* in Kolkata, *chawl* in Mumbai, *comunas* in Columbia, *katchi abadi* in Karachi, *kampong* in Jakarta, *iskwater* in Manila, *shammasa* in Khartoum, *umjondolo* in Durban, *bidonvilles* in Abijan, *baladi* in Egypt, *gecekoundou* in Ankara, *conventillos* in Quito, *favelas* in Brazil, *villa miseria* in Buenos Aires, and *colonias populares* in Mexico City.

Despite the richly varied physical, legal, social, political, and economic characteristics of slums, they tend to share a common genesis. With few excep-tions, they are the result of a perfect storm of deep poverty, corrupt leader-ship, institutional failure, and IMF-imposed Structural Adjustment Programs leading to a massive transfer of wealth from poor to rich.[14] The net and, for some experts, irreversible result is that cities of the global South have largely been converted from engines of growth and prosperity to dumping grounds for a surplus humanity. Resources that might have been invested in upgrad-ing public life are typically appropriated by the relatively powerful, leaving the urban poor to fend for themselves.

Until the debut of *Slumdog Millionaire,* winner of eight Academy awards in 2009, most Westerners were largely oblivious to the lived realities of the over one billion slum dwellers. The film uses the dilemma of an eighteen-year-old orphan from Mumbai's largest slum, on the verge of winning millions on an Indian version of "Who Wants to be a Millionaire" game show but suspected of cheating, to tell a Dickensian story of social mobility within a polarized world of wealth and poverty. Some viewers scorned the film as a tragic example of "poverty porn." Others applauded it as a stunning form of artistic expression that, rather than ennobling poverty, ennobled the poor. Where both groups could agree is that the film offered a rare and penetrating window into the human diversity, vibrant energy, and "ordered chaos" of informal urban settle-ments. In fact, a growing number of researchers, planners, and activists have begun to highlight the "positive" aspects of slum life, shaped not by oppres-sion and helplessness but by the collective intelligence and individual energy of thousands of resourceful people. In a startling reversal of "mission," they're approaching slums, not to fix poor residents, but to learn from them.

Learning from slums? The idea may not be all that outlandish, especially as one considers their distinctive built environment, local resource use, and cultural and social vitality. Slum dwellings are people's own solution to their housing needs, being independently built and incrementally upgraded by generations of residents who find ingenious uses for materials that would otherwise pile up in landfills. In the process, inhospitable lands are transformed into vernacular communities without the need for any master plan, zoning ordinances, construction laws, or technical expertise. The fact that eighty percent of settlement land is dedicated to home construction enables slums to have high densities without going higher than ground plus one or two stories. Living areas are multi-functional, providing a model of optimal space utilization.

All cities require a concentration of food, water, energy, and building materials, and by any measure, slums exemplify a low-energy way of life. Squatter settlements are designed for human beings instead of automobiles. Limited (often stolen) electricity powers a limited number of electrical devices. Clothes are washed by hand in cold water and then dried outside on a clothesline. Bathing is done with a bucket and cup. There are no industrial lawns or domesticated yards, only small organic gardens on family plots.

Slums are also vibrant, tight-knit, and mixed-use communities. In Mumbai's Dharavi slum (where *Slumdog* was shot), small businesses include everything from tea stalls and tailor shops to welders and furniture makers. In contrast to the isolation and bland design of gated subdivisions throughout the developed world, slums are organic and intensely human places. Children improvise games on the hundreds of lanes branching into bustling commercial areas. Most have strong local identities and a range of sites for face-to-face interaction. Central to their sense of meaning and well-being are "sacred spaces"—small temples, mosques or churches that provide a kind of spiritual health delivery system for residents struggling against chronic stress, depression, and alcoholism.

None of this is meant to idealize squatters as a new "revolutionary class" or to minimize the concentrated disadvantage that marks their daily life. There's nothing glorious about thousands of people being crowded into a single acre, the stench of untreated human and industrial waste flowing through open drains, high levels of typhoid and malaria, or child and bonded labor resulting from manufacturing jobs being subcontracted to the so-called "self-employed." Women, in particular, must raise children under the constant threat of eviction, infectious disease, and domestic violence. But what if the laudable aspects of these communities could somehow be disentangled from the heartrending parts? What if residents could organize themselves in ways that could instill hope, mend families, create jobs, foster educational opportunities, and improve sanitation and health? And what if Christ-followers from the global North could come alongside their sisters and brothers in the South in ways that strengthen local community improvement efforts?

## Learning through Solidarity

Thousands of "new evangelicals" graduate every year from religious and secular colleges and universities. Many of these have participated in the kind of off-campus service and study programs profiled in this text. They now find themselves considering longer-term service or even a career among the world's urban poor. While some choose to straightaway enroll in advanced studies, others realize that in order to maximize the benefits of graduate school, they need extended practical experience—the kind that produces a high level of intercultural competence, second language proficiency, and firsthand knowledge of development-related issues. Azusa Pacific University's Master of Arts in Transformational Urban Leadership (MATUL) was designed to provide students this opportunity, culminating in a professional graduate degree.[15]

The entirely field-based degree program is co-sponsored by entrepreneurial training institutions on four continents (Asia, Africa, South America, and North America). "Foreign" (American and other) students complete coursework side-by-side with "national" classmates enrolled through a host academic institution. Through a unique combination of conceptual and experiential learning, Christian leaders are prepared to launch vocations rooted in an exceptional awareness of the urban poor realities. The MATUL may well be the only graduate program in the world exclusively focused on the world's burgeoning slums and shantytowns.

Most masters or doctoral degree programs in development practice are largely classroom-based. Students learn *about* particular realities, and ways to address them, but without necessarily living and working *with* the people most affected by them. What these programs do well is synthesize expert conceptual knowledge from various disciplines to understand the complexity of the urban poor condition. Where most are deficient is in arranging circumstances whereby students join those theoretical understandings to an in-depth experiential awareness of the world's problems.

## Solidarity through Lifestyle

One of the MATUL program's central assumptions is that insight and understanding is revealed, not through physical distance and emotional objectivity, but by sharing in a significant way the experience of being marginalized, un-resourced, and perhaps even mistreated—i.e., through *solidarity*. Western students who participate in the MATUL program are expected to relocate to program sites within select global megacities, find housing with local families either in or adjacent to slum communities, and engage in intensive language learning for three to four months prior to beginning formal coursework through the hosting institution. Students embrace a style of being that puts them in direct and reciprocal relationship with those whose reality they wish to comprehend. Solidarity *with* residents becomes the basis for learning *from* them, "to receive," in the words of Henri Nouwen, "the fruits of the lives of the poor, the oppressed, and the suffering as gifts for the salvation of the rich." This is only possible when the primary bond of the knower to the known is one of empathy and love rather than dispassionate logic.

Of all the great Christian doctrines, it is perhaps the Incarnation that has been most neglected in its pedagogical theological significance. Jesus didn't remain in a sequestered religious or cultural "bubble," nor did he conduct "mission trips" from the heavens to earth. He became little, weak, minority, vulnerable, dependent, and misunderstood. He entered the world's pain, problems, and thought systems through direct, firsthand encounters that involved costly identifications (Phil. 2:6–8; Matt 20:26–28).

There are at least six core theological-pedagogical values within the MATUL educational design that express solidarity of lifestyle and a "radical esteem for the Incarnation":

- *Self-limitation* (vs. power preservation). Students take on to themselves some of the conditions and constraints of temporal existences radically different from their own.
- *Embodiment* (vs. detachment). Students are placed in direct, physical relationship *with* slum life rather than merely taught *about* it.

- *Involvement* (vs. distance). Students make an experiential commitment to *narrow the distance* between themselves and those who are "stranger" within their host communities (e.g. Muslims, Marxists, drug dealers, sex workers, etc.).
- *Collaboration* (vs. independence/exclusion). Students relate to community families and associations in ways that are caring, mutual, and reciprocal, and that reverse the traditional relationship of outsiders dispensing knowledge and time upon a "dependent" community.
- *Responsibility* (vs. passivity). Students re-imagine the ultimate purpose of a graduate education, away from the mere acquisition of knowledge, marketable skills, and personal security, and toward the *application* of those competencies in the transformation of poor communities.
- *Redemption* (vs. domestication). Students imbibe a simple ethical imperative: that they are here to make a difference, to mend the world, to make it a place of justice and compassion. Faith is not an acceptance of the *status quo*, but a protest against the world as it is in the name of the world as it ought to be.

## Solidarity through Service

Another aspect of solidarity, building upon a lifestyle of downward mobility, has to do with social analysis and reflective action. The forty-five-unit MATUL degree program includes five practical training (field internship) courses, each operating through community organizations based in the urban poor communities where students reside. For each course, each student completes forty hours of voluntary service under the mentorship of seasoned national practitioners. Areas of service include health care, small business development, educational centre development, compassionate outreach to vulnerable populations, and issues surrounding land rights.

The real lives of poor people are often rendered invisible by mainstream institutions. To understand *why* particular groups of people have been relegated to the margins of global society, detached study is inadequate. Knowledge easily becomes "inert"—memorized from texts or lectures but not actually tested through firsthand experience. Deep learning requires that we enter into a critical awareness of actual conditions, causes, and consequences as community residents experience them. The MATUL program facilitates this through a set of research and service collaborations within indigenous organizations, each one focused on a particular dimension of community pain and possibility.

But international service-learning, like tourism generally, is ambivalent. Under certain conditions, it can enrich the life of host communities while providing students valuable resources for re-shaping their world awareness and personal lifestyle. Under other conditions, it can be just another "been there, done that" consumer form made possible by wealth accumulated within a grossly unequal system. When this happens, service-learning tends to merely service that system, enabling volunteers to "take," actively—all the while remaining largely oblivious to the ways they might be negatively impacting the local culture, environment, and economy.

The unintended effects of sending large numbers of ill-prepared North Americans to non-traditional destinations have historically received precious little "air time" among education abroad professionals. This, too, is beginning to change. Two of the largest and most influential international education professional organizations (NAFSA and The Forum on Education Abroad) have formed task forces and subcommittees to consider how education abroad students might journey more mindfully. The Forum's "Standards of Good Practice" now guide global educators, not just in expanding students' intellectual and cultural horizons, but also in maximizing the benefit and minimizing the harm to the host culture and environment.

Over the last few decades, the larger tourism industry has also made efforts to ameliorate the negative effects of travel. Tourism strategies variously described as "green," "ethical," "responsible," "people to people," "small-scale," "sustainable," and "community-based" are attempting to expand the role of tourism to include the sustaining or enhancing of the geographic, social, economic, cultural, or spiritual character of a place. For study and service programs (like the MATUL) operating among poor rural and urban populations in the global South, "pro-poor tourism" takes it one step further, seeking to generate net long-term benefits for rural and urban poor—those typically left out of tourism development.[16]

## Learning toward Shalom

Concern for "standards of good practices" among global educators in the mainstream culture finds its parallel in the biblical vision of *shalom*. In the

Old Testament poetic and prophetic literature, shalom is used to indicate an earthly order where justice and delight mark all of one's relationships: with God, with self, with others, with nature. In shalom, the whole creation flourishes: crooked structures are made straight, desolate places come to life, swords are beat into plowshares, and all nature and humankind, together, delight in their Creator. Freedom, harmony, prosperity, and hope stand against injustice, hostility, poverty, and despair.[17] Although shalom is an explicitly religious vision, it overlaps in some significant ways with the modern concept of sustainability. Both envision a global society founded on respect for nature, human rights, economic justice, and a culture of peace. Both signify a particular quality of life. Where they diverge is in the weight given to the spiritual dimension—the transcendent meaning and motivation found in serving fundamental human values, both as an act of devotion to God and as the necessary basis for a sustainable world.

In the MATUL program, the vision of shalom provides a spiritual-social-ecological model with which residents of disenfranchised settlements can contemplate "what is" in light of "what ought to be." For students as well, the shalom perspective inspires faith in the ability of people, working together, to achieve an enhanced quality of life in the sectors being addressed through their five internships: housing/environment, primary health, education, small business development, and freedom for vulnerable populations.

Program participants are invited into each of these sectors of slum life through locally managed, grassroots organizations. In most cases, these organizations have themselves stepped into the gap of providing critical social services to persons left underserved by government programs. Though often operating with limited staff and shoestring budgets, most welcome foreign students willing to adopt learner-servant roles. Indeed, the organization is often the one offering a service to the learner, not vice versa.

A number of general principles guide student involvement with their internship organizations. Each guideline aims to help cultural outsiders maximize the potential good and minimize the potential harm resulting from their intervention in vulnerable communities. In a reversal of the assumptions most foreign change agents carry to the field, interns soon come to appreciate (1) that local residents are already quite knowledgeable of the various factors underlying their condition; (2) that many are willing to work hard to improve their condition; (3) that the impetus for change must originate *within* the community itself—through local families, neighborhood associations, and those allied in their development; and (4) that the role of outsiders is to learn from, serve alongside, and otherwise support local residents in their community improvement.

Within this assumptive framework, interns engage in study and service projects that support a vision of urban community life where social, spiritual, environmental, and economic factors produce a life system that is socially bearable, economically equitable, and environmentally viable, as well as spiritually satisfying. Such communities enable residents to lead harmonious, healthy, dignified, productive, and meaning-filled lives—both now and in future generations—without harming the natural world.

## Social Shalom

The MATUL program aims to connect student guests and community hosts in ways that narrow the gap between "us" and "them" and strengthen the bond of understanding and respect between strangers. Every program participant is potentially a bridge between peoples, enabling a two-way learning process that can be deeply rewarding for guest and host alike. Cultural appreciation opens the door to the forging of rare cross-cultural bonds and alliances based on a common commitment to community betterment.

As part of their commitment to social shalom, MATUL students seek to form mutually beneficial relationships with urban poor families, national students and instructors, and staff mentors within grassroots organizations. Instead of setting up a separate and self-sustaining "bubble" with other foreigners, students learn to adapt themselves to local cultural patterns and to communicate in and outside the classroom in the local language. Doing so acts to minimize their "footprint," both on local customs and on natural resources. Within their internship organizations, local populations define what their livelihood priorities are. They also determine how the financial resources, ideas, and effort brought in by foreign students might positively contribute to community improvement. Caring and reciprocal relationships between hosts and guests over a period of two years replace interactions that are transitory, non-repetitive, and oriented to satisfying only private goals.

## Economic Shalom

Global tourism, inclusive of its educational forms, is often touted as a powerful vehicle for generating new jobs and services, earning foreign exchange, and alleviating poverty. Tourist demand creates much-needed jobs in construction, light manufacturing, transportation, telecommunications, and financial services. Locals are able to then use their wages to buy food, farm machinery, medicines, and other items needed to improve their lives. New economic enterprises can even be established in isolated locations, stimulating much-needed infrastructural improvements.

These potential benefits, however, are not automatically fulfilled. Especially in the economies of third world cities, a relatively small amount of the non-wage revenues generated by tourism actually stays in the country. Much of it ends up being repatriated ("leaked") to Western firms that own and operate the airlines, hotels, car rental agencies, and food services that foreign travelers depend upon.

In an effort to promote economic shalom within slum communities, the MATUL is structured as a long-term partnership between APU and local academic institutions, specific host communities, and a network of grassroots organizations that support leadership development and the creation of education-oriented microenterprises (e.g., family stays, language coaching, subject lectures). Office and field staff is drawn almost exclusively from the local community. Food and fuel supplies, along with program equipment, are also locally sourced. Students live with, and disburse room and board payments directly to, local families. They patronize locally owned eateries, utilize public forms of transportation that employ poorer members of the community, and learn to pay a fair price to vendors operating in the "informal" sector. In these and many other ways, program participants seek to deliver economic benefits to host communities while multiplying opportunities for intercultural interaction.

## Environmental Shalom

Education abroad that is environmentally sustainable strives to minimize the negative impacts of travel on the ecosphere. This is a fairly recent aim, one that seeks to respond to climate change rooted in what Lester Brown describes as the Western-modeled "fossil-fuel-based, automobile-centered, throwaway economy." In the past, the natural world was perceived as trivial, merely the stage for the interplay of cultural actors, with no particular moral questions or obligations. This general disposition has begun to change. We now recognize that much of our environmental crisis, as well as the way out of it, is fixed in human behavior.

At the root of human behavior is a certain relationship between humans and the earth. Students enrolled in the MATUL program are urged to see themselves in fundamental solidarity, not just with their urban poor hosts, but also with nonhuman creatures and their habitats. All life is sacred, intrinsically valuable, and deserving of being treated as "subject" rather than "object."

Christian love in an ecological context may, at first glance, seem appealing. But it raises certain indelicate questions. One of these is whether the potential benefits of international travel, both for global learners and for local residents, might be outweighed by the associated financial and environmental costs.[18]

To compensate for the carbon dioxide that their round-trip travel to their program site creates, MATUL students are required to purchase "carbon offsets." An offset is a flight surcharge, paid to an offset company like Terra Pass, that funds projects—like tree planting, solar energy, landfill gas capture, and wind farms—calculated to help balance out the environmental impact of airborne journeys. Once at their field site, and for the duration of their program, participants are expected to embrace natural living patterns within host families. There they learn to consciously adjust their level of water and power consumption toward the local standard, expressing responsibility and self-restraint in moral consideration for the nonhuman creation.[19]

## Spiritual Shalom

As previously noted, many young adults are re-imagining spirituality in terms of a wider, non-institutional, and values-based vision of how the world ought to be. In profound contrast to the modern monoculture of hyper-individualization, profit maximization, and profligate disregard of social and environmental consequences, many are on a sacred quest to realize a sustainable and deeply satisfying existence rooted in global concern, reverence toward other species and lifeways, solidarity with the forgotten, and delight-filled communion with the God of creation. They intuitively know that any healthy society depends on fundamental purposes and ultimate meanings—what some call "spiritual capital"—to turn members outward and promote the common good. In biblical terms, spiritual shalom is the consummation of love in all relationships, "binding everything together in perfect harmony" (Col. 3:14).

Community internships invite MATUL students and community members, together, to pursue works of community transformation that serve as approximations of the harmony and healing anticipated in the New Creation

(Isa. 9:2–7; 11:3–9; 58:5–7; 65:17–25; Rev. 21–22). Grassroots organizations, many of them faith-based, are singularly able to harness residents' social and spiritual solidarity, providing foreign students a rare window into the sundry ways resource-poor residents act together to improve their communities. Acts of compassion and political advocacy, evangelism and Bible study, women's education and economic development—all of these, and more, serve as signs of a new reality that Jesus said was causing people to climb over each other and gladly sacrifice everything just to experience (Matt. 13:44–46).

## Conclusion

United Nations researchers estimate that sometime around 2050, the human race will attain its maximum population, level off, and then decline. This final build-out of humanity will coalesce with irreversible climate change, totally altering the conditions of human life as we know them today. This will take place in many of our lifetimes, but will be felt most dramatically in the city-slums of the South. Squattable land is running out. Third world labor markets are increasingly unable to absorb any more people. The future is uncertain. Will a new generation of slum dwellers simply resign themselves to the under-side of history? Or will they find ways to contest their abandonment and avert the slum clearance campaigns that are making way for modern shopping malls and office buildings?

There may not be a way back from the brink. But there are two good reasons to be hopeful. One is readily apparent in the resourcefulness and resiliency of the urban poor themselves. The other is the growing commit-ment of others (including Christian congregations and colleges) to walk the "narrow path" of costly identification with people in their actual situations. Transportation and communications technologies have shrunk distances. The spread of television and popular culture has infused common cultural ele-ments into previously isolated areas. And now the "Southern shift" in global Christianity, along with a burgeoning global network of national NGOs, has laid the foundation for strategic North-South partnerships.

Through the programs documented in this book, and many others, a rising generation of Christian internationalists are preparing themselves, both intellectually and experientially, to launch vocations dedicated to the inter-ests of "the least of these." Their capacity to see shalomic potential, rather than hopeless degradation, in the world's new urban habitations will enable them to catalyze new forms of advocacy and action in fields as diverse as global health, environmental policy, church leadership, and public administration. In so doing, they will supply what foreign policy expert Walter Russell Mead believes "has been sadly lacking in the world of U.S. foreign policy: a trusted group of experts, well versed in the nuances and dilemmas of the international situation, who are able to persuade large numbers of Americans to support the complex and counterintuitive policies that are sometimes necessary in this wicked and frustrating—or, dare one say it, fallen—world."

# CHAPTER TWELVE

# The Phenomenology of a Christian Environmental Study Abroad Program

CHRIS ELISARA

*Chris Elisara (MBA, International Economic Development, Eastern University, PA; Ph.D. Intercultural Education, Biola University, CA) is the founder (with his wife Tricia), and executive director of the Creation Care Studies Program (CCSP). CCSP is an independent Christian educational institution with campuses in Belize, Central America, and the South Island of New Zealand. Serving twenty-five institutions, and up to twenty-five students per semester in each location, CCSP serves a unique niche in Christian higher education as a semester-long multi-disciplinary environmental study abroad program. Through field-based stream, marine, and forest ecology courses, coupled with courses in theology, sustainable community development, environmental literature, and internships, CCSP serves biology and environmental science students equally well as arts and humanities majors with a passion for environmental stewardship.*

*Nicholas Wolterstorff's shalom-based education is the cornerstone of CCSP's theology, philosophy, and educational praxis. This chapter compliments an earlier publication exploring CCSP's brand of shalom-centered education by looking deeply at the relationship between shalom, environmental stewardship, and*

*CCSP's notion of an "earthy faith." Special attention is given to the ways CCSP intentionally cultivates an earthy faith through its pedagogical approach and practice of worship.*

Under the moon-shadow of snow-capped peaks, students and staff sit in a circle in the garden of the Old Convent—the Creation Care Study Program's New Zealand campus. Weary smiles and hushed words are exchanged under the yellow light of encircling tiki torches while patiently and reverently waiting for the day's last event—the semester dedication service. It's been a thrilling, but long and exhausting, first day of the semester.

After traveling halfway around the world, students are picked up at the Christchurch airport. Luggage is bundled under the requisite blue tarp to ensure everything is kept dry from New Zealand's capricious "sun showers" while students board vans for the three-hour drive north. As the group travels "100 K" down the left hand side of the two-lane highway the landscape, sky, light, and small towns zipping by the window whisper over and over again, "Believe it! You're really in New Zealand."

An hour from their new home, the travelers round a corner and everyone gasps at the sight: snow-capped mountains kissing a rugged coast and glacier-blue ocean. Breathtaking. The beauty before them is dizzying—something like the Israelites may have felt as they were about to step across the Jordan, or the Maori spying Aoetaroa for the first time from their Pacific-crossing canoes.[1] It's a mixture of, "Wow, I'm going to live in that good and beautiful place over yonder. I can't wait to get there, but what will it be like? What will I experience there?" They will know soon enough.

Soon after pulling into the gate and unloading bags, students find their rooms, rest a little, and then reconvene for dinner warmly wrapped up in coats, hats, and scarves. Fish and chips will be served on the beach only two miles from home under high mountains, a setting sun, rising moon, slight ocean breeze, and a cooling earth. Dinner begins with prayer and is followed by a spread of salty fish and chips dipped in sweet, runny Kiwi tomato sauce. The after-dinner entertainment is skipping stones on the flat calm bay. Someone jokes that the only thing that would make this unbelievable first dinner "perfect" would be if Courtnay, the program director, would call in our resident Sperm Whales to breach and frolic in the bay for our mutual pleasure. Heads nod, then someone wistfully adds, "OK Courtnay, whales are a big ask, so we'll settle for a pod of Dusky Dolphins."

The students' first New Zealand dinner slowly digesting and keeping them warm, their soft exhalations are visible in the chilly air as they sit waiting in the garden. Jet lag is wreaking havoc on mind and body, but the staff has decided no matter how tired and exhausted—and *everyone* is "knackered"—on the first night of the program, the new community will intentionally take time to dedicate the semester to God. So they do.

On the other side of the world, students attending CCSP's Belize program touchdown at the Philip S.W. Goldson International Airport on the outskirts of Belize City. They quickly disembark and load up into CCSP's converted school bus for the two-hour drive from Belize's eastern seaboard to its western border. On the drive "home," the landscape quickly changes from tropical Caribbean coast to mangrove-lined waterways. On a curve, the landform becomes tropical savannah. Around mile marker fifty-five the bus is speeding though limestone caste and lowland tropical rainforest, occasionally slowing down for speed bumps when passing through small villages. Arriving famished, students savor the national dish of rice, beans, and stewed chicken with fresh homemade flour tortillas for dinner. Toucans looking for an evening roost stop in a huge fig tree outside the dining room and make a croaking call. Enraptured students croak back, and an impromptu neighborly bird-human conversation breaks out. The semester is dedicated to God, and just like their fellow students in New Zealand, the Belize students crawl into bed at the end of their first day drained but satisfied.

Undeniably there are different experiences derived from the geographical and cultural differences between Kaikoura, New Zealand, and San Ignacio, Belize, however it is also undeniable there is a common CCSP phenomenology that transcends place and culture. But what exactly is the quintessential "CCSP experience" we purposefully seek to create, or better yet "curate,"[2] regardless of location? Why do we seek to curate *that* particular experience as constitutive of a Christian environmental studies program? And *how* do we curate the experience?

## Educating for Shalom

In the Old Convent's moonlit garden the newly assembled CCSP community dedicates their semester to God by praying:

> Christ, your cross speaks to both us and to our world. In your dying for us you accepted the pain and hurt of the whole of creation. The arms

of your cross stretch out across the broken world in reconciliation. *You have made peace with us. Help us to be your peace by sharing in your reconciling work. Help us to be part of, and agents for, your peace in this world.* May we recognize your Spirit disturbing and challenging us to care for the earth, and also particularly the poor for whom you have a special love. O Christ, the whole of creation groans. Set it free and make it whole. Set us free and teach us to be the people you have called us to be. In the name of Christ, Amen.[3] (emphasis added)

The highlighted portion of this prayer articulates the animating commitment at the center of CCSP's educational vision—the biblical concept of shalom. Our mission statement reads, "CCSP is a Christian organization whose mission is to educate students to *be a part of, and agents for, God's shalom,* particularly through understanding and caring for creation." So why do we curate the particular CCSP educational experience we do? Simply put, compelled by our theological, philosophical, and pedagogical convictions, we have shaped the CCSP experience in our best attempt to educate for shalom. Moreover, CCSP has chosen to focus on an oft-neglected dimension of shalom for evangelical Christians, namely, care of creation. At one level the relationship between shalom and creation care is broad and complex, but at another level it is quite simple: there is an inextricable relationship between human poverty and the health of ecosystems. In light of this fact, one of our highest educational aspirations is to sensitize students to the nexus of environmental injustice, ecological degradation, and poverty so they can apprehend that caring for creation is an act of loving our neighbor, and especially our neighbors suffering from poverty. Thus, within the first hours of each semester, students are not only introduced to the mission of CCSP, they are literally praying it right out of their student handbooks, and will do so repeatedly through the semester. CCSP's dedication service epitomizes what the handbook's editors describe as the "convergence of spiritual development and commitment to global engagement" fostered by quality study abroad programs. But this descriptor merely hints at what students will learn in experience after experience, and course upon course, for the rest of the semester.

Pedagogically speaking, in the dedication service, CCSP intentionally intensifies through ritual one of the most powerful liminal moments of the student's CCSP experience for the purpose of imparting to them as forcefully and effectively as possible what we consider to be the most important things to grasp about CCSP.[4] That is, the biblical truth of shalom, and that we are to be a part of and agents for it. A core set of beliefs, values, and truths essential to CCSP animates the experience we create in the dedication service, from its natural outside setting (which brings in elements of temperature, darkness, beauty, and sounds) to the content of the prayers, scriptures, and symbols within the service, and the service's participatory nature. Draw back a bit further and consider the dedication service in the context of the whole first day, and you will also perceive, as weary students intuitively do in the moment, how the dedication service fits into caring for basic human needs at a time when student and staff energies can only focus on the essentials. In short, the dedication service both signals and models for students CCSP's serious spiritual intentions for the semester, while simultaneously declaring that communing with God is a basic human need to which we must and will attend.

As we have striven to provide an educational experience equal to our biblical aspirations, Nicholas Wolterstorff's writings on biblical justice and education have influenced us greatly. We believe they display a vision adequate to the task and calling of Christian education; thus we will briefly explore Wolterstorff's contribution to CCSP in the following section.[5]

What does it mean to participate in the kingdom of God? What is the biblical vision of the Christian-in-the-world? Wolterstorff addresses these questions when he asserts the centrality of the biblical concept of shalom, which is the existential reality of the reign of God. The purpose of the Christian church is to pray and struggle for shalom, celebrating its presence and mourning its absence. Shalom is therefore also the goal of Christian education: to exhibit and equip for shalom. But what is shalom? According to Wolterstorff, the Scriptures describe shalom as God's desire for a broken and hurting world. It encompasses the whole breadth of our relationships, including those with God, self, others, and nature. This is no disembodied evangelical Gnosticism. Rather it is embodied individuals and communities in relationship with the earth in which they have been placed, and with the Author of the universe. Flourishing is at the heart of the vision of shalom: the God of life desires life in its fullest.

There are three key parts to Wolterstorff's understanding of shalom. The first is that shalom involves the *absence of conflict and violence*. Shalom, then, is a total commitment to seeking peace, both with and for humanity, and with and for the rest of creation. Second, shalom entails *doing justice*. Consequently, in an unjust world, shalom must include the attempt to put things right, acknowledging wrongs inflicted and seeking restoration. It includes a challenge to the oppressors and hope for the oppressed. It includes a liberation mandate that is concerned with the asymmetrical power structures dominating our world. Wolterstorff insists that Scripture makes it clear that

> the cries of the poor, of the oppressed, and of the victimized touch God's heart, and . . . the groans of God's created but now polluted earth bring tears to God's eyes. If a college is to commit itself to serving the God of the Bible it must commit itself, as an academic institution, to serve the cause of justice in the world. I find no detour around this conclusion.[6]

This twin emphasis on social justice and ecological stewardship is at the core of CCSP's work in creation care and is encapsulated in the term *earth justice*. We desire to teach about and for justice so that our graduates practice justice.

Lastly, shalom will only be complete when we have "*delight and joy*" in our relationships with God, others, creation, and self. It is not enough to be rid of violence and injustice. Only when there is enjoyment in who we are, and in everything with which we are in relationship, will shalom be fully realized. In these three ways, shalom is completeness.

Given shalom's biblical imperative, Walterstorff develops a model of Christian education that in earlier writings focused on three teaching tools to educate for shalom: reasoning, discipline, and modeling. An important shift in Wolterstorff's thinking, however, has been the addition of a fourth factor: the cultivation of empathy for the world around us. This fourth factor has also been central to CCSP's education for shalom.

Wolterstorff suggests that although empathy is not typically cultivated in educational praxis, it is critical that educators actively seek to do so. The most effective way to do this is by direct experience with victims of injustice:

> If people are to be energized to struggle to undo injustice, it is important that they listen to the voices and see the faces of the victims so that empathy can be invoked. . . . [R]eading books about injustice is, for most people, including myself, far less effective in energizing them to action than actually listening to the voices and actually seeing the faces of victims.[7]

Wolterstorff insists that the walls between school and life outside the classroom "must become much more porous than traditionally they have been," with teachers exploring ways "of bringing life into the classroom and of bringing the classroom to life."[8] Engaging in the world (and bringing the world into the classroom) is therefore one of Wolterstorff's key recommendations for leading students into empathetic and shalom-seeking relationships with the wounded world. With these convictions, Wolterstorff commends international study-abroad programs (like CCSP's Belize program) to developing countries. But as the editors of this book demonstrate, geographical location within a developing country is not necessarily a prerequisite for cultivating globally engaged students if the focus of the program within a developed country (e.g., Orvieto Italy, or San Francisco's urban core) intentionally "emphasizes formation of personal ethics, cultivation of empathy, the creation of deep communities, and commitment to social responsibility."

We fully embrace Wolterstorff's concept of empathy. To build further, we want to contribute two additional elements we see as congruent with Wolterstorff's perspectives. First, although his work primarily addresses the need for empathy with suffering humans, we want to extend these ideas to a wounded and suffering creation. Second, we also suggest that in stressed ecosystems, as in suffering individuals and communities, there may also be beauty and goodness to be understood and celebrated. This is, increasingly, an essential art.

Drawing on Wolterstorff's insights, we believe the following are essential characteristics that shalom-based education projects like CCSP's must embody. The first is, they must be faith-informed. By that we mean the program must encourage and inspire faith in the living God. It will intentionally seek to challenge and broaden "childhood" faiths. A vibrant spirituality will be part of this. Without it, as Leonardo Boff observes, religion is breathless and education runs the risk of abstracting God from real-life experience.[9] To this end, CCSP has shaped a spiritual focus around "general sacramentality,"[10] or more plainly put, an "earthy faith," which we will explore in greater depth in the next section.

Educating for shalom stresses Christian character, values, and virtues. I argue that education can be neither apolitical nor amoral. Rather, our politics must reflect what Jim Wallis calls "God's politics."[11] The God of the Bible has given us the task to struggle for justice for the marginalized and the vulnerable. Though sharpening students' intellects has its place, education cannot be merely intellectual. Therefore, the entire education institution must also embrace emotions, character formation, virtue building, and setting life goals and priorities.

Education for shalom also stresses engagement. As Brian Walsh instructs, and as Ron Morgan affirms in Chapter Eight of this volume, the appropriate biblical categories of Christian faith are neither optimism nor pessimism but rather prophetic critique and prophetic hope.[12] The earth and its inhabitants have many wounds. A Christian education must address these wounds and the reasons they exist. Additionally, it must articulate hope in the redeeming power of a God who calls us to respond by imagining and pursuing alternatives.

By placing shalom at the heart of our work, CCSP intentionally pursues a radical educational project. We seek to align our entire pedagogy with this goal.

## Why Cultivate an "Earthy Faith" When Educating for Shalom?

Our reading of Scripture leads us to the conclusion that the Christian faith *is* an earthy faith. We did not arrive at this perspective simply because our particular educational focus is creation stewardship. Rather, we agree with Eugene Peterson when he writes in *Leap Over a Wall: Earthy Spirituality for Everyday Christians* (1997), that God

> can never be dealt with in an antiseptic theological laboratory as a specialty of heaven, but only on this earth—"on *earth* as it is in heaven." Earth, and the conditions of earth—weather, digestion, family, job, government—define the context in which we deal with God.[13]

We believe that it is becoming increasingly critical for Christians of all traditions, and perhaps evangelicals in particular, to recover a faith at home in this world, a faith that perceives God working in this place, and a faith that works for the redemption of all creation. This is not a faith that simply plucks survivors from a sinking ship, but rather a faith viewed as participating in God's work of restoring the entire boat.

While much has been written on the necessity of an earthy faith,[14] the context of such a call is the crisis of (un)sustainability and ecological degradation facing our world, and the ambivalence, at best, of the church. Questions of environmental degradation are made all the more pressing because their effects are disproportionately borne by the poor and marginalized. There is, therefore, a critical need for a radical change in our relationship with the earth.

The onus rests on us to reorient ourselves so that the earth is cherished rather than exploited beyond its ecological limits.

Despite the ambivalence of the North American church toward this issue, there exists within the Christian faith, and the biblical text, the resources for a response. We agree with Bouma-Prediger when he writes, "The gospel is surely more than caring for the earth, but just as surely it involves nothing less."[15]

A central aspect of an earthy faith is an affirmation of the physical, material, and embodied—to affirm, as Larry Rasmussen reminds us, that "matter matters."[16] This affirmation is founded in Christology: Christ's life (the Incarnation of God on this earth), death (the power of God's love for the whole earth), resurrection (the eschatological hope in Christ for the earth), and reign (the rule of Christ over the whole earth), and as Walter Brueggemann also expertly exegetes, in the centrality of the earth, or "land," within Old Testament narratives.[17] An earthy faith sees humanity in intimate relationship with the earth. Rasmussen puts it thus: "Earth is bone of our bone and flesh of our flesh."[18] This acknowledgment is critical. No longer can we see ourselves separated from the earth. Instead, we are completely dependent upon and interrelated with the earth.

An earthy faith finds expression in a vibrant *sacramentalist spirituality* that makes space in our worship of God for our relationships of belonging to the earth. This sacramentalist perspective seeks to recover a vision of Christ in our neighbors, especially the poor and marginalized. It also acknowledges that only on this earth can we, as embodied persons, see, feel, touch, and sense the presence of God. But this spiritual perspective applies not only to humanity: all creation exists to voice worship to the Creator. Sacramentalist spirituality enables a reimagining of the world in which we can see fingerprints of the Creator God in creation around us. An earthy faith will also express itself through a desire to seek an *earth justice*, a justice that combines social justice and ecological stewardship in a desire to see shalom restored to all creation.

A sacramentalist spirituality and earth justice are critical for—and necessary expressions of—an earthy faith. They are also essential for empathy. A sacramentalist spirituality feeds into empathy through a reimagining of the world. One feels empathy for creation through seeing God's imprint in creation. Without an empathetic bond and a sense of urgency, the struggle for justice will never be entertained, and an earthy faith is hollow. Teaching for an earthy faith that pursues shalom will therefore situate the building of these empathetic relationships at the center of its pedagogy. As Bouma-Prediger makes clear, however, "We care for only what we love. We love only what we know. We truly know only what we experience."[19] This linking of love, knowledge, and experience echoes Wolterstorff's emphasis on the need for direct experience. Thus, together with sacramentalist spirituality and earth justice, empathy is at the heart of an earthy faith.

## A Quintessential CCSP Experience: Cultivating an Earthy Faith in Worship

In addition to our initial dedication service, the CCSP community worships together each week as a part of our weekly Sunday Community Night. The following is a worship service commonly used each semester in both Belize and New Zealand. Adapted from a service pioneered by Cityside Baptist Church in Auckland, New Zealand, it is highly experiential. The service consists of "kinesthetic worship" with worshipers encouraged to interact with certain earthy elements—water, earth, fire, and air—in their worship praxis. These elements are used to express worship to the Creator and also, particularly, to focus on the work of the Holy Spirit. The service draws heavily upon an earth (sacramentalist) spirituality and is primarily conducted outdoors so as to engage directly with creation. This particular service is also carried out in the second half of the semester, when students are more relaxed with each other, are already familiar with creation theology, and are open to a creative worship praxis.

Four stations are set up around the campus—all but one are outdoors. Care is taken to ensure that they are sufficiently apart so that each occupies a separate and distinct space. The service is conducted in the evening and, with the exception of the security lights and some table lamps set up at the various stations, the campus is completely dark. The community gathers at the veranda. The worship leader introduces the service, in the same way that all our services are introduced, with the following short liturgy:

Worship Leader:  Jesus Christ is the light of the World. [Light candle]
The light shines in the darkness and the darkness has
not overcome it.

All:  Light of the world, shine on us.
Light of the world, give us peace.

> Fire of life, heal this broken world with your love.
> Amen.

The worship leader then introduces the service:

> Throughout the biblical text created things are used as images, meta-
> phors, or tangible objects to provoke and direct readers to ponder the
> glory of God, the mission of His Son, and the work of the Spirit. The
> biblical text is so laden with these images that most times we pay little
> or no attention to them. Tonight we meditate on creation in order to
> meditate on, and worship the Creator.

> The format for the service is then explained. There are four stations.
> At each station there are instructions in the form of small laminated
> cards—though students and staff need not do anything they find
> uncomfortable. Worshipers are welcome to walk to the stations in
> any order they like, and spend as much time as they like at each sta-
> tion. However, after forty-five minutes, a bell is rung to indicate that
> it is time to meet together again. The walk between the stations takes
> place in silence, an act of worship itself. The journey therefore is indi-
> vidual, with each person visiting the stations in their own time and
> in their own order.

The worship leader then reads a prayer and says a blessing by New Zealand
poet, Anne Powell:

> Wild lover of a broken earth, we consecrate this time of worship to
> your glory.
> We do not see you, but we know you to be here:
> In your creation, in our worshiping community.
> Ground us in your presence; wash over us with your love;
> Burn in our minds; blow the breath of life into our doubting hearts.
> Holy Spirit, meet with us this night. Amen.
> And may the Maker of water and air and fire heal you who walk the
> earth. Go, walk in peace.

Positioned on a mound on the periphery of campus where it soaks in sun or
moonlight, the wind station offers sweeping vistas of farm paddocks, fences,
trees, and the distant horizon. Rarely at this location is the breeze completely

still. The instruction card contains a short translation of the Hebrew word "ruach" (wind, breath, spirit) and records the following biblical text:

> Do not marvel that I said to you, "You must be born anew." The wind blows where it wills, and you hear the sound of it, but you do not know where it comes or where it goes; so it is with every one who is born of the Spirit. (John 3:7–8)

Likewise, worshippers find there a poem by James K. Baxter. Instructions invite them to read the following words aloud three times softly:

> Lord, Holy Spirit
> You blow like the wind in a thousand paddocks
> Inside and outside the fences
> You blow where you wish to blow.

Finally, the following invitation is offered:

> Feel the breeze, faint or blustery as it is. Ponder this question: How big is your God?

The instruction card at the water station records the following biblical text and commentary:

> Jesus said: "The water that I will give will become a spring of water, welling up for eternal life" (John 4:14). The well is deep. The tap is on full. The river of God overflows. We are flooded with the gifts of the Holy Spirit. It is poured into us, over us, around us. Drink deep, delighting in God's extravagant abundance.

The instruction card invites worshipers to pour themselves glasses of cold water and to reflect on the dry things in their lives and relationships. The card then invites them to drink half the glass and pour the other half onto the earth; to wash their own feet in a tub of water and know that Christ has made them clean; to say a prayer for those who are unable to enjoy clean drinking water and other basic needs; and finally to pray that Yahweh's justice will be done in this earth.

The fire station is the only indoor station. It is set up in the classroom. The room is lit solely with candlelight. A centerpiece—a table spread with unlit candles and the words "Jesus will baptize you with the Holy Spirit and fire" (Matt. 3:11) written above it—occupies the front of the room. On the floor, in-between the entrance way and the centerpiece, a poem is written in large writing. It too is illuminated by candlelight. The poem by New Zealander Joy Cowley reads:

It just happens
a suddenness inside me and then a presence
of wind and flame burning, burning,
and I cover my eyes with my fears
knowing that I am too small and too frail
to bear this firestorm of love.

Worshipers are invited to light a candle at the centerpiece and reflect on how a small flame can start a bigger blaze. The following prayer is suggested:

O Lord God, Firestarter,
You are a wild forest-fire,
You are a flash of lightning in the night sky,
You are a blazing, burning, flaming star.
You are a fire burning in the hearth; you warm the whole house.
You are a flickering candle; you cast light to all the dark corners.
Come anew, O Flame of Love,
Melt my cold heart, set my life on fire.
Amen.

The worshipers receive a final thought, from another card, before they leave the station: "A fire bursts out—contagious, unpredictable, dangerous. Flames leap across with unquenchable desire."

The earth station is the only station where the worship leader is present. As each worshiper comes to the station they are greeted with the following words:

You are 'adam from 'adamâ.[20]
You are human from humus.
You are an earth-creature.
Dust from Dust—you were made from the earth.
Dust to Dust—to the earth you will return.
And from the earth you will rise again
when Christ comes back in full glory
to consummate His kingdom on this earth.

You are connected to the earth,
You are dependent on the earth,
You *are* earth.

They are given the following biblical texts on the instruction card:

The earth is the LORD's, and all that is in it. (Ps. 24:1)

The LORD God formed man from the dust of the ground, and breathed into his nostrils the breath of life; and the man became a living being. (Gen. 2:7)

Worshipers are then asked to take their shoes off and step into a pile of mud. They are told to pick some up in their hands, roll it around a little, and enjoy being a part of the earth God loves. As each worshiper leaves, they are painted with a muddy cross on the forehead and the worship leader says the following:

Christ died for the world He loved.

Christ's resurrection offers hope for all that is.

Christ will come again to make all things whole.

At the end of forty-five minutes, when everyone has had a chance to visit all four stations, a bell is rung and the worshippers gather back again at the veranda. A quiet conclusion to the service is provided. Each worship time we share we conclude with the following short liturgical refrain:

Worship leader: Father, watch over us and care for us.
Holy Spirit, inspire us with faith, hope, and love.
Christ, give us strength and courage to follow you.
All: Give us your peace. Amen.

This case study illustrates in a concentrated example the variety of ways CCSP seeks to facilitate and practice a sacramentalist faith. The service is built on the use of Scripture, direct experience of nature, carefully thought through activities and prayers, and "out of the box" creativity. Rather than blocking creation out during our worship, we seek to see the fingerprints of God within the world.

If successful, our hope is that students will commune and respond deeply to God. We also desire that they will add what they learn from participating in this worship service to what they are learning in other areas of the program to cultivate a robust and vibrant earthy relationship with the loving creator God—ecological literacy; capacity for "deeply-seeing" social, ecological, economic, spiritual, and other interconnections in reality; the necessary core virtues, or "habitual dispositions we must exhibit to be faithful earthkeepers," which, following Steven Bouma-Prediger's lead, are peaceableness, justice, compassion, wisdom, and attuning their biblical worldview to a robust theology of creation and creation care . . . which in turn seeks to live in authentic community with the wider communities of town, region, and nation.[21]

Many of our students' trajectories have been challenged and sometimes transformed as part of their involvement in CCSP. Naturally, the level of change has been different in each individual, with no one student's metamorphosis identical to another's. Change has taken place in all our students, though not always in the ways we had intended. This is something we cherish. Our goal is to help students be a part of God's work in this world. We hope that students will pick up and draw upon an ethic of ecological stewardship and social justice in their everyday life, but to be an authentic expression of faith it must come from within them. We can only help create the space in which such an ethic could be planted; whether it will come to fruition or not is something over which we have little control. Nevertheless, the value of studying abroad with CCSP for a semester is in providing the opportunities and impetus for our students to mature into Christians who will work for shalom in their daily lives.[22]

# CHAPTER THIRTEEN

# The Study Service Term

## An Alignment of a Religious Tradition
## with an Academic Program

### Thomas J. Meyers

*Thomas J. Meyers (Ph.D. in Sociology, Boston University) is Associate Academic Dean, Director of International Education and Professor of Sociology at Goshen College. In his international education role, he supervises Goshen's study abroad programs in Africa, Asia, and Latin America. Goshen College requires all students to complete a semester of international education, and the majority of them travel to a developing country. Thomas regularly travels to each site where a faculty leader is in residence. Prior to becoming an administrator, he led eight groups of students to Guadeloupe in the West Indies and Ivory Coast in West Africa.*

*This chapter describes the integration of a theological tradition and a study abroad program known as the Study Service Term (SST). For more than forty years, Goshen College students have been studying and serving alongside people in societies that are significantly different than their own. For Mennonites, the Incarnation of Jesus Christ is understood as an act of crossing over into the human realm, with all of its frailties. With great humility and respect for the other he entered homes, broke bread with people, worked on their boats and in their carpentry shops. In this tradition students participating in the SST program are asked to cross over into the lives of their hosts and to gain a global perspective on the human condition.*

## Goshen College Begins a Bold New Initiative in International Education

On the morning of September 12, 1968, fifty-two Goshen College students stepped onto a Greyhound bus bound for Miami, Florida. Several days later, they boarded airplanes for their final destinations of Costa Rica, Guadeloupe, and Jamaica. Three sets of Goshen College faculty leaders met them at the airports in San Jose, Pointe-á-Pitre, and Kingston for a semester of study and service. Goshen had just begun an experiment that at the time was nearly unprecedented in higher education. At that juncture, and to this day, the college began to require all of its students to complete a semester of international education. For forty years, international education has been at the core of the general education program at Goshen College. Thirteen hours of credit in language, history, cultural study, the arts, and natural science have been incorporated in international education. To meet this requirement more than eighty percent of the student body has traveled to a country with cultures that are "significantly different than those of North America."[1] Current locations include Cambodia, China, Egypt, Jamaica, Nicaragua, Peru, Senegal, and Tanzania.

All Goshen College faculty are encouraged to go abroad for at least one semester during their tenure at this institution. Many have spent more than a year developing a program along with national country coordinators and working with multiple groups of students. The structure of the program has remained relatively unchanged in forty years. Faculty and their family are in place in a large city (often but not always the capital of the country) and greet students upon arrival. Students spend the first half of the term in a study program of language and cultural classes taught by professors from the host country. They live with a national family and commute to and from a central meeting point via public transportation. At the midpoint in the semester, they are sent out in groups of two or three to a smaller town or village in the interior of the country where they live with a second family and work—in a clinic assisting nurse midwives in Senegal, with a reforestation program in Nicaragua, developing a computer program for a guinea pig farmer to track his production in Peru, interviewing victims of landmines in Cambodia, and so on.

The Study Service Term was born in the shadow of both the Vietnam War and the emergence of the Peace Corps, at a liberal arts college that is deeply rooted in a denomination with a long legacy of emphasizing service. Indeed, the motto of Goshen College is "culture for service." Long before service-learning became a popular phrase in academe the college attempted to wed a strong academic tradition with service-learning, within a particular theological context. Former Goshen College President Lawrence Burkholder described our form of service as "service seeking understanding." At a national conference on international education in 1989, Burkholder said:"What I am referring to is a basic commitment to a life of service—not simply to tearful and ephemeral responses to pictures of starving children in Sudan or the homeless freezing to death on the streets of New York City. Service without a philosophy or a theology or a tradition of service is likely to be short-lived, erratic, superficially emotional, and fragile when the going gets hard."[2]

## Service as an Expression of the Incarnation

Among the many metaphors that have been used to describe our Study Service Term is incarnation. As my predecessor Dr. Wilbur Birky put it,

> Let us propose the Incarnation as an act of divine imagination rooted in a profound realization that even God could not know and understand the human condition completely without entering into it, to experience it in the body. That was a true cross-cultural experience. So a description of at least the early parts of Jesus' incarnation applies aptly to the SST experience: it is to give up one's customary place of comfort to become as a child, to learn a new language, to eat in new ways, to be received into a new family, to work in the mundane "carpentry shop," to experience frustration and success, and to learn to serve in the very "thick" of life. This is service-learning in the context of crossing over into the life of the "other." If necessary for God, how much more so for us is this knowledge by experience for compassionate action.[3]

Birky's insights borrow from a long tradition within the Mennonite church that recognizes the profound importance of Christ's humanity and the example of his life in the world of his day. Mennonites descend from the Anabaptist wing of the sixteenth-century century Protestant Reformation.[4] Among the important intellects of the Anabaptists movement was Pilgrim Marpeck.[5] Marpeck insisted that to be a Christian is to be actively involved in meeting human need wherever one confronts it. This position was a logical outcome of his understanding of the Incarnation. For many in his time, the Incarnation was simply a reflection of the inner transformation of all believers. There was little need for an external expression of the internal, even to the point of suggesting that public church ceremonies such as church services were no longer necessary. Marpeck's response to the so-called Spiritualists was that there can be no separation between external and internal expression of faith. The two are inextricably linked. In Christ, both the internal transformation of the believer and the external manifestation of love of one's neighbor become congruent. In a recent article about Marpeck's theology Reardon summarizes Marpeck's argument in the following paragraph:

> ". . . in the revelation of Christ, God has first given Himself to be known so that they may all believe in Him and have eternal life." This revelation takes place within physical existence. It is an embodied revelation, thus Marpeck avoided any attempt to separate the "physical voice of Christ" (the spoken embodied words) from the "Spirit and Life". Christ's physical nature was a reality, and because of this incarnational reality, Christ was able to meet our physical reality and engage in the signs of our existence. This is important because Marpeck takes seriously the state of our embodiment. We must use the "elemental voice" while in the flesh. Thus, to communicate the spiritual, God must appropriate the physical and unite them. In an incarnational existence, the "spiritual reality is not hopelessly unknowable but is available because of Christ's incarnation and the presence of the Holy Spirit in the believer.[6]

With this understanding of the dual nature of the Incarnation, Marpeck's thinking follows a natural progression to suggest that, like Christ, the believer must have an active presence in the face of human need that expresses both inner transformation and a desire to make very explicit the attempt to be a disciple and to follow the model of Christ's active intervention in the world. Along with like-minded sisters and brothers, the believer must take his or her social responsibility seriously. In a dissertation on Marpeck, one scholar observes that, "Marpeck conceived of a transformed community of transformed persons, transforming the larger human community. . . . The believer served not only the body of Christ but also the whole world."[7] In his own life, Marpeck carried out this belief system by his own acts of charity that included aiding refugees, covering debts of the indigent, and providing firewood not only for local residents of cities in which he lived, but even on occasion for soldiers who pillaged those same cities. As Klassen notes, "in this situation, the issue of social justice and loving the enemy took on a concreteness that went beyond the theoretical. Marpeck's solution was to provide wood for all and in that way eliminated the need for occupying soldiers to break into homes and use furniture for firewood."[8]

As most people lack Marpeck's eloquence, Mennonite are often more inclined to imitate his behavior and reach out to others as an expression of their faith. For many, a life of service and a commitment to discipleship is at the heart of what it means to be faithful. In his classic essay on the Anabaptist vision, former Goshen College Dean Harold S. Bender observed that discipleship is the very essence of what it means to be Christian: "The Anabaptists could not understand a Christianity which made regeneration, holiness, and love primarily a matter of intellect, of doctrinal belief, or of subjective 'experience,' rather than one of transformation of life. They demanded an outward expression of the inner experience."[9]

## Host Families and Service: Discomfort and Dislocation

Goshen College students and faculty have many opportunities to put into practice the faith tradition that has come down to them from the Anabaptists. Similar to Catholic students who have the opportunity to engage their tradition in the Angelicum program in Rome (described by Briel elsewhere in this volume), Goshen students come face-to-face with the theological legacy of the Mennonite Church as they spend six weeks in a metropolis and then six more in a rural village in a developing country. This program provides ample opportunity for the Goshen student to actively engage the people of the culture that they are entering and, wherever possible, cross over into the lives of others.

As described so often in this volume, for many students, crossing over involves an initial experience of dislocation and discomfort. This experience begins the moment they touch the ground in their adopted country. Riding in a bus or taxi from the airport in a place like Abidjan or Dakar includes an initial exposure to sensory overload; new sights, sounds, and smells. Students often feel a visceral response to the beggar who was tragically deformed by disease and is standing outside of the bus at an intersection. Or as they look out of the window of their vehicle, students realize that trash is not scrupulously picked up on a regular basis and that their hosts constantly deal with the residue of modern commercial life, such as the omnipresent plastic bags that litter the streets of their new city. The student must begin to come to terms with their taken-for-granted assumptions about access to health care or sanitation services.

The challenges of crossing over become even more apparent as students move in with their host families for six-week stays. Students quickly discover that someone may have given up their bed in a crowded household, or that someone has even left the house to make room for them. Occasionally the hospitality they experience is almost overwhelming. While on service as teachers in a school in northwestern Tanzania, two students lived in a home where a teenage boy died after a brief illness with a relatively benign (for us) tonsil infection. One of them reflected (in the following excerpt from her journal) on the hospitality they received even in the face of tragedy:

> In the days and weeks following his death, the house was constantly bombarded with visits from neighbors, school friends, and relatives all wanting to sit with the family and mourn together. Neighbor women, distant relatives, and friends volunteered to manage meals for the large number of guests coming in and out of the house and a collection plate circulated for people to pitch in to buy a cow to slaughter for the funeral party. Laura and I tried to assist as best we could but often found it more helpful to stay out of the way of the business and preparation. However, in the flurry of guests, preparation, and her own grief, a host grandmother, who was raising her orphaned grandson and his siblings, stepped out of her own grief and distress to ensure that we were properly fed, that we weren't over exhausted by the activity, and that we were able to sleep well. Her mindfulness and concern in the midst of her own grief was a powerful and very humbling statement of hospitality and compassion that moved me to tears.[9]

At Goshen, we often talk about service having more to do with being than doing. It includes being a different kind of North American than people in other parts of world experience directly via tourism or indirectly through the media, one who adjusts to the host culture and places few demands upon it, including using the local language rather than English. One who moves across the difficult boundaries of gender, race, and class—or as Holt describes elsewhere in this volume, one who develops "relationships beyond borders." In essence, we ask our students to be people who embody the Incarnation.

At times our hosts are puzzled and even surprised that we truly want to enter their homes, eat their food, sleep in their beds and participate in their family lives. When we first started sending students to homes in Nanchong, a city in central China, people there remarked over and over again about the fact that the students were not in hotels (like most North American visitors to the city) but were actually living in Chinese homes. In West Africa when I went to a small village in central Ivory Coast to ask permission to visit for a weekend with a group of students, a village elder took me to a house and pointed to the bed and said, "Can you sleep there? Can you eat our food?" When I replied that we would be honored to spend time in their homes he said to me, "White people first came here to enslave us, later they came to force us into working for them, and now you want to sleep in our homes." He was clearly astonished.

For students, the experience of dislocation takes many forms. When I took students to the village in Ivory Coast, one of them had to grapple with the investments he had in U.S. companies that process chocolate. Ivory Coast is the world's leading producer of cocoa. In his journal, the student wrote: "I knew before coming here that the U.S. exploits developing countries and that as a stockholder in the chocolate industry, I am directly apart of this exploitation. How do I, within myself, reconcile what I see and what I feel? My pragmatic, economic, U.S. American mind wants that village to keep producing cocoa and not change. But I see how the people work for me and the returns they get and I am ashamed."[10]

Ten years after her SST experience in Guadeloupe, another student wrote the following in a Goshen College publication:

> "My service placement in a home for "delinquent" girls . . . provoked reflection. Trying to make myself useful by initiating games and teaching macramé, I observed public social workers beating and berating the girls. In my mind surfaced issues ranging from individual learning styles to culturally determined notions of violence and, in the words of one of my leaders, the systemic nature of evil. Much as I would have liked, I could not sidestep questions about my personal complicity and potential to contribute to change, not to mention how my desire for change might stem from cultural assumptions as much as from what I still hold to be important concepts of justice. At times these issues seemed overwhelming . . . ."[11]

Living with host families for three months raises many questions about inequality and the assumptions that go along with the privileged position of many North Americans. A student in Ivory Coast received a letter from the family that he lived with in the capital, Abidjan, with the news that a child had died at birth. He had moved to the northern city of Ferkessedougou to assist health care workers in a hospital that is one of a few medical facilities serving the northern half of the country. He wrote the following entry in his journal:

> Friday morning I received a letter . . . from my family in Abidjan. . . . How happy was I to read of my new sister Gloria?! And how shocked was I to read that she had died unexpectedly three days after her birth?! I guess living in a continent with an infant mortality rate of 10%, one should logically expect that if one lives with ten children, (like I have during my time here) that one will die. One did. But that logic doesn't quiet in any way the shock I feel right now. I never knew Gloria; I never will. I have only known her family for six weeks.
>
> When I told people at the hospital the news, the response was "that happens." I guess it does—everywhere. Being middle-class American, I have been conditioned to believe that when a baby is born, it will live. Even though I'm living here in Cote D'Ivoire right now, I guess accepting the realities of life is more difficult than I expected.[12]

Spending time in remote rural village health clinics, soup kitchens, or working in a villagers fields, students have opportunities to connect this sense of discomfort and dislocation with some important theological insights. A student who recently returned from a semester in Peru reflected on his experience in the following excerpt from a paper, in which he compares some of the experiences in his service assignment in a coastal town of Northern Peru to those of Saint Peter, particularly Peter's moments of denial at the end of Christ's life. This student worked with youth in a drug prevention program. Drug addiction is an enormous problem in the city of Chimbote. He writes:

> One day as we were leaving . . ., a neighboring youth center, a small boy passed by the door. We occasionally saw him around the area. He was always dirty with holes in his pants, smudged cheeks, matted hair, and carried a palette stuck full of candied apples small enough to be apricots. He sold them for less than a (Peruvian) sol, about thirty cents. This time though, he was crying. He shuffled slowly through

the dust; flies hovered over his tray hoping for a chance to land on the fruit. Javier, our social worker and guide, followed a fellow student and me over to the boy. "Que paso hijo?" he asked. Children in such poverty are often socially awkward or stunted. They are often abused by their parents or neighbors and so answering us was hard for him. After a few mumbled replies we gleaned that the (local youth) gang was hanging out at the corner as he turned down our road, and had slapped him across the head. We asked if they had taken his money or any apples. Satisfied that they hadn't, though completely powerless if they had, we left and let him go on his way.

I told Javier, "That's horrible that they would treat a child like that!"

But he responded that I didn't know the half of it. "That boy works selling apples while his parents sit at home. They take the money he makes and buy coke to get high during the day." I was shocked into silence. My Spanish did not have the appropriate vocabulary to express the anger that welled in my heart while my eyes began to swell. We walked quietly back along the dirt roads pitted with washing water, urine, and crawling with stray dogs. A weakness comes to the knees in the face of such injustice. The gravity of human fallenness pulls even the strongest from their feet. Powerlessness crushes pride and security, and in the humility found by the commonality shared between myself all the fallenness around me, the space thinned and I saw God. Though I was in no way responsible for that child's abuse, Jesus could look me in the eye and ask, in light of my lack of effort and focus on self-comfort, "do you love me?"

My host family in Chimbote was a broken one. My host mother worked with the parish outreach programs. . . . she would often tell me family stories over dinner. They were always sad and about the failures of her children or family. She loved the parish though and was thrilled with my work there. Before I left I gave her a bar of chocolate as a parting gift. I had given her other things during my stay, like chocolate chips, greeting cards and pictures of Illinois, but this one was too much. She tried to reject my offer, but found me insistent, so she made off to her room for a moment and returned with a woven hanging of the *Virgin de Guadalupe*. She gave it to me. I steadfastly refused! I knew the meaning of such icons to the religious of Chimbote. She said the rosary every evening. Tears filled her eyes and she pleaded with me. "You must take this. Look at my family. My daughter is gone, the other is crazy, my first son doesn't care and my second is a Protestant! I have no one to give my things to. Do not worry; I have my Corazon de Jesus and other virgins. I will die soon; you must take this and carry my faith on." Tears brimmed along my eyes as well as I reached for the tapestry that now hangs above my bed. As Jesus called Peter—such a rash and flawed disciple to carry the mantle of Jesus' mission—my host mother gave me—a reluctant servant—the essence of her faith, that I could carry it forward.

I will admit to a certain relief as I left the dirt roads of Chimbote. There was no less pain that I could see after my stay. Service is not so much about giving as it is receiving.[13]

## Learning to Live Out of Control

One of the important lessons that both students and faculty learn while living in a developing country is to learn to give up a sense of control over one's life. Academics are used to being in control, they decide what text to use in a course, organize syllabi, and choose strategies for evaluation of student work. In the context of the developing world this sense of being in control is frequently challenged, and in the process, we begin to understand that much of the world lives in a perpetual state of feeling out of control of their destiny. One poignant example stands out from my first term in West Africa. On the night of January 11, 1994, the CFA (currency of much of former French West Africa) was devalued by fifty percent. My custom was to get up early and go and purchase several baguettes from the local bakery for my family's breakfast. Instead of the usual morning greetings, I experienced the anger and resentment of people who had literally lost half of all of their money over night. My white skin associated me with the international monetary policies of France which had dramatically changed many lives. In spite of my innocence, I represented those with the power to affect the destiny of millions of Africans. In that moment on the street in Abidjan, I felt the weight of four hundred years of colonial oppression.

That experience took me back to my own SST days. I have an indelible image in my mind from my service experience in the northwest of Haiti. In the town where I was living, a woman who had experienced an epileptic seizure was brought to the rudimentary health clinic. While thrashing about in a seizure, she had rolled into an open fire, severely burning her abdomen. Her family was asked, why did you wait eight days to bring the woman to the clinic? Their simple but profound answer was that they did not have clothes to put on her. It took eight days to find a dress before they could bring her to the clinic. I saw her the day she arrived, and again several weeks later, the day before she died of pain and starvation. In addition to suffering the acute anguish of a burn where there was no pain medication, she could not process food and so she literally starved to death. She could not speak, but her eyes cried out to this white face, surely you can do something for me. I could do nothing.

The experience of dislocation and discomfort causes many students to think about issues of power and privilege in new ways. As one faculty member notes, "disorientation, when it does not overwhelm, contributes toward humility and receptivity. Disorientation engages students, draws them out, and makes them open and vulnerable–teachable. Newness, in this form temporarily removes traditional foundations, including the safety of home and the certainty of one's cultural truths, teaching students skills essential for entering a postmodern world."[14]

## Lessons Faculty Learn on SST

Living and working with students, faculty are also challenged to live out the Incarnation in their roles as professors and mentors in a culture and language that is often very new to them. Many return to Goshen College with new insights about their adopted country but also about teaching and learning. One faculty member describes the way SST leadership transformed her approach to both teaching and learning in the following manner:

> Previously my conception of teaching and learning was that the teacher was responsible to be strong not weak; to be informed, not confused; to be loving and perceptive of students, not needful of love and perceptivity . . . But in Costa Rica, I was not an expert. I was not always strong. I was not always loving and culturally perceptive . . . Honesty about painful feelings and confusion did not appear to destroy their inner security nor did it seem to cause a lack of trust. Walking the same road as they did each day made us into co-learners. . . . One enduring result of SST in my personal life has been this basic challenge to my theories of teaching and learning.[15]

There are many other ways that faculty have learned to be humble in the face of adversity and to allow coworkers from the host country to be truly partners in the educational process. Every SST leader works closely with an in-country coordinator, university faculty and a network of host families and agency administrators. They spend many hours riding in cars, buses, and walking dusty dirt paths with people they depend upon. These colleagues offer a window into the culture that is invaluable; they are frequently the interpreters of situations and events that North Americans may find difficult to comprehend. North American university faculty are among the most fiercely independent group of workers on the planet. They tend to be extremely self-reliant. In our program, faculty have to give up that independence because the tables are turned and the faculty members become students themselves. Their colleagues are their teachers, and they must turn to them with some regularity to explain the complex dynamics of relationships between students and host families or the current political controversy in a particular country.

Students observe these relations with host nationals. They know when things are going well and quickly pick up on tensions that may occur in a program. Referring to his experience in the Dominican Republic one leader observed, "More than anything else, I learned to love the Dominican culture, both because I thought it was essential to communicate that love for Dominicans (for students' sake) and because I genuinely came to love the people, the land, and the culture."[16]

Another colleague described the experience of learning a great deal about grace via her connections with Central Americans. She said, "I don't think SST changed who I am or changed my teaching but some of the experiences touched me deeply. Like living in a thirty year old body speaking three year old Spanish. There is a certain kind of humility and aloneness (that one feels with limited language ability) but there is also a certain kind of grace you feel when people accept your three year old Spanish." Later in our conversation she added, "at one point in the year I felt inadequate and absolutely alone in the world. At that point I heard a voice in me say, the culture will support you if you allow it and it was true the culture carried me."[17]

## Service-learning as Praxis for Life

From the beginning of the SST program, Goshen College has attempted to integrate study and service. Students must attempt to understand the history and culture of a society first, and then move into service-learning assignments. The explicit intention has been that field experience must be informed by serious investigation of the culture. Service and learning are integrated and service becomes the praxis that can lead to transformation. For some, the long-term effect of SST is a complete turn-around in their life plans. In a recent survey of Goshen College alumni who participated in SST, ninety-two percent of respondents said that "SST was one of my most important life experiences."[18] Alumni commented on some very specific ways that they had been transformed by their SST experience.

China was the beginning of a journey which changed the way I looked at myself and the way I relate with the people around me.[19]

Today I am an Associate Professor of Political Science at Northeastern Illinois University. Given the big impact of SST on my life, I decided to pursue graduate studies in comparative politics, in large part because of my SST experiences in Honduras and Nicaragua.[20]

(After SST,) I was called to learn Spanish to help the stranger in my land better understand how to survive in my U. S. world. I went on to get a degree in nurse-midwifery and practiced in a small neighborhood health center in Chicago for more than 10 years, providing prenatal care and family planning to Mexican women and teens.[21]

At the summer music camp in Leogane, (Haiti) I taught violin to handicapped (blind) and non-handicapped students, using the French language, which I had studied four years in high school and at Goshen College. I loved the experience. The students were talented, eager to learn, and disciplined.

After Goshen College, I went on to Illinois State University in Normal to earn a master's degree in music education and to become a registered music therapist. To this day I play violin and utilize music therapy at hospitals and long-term health facilities. I also lead drumming circles that use exotic instruments from around the world to allow creativity, self-expression and a culturally influenced experience.[22]

# Conclusion

Living out the Incarnation is fundamental to Mennonite understanding of what it means to be a Christian. As Christians, we are called to discipleship. Every believer is called to a life of service, to bear witness to inner transformation by offering the cup of cold water to the thirsty or shelter to the homeless. SST is designed to develop knowledge from experience that leads to compassionate action. For many students and faculty members, SST is transformational. They begin to see themselves and the other from a global perspective. Many gain profound insights about faith while struggling with their status as privileged people living among the powerless. They experience dislocation and discomfort as they struggle with their positions in the world order.

While living with their hosts and working alongside of colleagues in a service-learning project, all who participate in SST experience a tremendous amount of hospitality. They realize at some point in their term that they are being served far more than they serve. They also realize that much of the world lives daily in a context where the people have relatively little control over their life circumstances.

There is good evidence that many Goshen College students have been transformed by the experience of spending three months in a developing country. At the very least they have gained insights about one other society beyond our borders. For some reflecting on their experience abroad has had impact on major life decisions such as where to live, how to respond to environmental degradation, and vocational choices. Many have chosen a life of service which includes continued work and travel abroad. All have had the opportunity to understand the Incarnation in new ways.

The Goshen College Study Service Term was a by-product of a particular moment in history and the adaptation of a particular theological tradition to a novel program in higher education. On SST students and faculty enter the world of the disenfranchised, the poor, or the stranger, try to understand them, and wherever possible, assist them.

# Toward Successful Transformations

RONALD J. MORGAN

In the United States today, there is a growing concern across much of academe that the university experience be more holistic than in the past, narrowing the gap between theory and experience, between concepts and commitments, between educating citizens and training professionals. The rapid globalization of communications and economic activity over the past generation has added to this mix, stimulating U.S. institutions to provide a previously unimagined array of "study abroad" opportunities for their students. The motivations behind this rapid expansion of international study options are several. At a minimum, there is the pragmatic recognition that tomorrow's graduates, in every field of study, will have to compete in this global marketplace, a consideration that forces institutions to provide international opportunities if they are to successfully recruit those who will become tomorrow's graduates. Beyond such pragmatic concerns, however, thoughtful and creative educators are recognizing that the study abroad setting offers almost unlimited potential for the kind of integrative, holistic learning they are seeking to facilitate on their U.S. campuses. And they are working tirelessly, as well as collegially, to create programs and experiences that tap that potential.

The contributors to this volume have been profoundly influenced by all these developments across the landscape of U.S. higher education. But as Christian educators, we go a step further, aspiring to faith-tinged sorts of transformations at the edge of the world. While it would be accurate to say that we seek to encourage students' spiritual growth *as well as* their development as global actors, such a statement falls short of our deeper intentions. Rather than content ourselves by helping students grow in these *two* ways, we aim to do more. Ultimately, we hope to form a generation of Christian believers whose faith exerts a major influence on their posture vis-à-vis the wider world, and whose global awareness and broadened perspectives will leaven their self-understanding as followers of Christ.

The subtext of all these essays is that such profound transformations are more likely to occur in study abroad settings than in the more familiar context of the U.S. campus and classroom. In a 2006 article entitled "Being is Believing? Out of the Box (Subversive) Education," Philip Fountain and Chris Elisara presented "a case study of how space, place, and location have bearing upon what Wolterstorff has termed a 'shalom' model of education." In arguing for the pedagogical advantages of "being there," Fountain and Elisara argued that "direct experience facilitates a rich learning space in which empathetic bonds—so critical for inspiring understanding, action, and engagement—can seed and flourish."[1] With Fountain and Elisara, we affirm the advantages that are inherent in "being there," particularly for effecting the sort of deep personal transformations envisioned by the contributors to this volume. At the same time, we endorse their suggestion that some of those pedagogical advantages can probably be applied to on-campus curricula. Our goal here is not to belittle the traditional classroom setting; rather, by choosing to participate in this book project, our aim is to stimulate readers (and ourselves) to tap the rich potential of the study abroad setting.

Each study abroad program and pedagogical methodology described in the preceding chapters shares with the others a concern for training Christian students to "see" the world in deeper ways, ways that evince greater nuance, self-awareness, and empathy. "Being there" is crucial to this training process, for by allowing students to set aside the lenses formed by their native environments and positioning them to "see" from other vantage points, the study abroad setting provides what one Abilene Christian student called "a perfect storm for radical change in my identity." Our aim is that our Christian students learn to see more than "the world" in deeper ways; we wish to sharpen each one's perspectives on self, native culture, and personal circles of influence and fellowship. While the essays in Parts III and IV of this volume have highlighted efforts to encourage growth in empathy and solidarity with the cultural other or with the world's poorest peoples, we are skeptical that such projects will be very efficacious without the types of transformations of outlook described in Parts I and II.

All such discussions, of course, point to serious challenges that Christian universities must face if they wish to foster deep transformations through their study abroad programs. In these final pages, I wish to highlight some of those challenges under two broad headings—institutional and pedagogical—before closing with a brief proposal for defining success.

Institutions are by nature bureaucratic entities in which departments compete with each other or produce work that overlaps the work of the others because, frankly, they too often have no idea "what the other hand is doing." If Christian institutions are to conceptualize and deliver deeply transformative off-campus programs, there will need to be a broad institutional commitment to that vision. While study abroad directors *in situ* can certainly create thoughtful, spiritually provocative experiences for students who join them in places like Tanzania, Thailand, or inner city America, the transformative potential of their programs will certainly be affected, for good or for ill, by the level of shared commitment on their U.S. campuses. Those who oversee international programs on the home university campus, together with on-site directors, need to facilitate campus-wide dialogue and prayer on these matters, while building broad coalitions of administrators, academic departments, student-life professionals, and campus recruiters who share a vision regarding the desired goal. Out of these commitments, the campus community will need to grapple with fundamental questions, the answers to which will largely determine how deep their programs may be able to go.

While there are numerous questions that universities must face, a few will suffice for our purposes here. First, curriculum committees should do their best to help study abroad directors take maximum advantage of "being there." Rather than limiting potential for dynamic learning experiences by inflexibly imposing on-campus core courses or strict course sequences, they should encourage and facilitate the sort of creative innovation that will take maximum advantage of the specific study abroad setting and the teaching fortes of *in situ* instructors. A second crucial matter regards the appointment of visiting faculty members who constantly rotate onto the study abroad site. For example, how will the university balance the priority of offering students the greatest potential for a deeply transformative study abroad experience with the tendency to treat the visiting faculty opportunity as a perquisite to be rotated among individuals and academic departments? Once selected for such short-term roles, what training will faculty members receive prior to going abroad, so that they will share and contribute to the university's goal of spiritually transformative education? Another big question the Christian institution must confront involves the role of marketing and recruitment in forming the expectations of students who may go abroad: to recruit by promoting superficial tourism rather than pilgrimage (as John D. Barbour discussed in Chapter Two) will undermine the university's goal of fostering serious spiritual and personal growth. What mission statement do students find at the university's study abroad web site or in printed recruitment literature? What *visual* images invite them to consider a semester abroad? Finally, the campus community must develop effective structures for encouraging continuity between students' time abroad and their return to the home campus (see approaches described by Montgomery and Docter in Chapter Seven). Such continuity is crucial for two reasons. On the one hand, because virtue is fostered in community, the commitments that an individual has made abroad may well fade unless they are nurtured and processed upon return to campus. On the other hand, the broader campus community misses an opportunity for significant enrichment unless we engage returning students as ambassador for global commitments.

A careful reading of the foregoing essays uncovers pedagogical challenges as well. In the first place, there exists a danger, acknowledged by John Barbour in Chapter Two, that by inviting students to critically scrutinize their home cultures while encouraging them to practice openness to other cultural viewpoints, we may engender in them debilitating relativism or cynicism. Of course, we must challenge the ethnocentrism and cultural naiveté that many students take with them when they journey abroad; at the same time, we do them no good if we teach them to replace their narrow worldviews with "open-minded" assumptions that all cultures are equally good, and therefore must be uncritically embraced as they are. The difficult but navigable terrain is that which lies between such extremes, a near no-man's-land where judgment is suspended, to be sure, but not altogether abandoned. Students can discover, as they struggle through this tough terrain, that approach and empathy need not always result in unequivocal embrace.

This brings us to a second important pedagogical challenge that emerges from many of the essays in this volume. That challenge involves the place of scripture, prayer, and collective worship, those traditional vehicles for individual and collective spiritual growth, in the ethos of the Christian study abroad program. While there is probably much space for growth in this area, it has been gratifying to see study abroad practitioners placing so much emphasis on theological reflection, exploration of spiritual heritage, and shared worship experiences. Such practices, when enriched by face-to-face participation with local communities of the global church, should help students develop the blend of joyful receptivity and critical discernment that we aim to instill in them.

Finally, an institution that seeks to form globally engaged Christians must consider what it will call "quality" and how it will define "success." There will be temptations, born from the real or perceived need to compete with other institutions, to equate quality with cash and flash, or to measure success in raw numbers. But the types of success envisioned by contributors to this volume will be difficult to measure. While we might create an instrument for measuring levels of global "competencies" among our graduates, it will be more difficult to assess the deepening of Christian commitment or the reformulation of personal identities.

Nathaniel Taylor's 2005 article for *Books & Culture* is instructive here. A recent graduate of Bethel University (Minnesota), Taylor reflected on how his undergraduate education compared with that described by Ross Gregory Douthat in a book called *Privilege: Harvard and the Education of the Ruling Class*. Taylor describes the dilemma of mission and philosophy faced by a whole spectrum of faith-based learning institutions. On the one hand, we often measure our success according to the quantifiable marks preferred by the "top" institutions: size of endowment, admittances to top graduate schools, or earning power of graduates. But on the other hand, as Taylor observes regarding his alma mater, we aspire to a definition of success "constrained by the calling of God to live in the Kingdom of Heaven." As Taylor acknowledges, however, such a definition is difficult to quantify:

In God's kingdom success is not measured by the percentage of alumni that give money or which former students walk the halls of power or the latest academic research. In God's Kingdom success is loving God and loving your neighbor and giving hope to the hopeless

and blessing your enemies. Unfortunately for Bethel, these are difficult things to measure and even harder to execute. How do you help
students see the Kingdom of God? Where is the course that trains
Samaritans to be good?"[2]

For those of us who are committed to nurturing Christians whose faith will
inform their global commitments, and whose engagement with the wider
human family will deepen and enrich their knowledge of Christ, Taylor's
observation is spot on. Goals like ours will be hard to measure; they will be
difficult to achieve. But such is the nature of our calling as university educators
whose allegiance is to the Kingdom of God. Happily, that calling invites us to
a life of joy, purpose, and fruitfulness at the edge of the world.

# Liturgies for Study Abroad

JANINE PADEN MORGAN
(Abilene Christian University, Abilene, Texas; ACU in Oxford)

Worshipping in community is a meaningful, yet often underestimated, way to form global Christians. In worship, we are transformed both as individuals and as a community; as we align ourselves with God's character, we become increasingly concerned with God's own concerns. For this reason, we have felt it important to make available two model worship services (or liturgies) specific to, but not limited to, the needs of students in study abroad programs. A collateral effect of making worship strong within a community is that it serves as glue to hold the community together when the inevitable difficult times arise.

As a semester develops, students go through some predictable phases to which liturgies can minister. As they arrive and settle in, they need to be warmly welcomed and reassured of God's presence in distant places. As the semester progresses, they need to be reminded of God's purposes for them within the new communities to which they now belong—whether by being involved in their adopted cities or with each other. Finally, toward the end of the semester, they need to express thankfulness to God, looking back to memorialize the experiences of the semester.

# Liturgy of Beginning:
## A Memorial to God's Presence in Distant Places (Part A)

*This is a liturgy for the beginning of the study abroad experience—ideal during the second week. For this service you will need:*

- River stones, markers or Sharpies, candles. Cover a central table in small stones with candles lit throughout.
- If you share the Lord's Supper, communion bread and wine. Place the bread and wine in the middle of the stones on the table.

### WELCOME / CALL TO WORSHIP:
*The Emmaus Prayer*

**Leader:** *That this evening may be holy, good and peaceful,*
*let us pray with one heart and mind:*

**All:** *Lord Jesus, stay with us,*
*for evening is at hand and the day is past.*
*be our companion in the way,*
*kindle our hearts, and awaken hope,*
*that we may know you as you are revealed in scripture*
*and in the breaking of bread.*
*grant this for the sake of your love toward us.*
*Amen.*

### PRAYER & WORSHIP SONGS: *(Emphasis is on God's presence)*

### SCRIPTURE READING: *Genesis 28:5, 10–22*

*Unpacking the Text: Reading for Knowledge*
- What do you notice?
- What are the circumstances in Jacob's life when the dream occurs?
- What is he experiencing?
- What aspect of God is revealed through the dream?

- How does Jacob respond to God's revelation?

*Lectio Divina: Reading for Meaning*
*The leader rereads the above passage—once out loud, and a second time allow them to reread it quietly to themselves.*

*Leader: As you read, notice what phrase or word stands out to you.*
> *Meditate for a minute on this phrase/word from the text that is meaningful to you personally right now.*
> *After a minute or so, ask them to call out the phrase or word that captured their hearts.*

*Stone Meditation (with background music):*
Take a stone, hold it. Feel its weight and its texture. Really notice the stone in your hand. What color is it? Heavy/light? Smooth/rough?
> Write on the stone the word or phrase that you meditated on above.
> Keep this stone with you—in your pocket as you travel, on your desk.
> Don't lose it, as we will bring the stones back at the end of our journey together.
> Let it be a reminder of the God who is with you wherever you go.

*Prayer Of Intercessions: These are suggested topics for prayer. Prayer can be prompted by the leader who asks people to call out names and/or places of concerns. Allow a minute or so for each section.*

- All who travel
- Refugees and asylum seekers who are displaced because of war or famine
- All who have unresolved family issues
- All who miss friends and family

*Prayer: (Ps. 139:1–12)*
*Divide group into two and read antiphonally (one side, odd verses; the other, even verses), with the final refrain, verses 23–25, read in unison*

*All:*    [23] *Search me, o God, and know my heart;*
> *test me and know my anxious thoughts.*
[24] *Point out anything in me that offends you,*
> *and lead me along the path of everlasting life.*

[25] *You go before me and follow me.*
   *You place your hand of blessing on my head.*

## DISMISSAL & BLESSING:

*Leader: Jesus places a hand of blessing on each of your heads. He reminds us in his very last words in the book of Matthew: "Surely, I am with you always, to the very end of the age." (Mt. 28:20)*

*Go in peace to love and serve the very real, the very present Lord.*

# Liturgy of Ending:

## A Memorial to God's Presence in Distant Places (Part B)

*This is a liturgy for the end of the study abroad experience—ideal during the last week. For this service you will need:*

- *Leaders, from all the faculty and staff.*
- *The river stones, marked with a personalized word, from the Part A of the Liturgy of God's Presence. A plant saucer (16" circumference). Prior to the service, you may need to provide some additional stones with markers to write on, as (inevitably) some will have gotten lost.*
- *If you share the Lord's Supper, communion bread and wine. Place the bread and wine in the middle of an empty table.*

### WELCOME / CALL TO WORSHIP:
*Emmaus Prayer*

**Leader:** *That this evening may be holy, good and peaceful,*
*let us pray with one heart and mind:*

**All:** *Lord Jesus, stay with us,*
*for evening is at hand and the day is past.*
*Be our companion in the way,*
*kindle our hearts, and awaken hope,*
*that we may know you as you are revealed in scripture*
*and in the breaking of bread.*
*Grant this for the sake of your love toward us.*
*Amen.*

**Prayer:** *Adapted from Ephesians 3:14–19*
*Leaders pray antiphonally between members of the faculty and staff.*

When we think of this time together, we can't help but pray to the Father, the Creator of everything in heaven and on earth, in deep thanksgiving.

We pray that from God's glorious, unlimited resources he has empowered you this semester and will continue to empower you with inner strength through the Spirit.

We pray that Christ has continued to make his dwelling place in your hearts as you have trusted in him in some of the difficult and challenging places of the semester.

We pray that your roots have grown down deep into God's love and have kept you strong.

We pray that, together with our study-abroad community and with the community here in [city, country], your understanding of God has grown, that you begin to know how wide, how long, how high, and how deep his love is.

May you continue to experience the love of Christ throughout your life, though it is too great to understand fully.

We pray that one day, each of you will be made complete with all the fullness of life and power that comes from God.

*All:*     *Amen.*

*Scripture Reading:* Genesis 32:22–30; Genesis 35:1–4; 6–7; 9–15

*Unpacking the Text:* Reading for Knowledge

- What do you notice?
- What is going on in Jacob's life when the wrestling match occurs?
- What could wrestling with God imply?
- Where in the semester have you seen the face of God? Wrestled with God? Identity become stronger/weaker? What name might you have now?

*Lectio Divina:* Reading for Meaning

*The leader rereads the above passage—once out loud, and a second time allow them to reread it quietly to themselves.*

*Leader: As you read, notice what phrase or word stands out to you.*
   *Meditate for a minute on this phrase / word from the text that is*

*meaningful to you personally right now.*
*After a minute or so, ask them to call out the phrase or word.*

**Stone Meditation** *(with background music):*

- Take your stone from the beginning of the semester. Hold it in your hand. Feel again its weight and its texture. Really notice it anew in your hand. What color is it? Heavy/light? Smooth/rough?
- Reflect a minute on the word or phrase that you wrote on the stone those months ago. Did you notice it at all throughout the semester—did it remind you of something important?
- With our stones, we will build an altar together. Place your stone in a cairn-like pile on the saucer, speaking out the word written on it, sharing (or not) why this word was particularly meaningful throughout the time here.

  [Allow time for everyone to place their stone]
- *At the conclusion, you may pour water over it; say some words similar to this:*

Like Jacob, we anoint this "altar" as a memorial to this place, a place far from home where we encountered God. Our identities are enriched because of this experience. Our understanding of God has changed; our understanding of ourselves has changed; and our understanding of others has changed. And we are thankful.

**Intercessions:** *(The prayer can cover some of the following topics.)*

- For the blessing each person has been throughout the semester
- For continued relationships with each other upon their return
- For their host country and friends made there
- For the reunion with friends and family upon their return, especially if there is difficulty at home
- For continual remembrance of the ways that God has been present in our lives this semester

## COMMUNION:

*[For our final communion service of the semester, typically the faculty/staff stand in twos or threes, speaking a blessing on each student as they come forward to receive bread and wine from them.]*

## Closing Prayer:[1]

*Leader:* Creator of the world, eternal God,

*All:* We have come from many places for a little while.

*Leader:* Redeemer of humanity, God-with-us,

*All:* We have come with all our differences, seeking common ground.

*Leader:* Spirit of unity, go-between God

*All:* We have come on journeys of our own,
to a place where our journeys have met.

*Leader:* So here, in this shelter house, we have taken time together.
For when our paths crossed here, there has been much to share
and celebrate.

*All:* We thank you for this our community, our three-in-one god,
yourself the pattern of all community. amen

## Taking a Stone With You:

*Leader:* God dwells in the midst of his people, tabernacling with us wherever
we go. As we have built an altar, so we take a bit of it home with us.
The stone you now pick up, may have been [Ashley's] memorial stone;
but now it represents each other in community. This then becomes a
symbol, not only of God's faithfulness to us as individuals, but serves
as a reminder of our community this semester, centered on Christ's
presence in ourselves and in those around us.

[Time for people to pick up a stone and hold it.]

## Dismissal & Blessing

*Leader:* May the grace of Jesus Christ, the love of God, and the communion of
the Holy Spirit be with us all, this night and always.
Go in peace to love and serve the Lord,

*All:* In the name of Christ, amen.

# Endnotes

Introduction—Cynthia Toms Smedley (University of Notre Dame, Notre Dame, Indiana; Center for Social Concerns)

1. Jon Wergin, foreword to *Putting Students First: How Colleges Develop Students Purposefully* by Larry Braskamp, Lois Calian Trautvetter, and Kelly Ward (Bolton: Anker Publishing Co., 2006), xi–xii. The second half of the quote, by Frederick Buechner (*Wishful Thinking: A Seeker's ABC*), was used within Braskamp's book, 212.

2. Darryl Tippens, "Scholars and Witnesses: The Christian University Difference," in *The Soul of a Christian University: A Field Guide for Educators*, ed. Stephen T. Beers (Abilene: Abilene Christian University Press, 2008), 21–35.

3. Oxford English Dictionary 3rd edition, item currently as of Second Edition 1989 revision, (Oxford University Press, 2009), retrieved October 17, 2009 <http://dictionary.oed.com/entrance.dtl>. Also found in Max Weber, *Economy and Society: An Outline of Interpretive Sociology* (Los Angeles: University of California Press, 1978), 462.

4. Mark A. Noll, *The Scandal of the Evangelical Mind* (Grand Rapids: Eerdmans, 1994), 7.

5. Canadian Conference of Catholic Bishops, *Statement on the Formation of Conscience*, Canadian Catholic Conference, December 1, 1973.

6. Catechism of the Catholic Church, "The Formation of Conscience" (Citta del Vaticano: Libreria Editrice Vaticana, Part III, Sect. 1, Ch. 1, Article 6, 1783), publication 1993, retrieved October 6, 2009 <http://www.vatican.va/archive/catechism/p3s1c1a6.htm>.

7. Neil Howe and William Strauss, *Millennials Rising: The Next Great Generation* (New York: Random House Publishing, 2000), 288.

8. Robert Wuthnow, *Boundless Faith: The Global Outreach of American Churches* (Berkeley: University of California Press, 2009), 25.

9. Daniel Obst, Rajika Bhandari and Sharon Witherell, "Meeting America's Global Education Challenge: Current Trend in U.S. Study Abroad & The Impact of Strategic Diversity Initiatives," *Institute of International Education Study Abroad White Paper Series* 1 (2007).

10. Karen Fischer, "Study-Abroad Directors Adjust Programs in Response to Recession," *The Chronicle of Higher Education* 55.26 (2009), A25.

11. Higher Education Research Institute, "The Spiritual Life of College Students: A National Study of College Students' Search for Meaning and Purpose" (Los Angeles: University of California, 2004).

12. Rebecca Winters, "Education: Higher Learning," *Time* 163.5 (2004): 58-61.

13. James A. Patterson, *Shining Lights: A History of the Council for Christian Colleges & Universities* (Washington D.C.: Council for Christian Colleges & Universities, 2006).

14. Sharon Daloz Parks, *The Critical Years: The Young Adult Search for Faith to Live By* (San Francisco: Harper and Row, 1986).

15. K. S. Gray, G.K. Murdock, and C.D. Stebbins, "Assessing Study Abroad's Effect on an International Mission," *Change* 34.3 (2002), 45–51, and B. K. Reinhard, "Study Abroad: Measuring the Effects of a Semester of Study Abroad on the Faith Development of Undergraduate Students" (Thesis, Saint Louis University, 2005).

16. Larry Braskamp, Lois Calian Trautvetter, and Kelly Ward, *Putting Students First: How Colleges Develop Students Purposefully* (Bolton: Anker Publishing Co., 2006).

17. Mary M. Dwyer, "Charting the Impact of Studying Abroad," *International Educator,* NAFSA Association of International Educators 14 (2004): 14-20.

18. David Comp, *Research on U.S. Students Study Abroad: An Update,* Volume III, 2001–2003, With Updates to the 1989 and Volume II Editions 2000–2003, retrieved May 16, 2009 <http://www.globaled.us/ro/book_research_comp.htm>.

19. J. Kinzie, "10 Years of Student Engagement Results: Lessons from NSSE," paper presented at the HLC-NCA Annual Meeting, Chicago, 2009.

20. The Higher Education Research Institute (2004).

21. R. Michael Paige, Elizabeth M. Stallman, Jae-Eun Jon, and Bruce LaBrack, "Study Abroad for Global Engagement: The Long-Term Impact of International Experiences," presented at the NAFSA Conference, May 29, 2009. Retrieved November 6, 2009 <http://cehd.umn.edu/projects/sage/news.html>.

22. Gay Holcomb and Arthur Nonneman, "Faithful Change: Exploring and Assessing Faith Development in Christian Liberal Arts Undergraduates," *New Directions for Institutional Research* 122 (2004): 93-103.

23. Brian Reinhardt, "Study Abroad: Measuring the Effects of a Semester of Study Abroad on the Faith Development of Undergraduate Students" (Ph.D. diss., School of Saint Louis University, 2005), 8–9.

24. Bruce W. Speck. "What Is Spirituality?" *New Directions for Teaching and Learning* 104 (2005): 3-13.

25. Wayne Teasdale, *The Mystic Heart: Discovering the Universal Spirituality in the World's Religion* (New World Library, 2003), 4.

26. Alexander W. Astin, "Why Spirituality Deserves a Central Place in Liberal Education," *Liberal Educator* 90 (2004): 34-41.

27. Tippens, *Soul,* 33.

28. United States Conference of Catholic Bishops (Washington, D.C.: USCCB, 1998) and *Faithful Citizenship: A Catholic Call to Political Responsibility* (Washington, D.C.: USCCB, 2003). USCCB Publishing, Washington, D.C.

29. USCCB, *Faithful*, 2003.

30. Mark Radecke, "Service-Learning and Faith Formation," *Journal of College & Character* 8.5 (2007): 1-28.

# Part I
## The Journey Inward

Cynthia Toms Smedley (University of Notre Dame, Notre Dame, Indiana; Center for Social Concerns)

1. Thomas Merton, *Love and Living* (San Diego: Harvest Book Publishers, 1979), 3–4.

Chapter One: Doors to Transformation—Janine Paden Morgan (Abilene Christian University, Abilene, Texas; ACU in Oxford)

1. Victor Turner, "Liminality and Communitas," in *The Ritual Process: Structure and Anti-Structure*, ed. Victor Turner, Roger Abrams, and Alfred Harris (Chicago: Aldine Press, 1969), 94–97, 106–113, 125–129.

2. James Fowler, *Stages of Faith: The Psychology of Human Development and the Quest for Meaning* (San Francisco: Harper Collins, 1995).

3. Walter Brueggemann, *The Message of the Psalms* (Minneapolis: Augsburg Press, 1984). Murray S. Decker successfully applies this three-fold paradigm to the movement of cross-cultural adjustment and culture shock of student mission interns. See Decker, "Student Sojourners and Spiritual Formation: Understanding the Intersection of Cross-Cultural Adjustment and Spiritual Disorientation," in *Effective Engagement in Short-Term Missions: Doing it Right!*, ed. Robert J. Priest (Pasadena, CA: William Carey Library, 2008), 559–89.

4. Miroslav Volf, *Exclusion and Embrace: A Theological Exploration of Identity, Otherness, and Reconciliation* (Nashville: Abingdon Press, 1996).

5. Reading these texts as narrative—as opposed to privileging the concerns and methods of textual criticism—grants a degree of freedom, allowing the character sketches to inform us today. Theologians Bruce C. Birch, Walter Brueggemann, Terence Fretheim and David L. Petersen concur: "At its most fundamental level such [narrative] reading and interpretation means taking seriously the claim of the text that it is speaking about encounter and relationship with God" [*A Theological Introduction to the Old Testament* (Nashville: Abingdon Press, 1999), 17].

6. Brueggemann, *Psalms*, 25.

7. Turner, "Liminality," 113.

8. Andreas J. Kostenberger and Peter T. O'Brien, *Salvation to the Ends of the Earth: A Biblical Theology of Mission* (Downer's Grove, IL: Apollos Press, 2001), 29.

9. Fowler, *Stages*, 173.

10. To be precise, the mark that God gives Cain is not his restless wandering, which was his sentence. But because "restless wandering" in Cain's mind was a death sentence, Yahweh mitigates the death threat by putting a mark on Cain in order to

protect him from being killed. In so doing, ironically, it is Yahweh who becomes Abel's brother's keeper (Birch et. al., *Theological Introduction*, 58).

11. Volf, *Exclusion and Embrace*, 41.

12. In a recent work entitled *Acedia and Me* (Riverhead, 2008), Kathleen Norris describes acedia as the "soul-sickness" of our age.

13. John Barbour, "The Moral Ambiguity of Study Abroad," *Chronicle of Higher Education*, 53.7 (2006).

14. G. K. Chesterton (*Illustrated London News*, 4/28/1928).

15. Birch et.al., *Theological Introduction*, 91.

16. Brueggemann, *Psalms*, 21.

17. Brueggemann, *Psalms*, 53.

18. Fowler, *Stages*, 114.

19. Ronald Grimes, *Deeply into the Bone: Reinventing Rites of Passage* (Berkeley: University of California Press, 2000), 13.

20. Johannes Blauw, *The Missionary Nature of the Church* (NY: McGraw-Hill, 1962), 41.

21. Brueggemann, *Psalms*, 51–53.

22. In a nod to Anne Tyler's novel, *The Accidental Tourist* (Ballantine Books, 2002).

23. Arnold van Gennep, *The Rites of Passage* (Chicago: University of Chicago Press, 1960), 23.

24. Volf, *Exclusion and Embrace*, 39; italics mine.

Chapter Two: Students Abroad as Tourists and Pilgrims—John D. Barbour (St. Olaf College, Northfield, Minnesota; semester in Asia)

1.  Four studies of religion and higher education all use St. Olaf College (sometimes disguised with a pseudonym) as an example. See Richard Hughes, ed., *Models for Christian Higher Education* (Grand Rapids: Eerdmans, 1997); James Tunstead Burtchaell, *The Dying of the Light: The Disengagement of Colleges and Universities from their Christian Churches* (Grand Rapids: Eerdmans, 1998); Robert Benne, *Quality with Soul: How Six Premier Colleges and Universities Keep Faith with Their Religious Traditions* (Grand Rapids: Eerdmans, 2001); and Conrad Cherry, Betty A. DeBerg, and Amanda Porterfield, *Religion on Campus* (Chapel Hill: University of North Carolina, 2001).

2.  Anthropological studies of tourism include Dean MacCannell, *The Tourist: A New Theory of the Leisure Class*, second edition (Berkeley: University of California Press, 1999); John Urry, *The Tourist Gaze*, second edition (London: Sage, 2002); Edward M. Bruner, *Culture on Tour: Ethnographies of Culture* (Chicago: University of Chicago Press, 2005); Jeremy MaClancy, *Exotic No More: Anthropology on the Front Lines* (Chicago: University of Chicago Press, 2002); and Valene Smith and Maryann Brent, *Hosts and Guests Revisited: Tourism Issues of the 21$^{st}$ Century* (New York: Cognizant Communications, 2001).

3. Tourism can be good or bad, either a journey that is educational, enjoyable, and beneficial to both the traveler and the host country, or the performance of the "ugly American" stereotype, when travelers from the United States act as if their wealth entitles them to exploit another culture. For thoughtful advice on how to make tourism politically and ethically responsible, see Rick Steves, *Travel as a Political Act* (New York: Nation Books, 2009).

4. Alain De Botton, *The Art of Travel* (New York: Pantheon, 2002); Sean O'Reilly, James O'Reilly, and Larry Habegger, *Travelers' Tales China: True Stories* (San Francisco: Travelers' Tales, 2004); and James O'Reilly and Larry Habegger, *Travelers' Tales Thailand: True Stories* (San Francisco: Travelers Tales, 2004).

5. George Gmelch, "Let's Go Europe: What Student Tourists Really Learn," in Sharon Bohn Gmelch, ed., *Tourists and Tourism: A Reader* (Long Grove, IL: Waveland Press, 2004), 426. An even more pointed critique of current student travel programs is Anthony Ogden, "The View from the Veranda: Understanding Today's Colonial Student" in *Frontiers: The Interdisciplinary Journal of Study Abroad* 15 (Winter 2007–08): 35–55.

6. The last two essays are Peter Walker, "Pilgrimage in the Early Church," Craig Bartholomew and Fred Hughes, eds., *Explorations in a Christian Theology of Pilgrimage* (Burlington, Vt: Ashgate, 2004), 73–91, and Graham Tomlin, "Protestants and Pilgrimage," in the same volume, 110–25.

7. If I were to teach this course again, I would emphasize more the possibilities for service in travel, and link this to Christian ethical values and principles such as those formulated by Thomas Meyers in his essay in this volume.

8. St. Olaf's semester-long faculty-accompanied programs each have a discretionary fund of several thousand dollars that can be used for service projects or charitable donations. Alumni of the programs who want to "give back" to the areas in which they studied contribute these funds. Establishing such endowments is a concrete step that other Christian institutions could take to address social problems in the countries that host our programs, and would support the student-initiated service projects I advocate.

9. Mary Midgley, "Trying Out One's New Sword" in *Heart and Mind: The Varieties of Moral Experience* (New York: St. Martin's Press, 1981), 69–75. Also see Mary Midgley, *Can't We Make Moral Judgments?* (New York: St. Martin's Press, 1991) and Louis P. Pojman, *Ethics: Discovering Right and Wrong*, second edition (Belmont, CA: Wadsworth, 1995), chapters 2 and 3. On the issue of judging and not judging in a very different context, see John D. Barbour, "Judging and Not Judging Parents" in *The Ethics of Life Writing*, ed. Paul John Eakin (Ithaca: Cornell University Press, 2004), 73–98.

10. Bernard Adeney, *Strange Virtues: Ethics in a Multicultural World* (Downers Grove, Il: InterVarsity Press, 1995), 188–90.

11. I wish to thank DeAne Lagerquist, Edward Langerak, Douglas Schuurman, and Bardwell Smith for helpful responses to a draft of this essay.

## Chapter Three: Reflection as a Means of Discovery: Where is God in the Experience?—Andrea Smith Shappell (University of Notre Dame, Notre Dame, Indiana)

1. For more information about the Center for Social Concerns, you can go to http://centerforsocialconcerns.nd.edu/.

2. Anton Boisen, *The Exploration of the Inner World* (New York: Harper & Row, Harper Torchbooks, 1936), 135.

3. Hiltner authored five hundred articles and ten books, including *Pastoral Counseling* (New York: Abingdon Press, 1949) and *Theological Dynamics* (Nashville: Abingdon Press, 1972).

4. Both books have been reprinted in Henri J.M. Nouwen, *Ministry and Spirituality* (New York: Continuum, 1996).

5. Patricia O'Connell Killen and John De Beer, *The Art of Theological Reflection* (New York: Crossroads, 1995), 19.

6. Ibid, 16.

7. Ibid, xi.

8. Henri Nouwen, "Becoming the Beloved," *Hour of Power with Robert Schuller* #1178, 1992.

9. L'Arche, founded in France by Jean Vanier, unites core members, people who have disabilities, with assistants in a profound experience of community. L'Arche communities have spread to many locations throughout the world.

10. Robert Kinast, *Making Faith-Sense: Theological Reflection in Everyday Life* (Collegeville, MN: The Liturgical Press, 1999), 20.

11. Michael Himes, et. al, *Doing the Truth in Love* (Mahwah, NJ: Paulist Press, 1995), 50–52.

12. Donald McNeill, Doug Morrison, and Henri Nouwen, *Compassion: A Reflection on the Christian Life* (New York: Doubleday, 1982), 64.

13. John Paul II, "Sollicitudo Rei Socialis" #38 in O'Brien and Shannon, eds., *Catholic Social Thought: The Documentary Heritage* (Maryknoll, NY: Orbis Books, 2002).

14. Peter Heniot, S. J., and Joseph Holland, *Social Analysis: Linking Faith and Justice* (Maryknoll, NY: Orbis Books, 1983).

15. Jon Sobrino, *The Principle of Mercy* (Maryknoll, N.Y.: Orbis Books, 1994).

## Chapter Four: Seizing the "God Appointments" When There Is Cultural Disorientation in a Study Abroad Program—Lon Fendall (George Fox University, Newberg, Oregon; semester in Bolivia-Paraguay)

1. This chapter focuses primarily on the Santa Cruz location, even though the program in 2009 had to be relocated to Asuncion, Paraguay, because of a U.S. State Department travel warning in place for Bolivia at the time travel arrangements needed to be made.

2. Murray S. Decker, "Student Sojourners and Spiritual Formation: Understanding the Intersection of Cross-Cultural Adjustment and Spiritual Disorientation," in *Effective Engagement in Short-Term Missions: Doing it Right!*, ed. Robert J. Priest (Pasadena, CA: William Carey Library, 2008), 559–89.; Jack Mezirow, "Transformation Theory of Adult Learning," in *In Defense of the Lifeworld: Critical Perspectives on Adult Learning*, ed. Michael R. Welton (State University of New York Press, 1995), 50.

3. Decker, "Student Sojourners," 562–567.

4. Decker, "Student Sojourners," 585.

5. "South American Studies Center, George Fox University," September 14, 2004.

6. Norris Friesen and Wendy Soderquist Togami, "Collaboration to Labor Together," in *The Soul of a Christian University: A Field Guide for Educators* (Abilene: Abilene Christian University Press, 2008), 117–121.

7. Mezirow, "Transformation Theory," 51.

## Part II
## Inward Journey to Outward Living: Community as Teacher—

Cynthia Toms Smedley (University of Notre Dame, Notre Dame,

Indiana; Center for Social Concerns)

1. Robert P. Lynch and N. Papanicolas, "How the Greeks Created the First Age of Innovation: Tracing the Roots of Synergy and Co-Creativity, 2007," 1.33. Online paper: http://www.enginesofinnovation.com/html/publications.html (accessed October 28, 2009).

2. John V. Taylor, *The Primal Vision* (London: SCM Press, 1963).

3. Henri J. M. Nouwen, Donald P. McNeill, and Douglas A. Morrison, *Compassion: A Reflection on the Christian Life* (New York: Random House Publishers, 1982).

Chapter Five: New Monasticism Meets Renaissance Bottega: Gordon College's Semester Program in Orvieto, Italy—John Skillen (Gordon College, Wenham, Massachusetts; semester in Orvieto, Italy)

1. Nicholas Wolterstorff's *Art in Action: Toward a Christian Aesthetic* (Grand Rapids, MI: Wm B. Eerdmans, 1980) remains a valuable introduction to the problem of a false dichotomy between art for art's sake and art's usefulness.

2. Modern classics such as Dietrich Bonhoeffer's *Life Together* and various books by Thomas Merton and Henri Nouwen serve as recommended reading for the program. Kathleen Norris's popular memoir *A Cloister Walk*, and her recent *Acedia & Me: A Marriage, Monks, and a Writer's Life* are attractive and accessible to students. Among the growing number of books and essays using the phrase "new monasticism," the recent book of essays entitled *School(s) for Conversion: 12 Marks of a New Monasticism* (edited by The Rutba House, from Wipf and Stock Cascade Books, 2005) is especially helpful. *The Benedictine Handbook* edited by

Anthony Marett-Crosby OSB (Collegeville, Minn: Liturgical Press, 2003) is a very useful resource for newcomers to historical understanding of the early monastic shaping of life, as is Jean Leclercq's classic *The Love of Learning and the Desire for God: A Study of Monastic Culture* (New York: Fordham University Press, 1982). And something like Alasdair MacIntyre's final paragraph in *After Virtue* (2nd edition, University of Notre Dame Press, 1984) hovers behind the program: "What matters at this stage is the construction of local forms of community within which civility and the intellectual and moral life can be sustained through the new dark ages which are already upon us. . . . We are waiting not for a Godot, but for another—doubtless very different—St. Benedict."

    An earlier draft of this essay, sprinkled with photographs, was posted in the online journal of the Studio for Art, Faith & History: http://safhpalimpsest.blogspot.com/.

3.  I like the title of a helpful book from a Roman Catholic perspective: *Contemplation and the Charismatic Renewal*, edited by Paul Hinnebusch (Paulist Press International, 1986).

---

## Chapter Six: An Intentional Roman Catholic Community: Integrating Faith, Reason and Service at the Heart of the Church—Don Briel (University of St. Thomas, St. Paul, Minnesota; semester in Rome)

1.  See the section on Catholic Studies in *Catholic Education: A Journal of Inquiry and Practice*, Vol. 12, No. 3, March 2009. Essays include Anthony J. Dosen, C.M., "The Development of Catholic Studies Programs in American Catholic Universities," 360–67; James L. Heft, S.M., "Almost No Generalizations: Reflections on Catholic Studies," 368–83; and Don J. Briel, "Catholic Studies at the University of St. Thomas," 384–98.

2.  Evelyn Waugh, *Brideshead Revisited: The Sacred and Profane Memories of Captain Charles Ryder* (Boston: Little, Brown and Co., 1979), 86.

3.  John Paul II, Discourse to the "Institut Catholique de Paris," 1 June 1980: *Insegnamenti di Giovanni Paolo II*, Vol. II/1, p.1581, in *Ex corde ecclesiae*, I.1:9–11.

4.  John Henry Newman, "Abuses of the College: Oxford," in *Historical Sketches*, vol. 3 (London: Longmans, Green and Co., 1909), 179.

5.  John Henry Newman, "Intellect, the Instrument of Religious Training," in *Sermons Preached on Various Occasions* (London: Longmans, Green and Co., 1894), 13.

6.  Alasdair MacIntyre, "Catholic Universities: Dangers, Hopes, Choices," in *Higher Learning and Catholic Traditions*, ed. Robert E. Sullivan (Notre Dame: University of Notre Dame Press, 2001), 10.

7.  Benedict XVI, Address of Pope Benedict XVI, "Meeting with Members of the Academic Community," Vladislav Hall, Prague, 27 September 2009.

8.  MacIntyre, "Catholic Universities," 16.

9.  John Paul II, *Ex corde ecclesiae*, I.2:10–12.

# Part III
## Coming Face to Face with the Social Other:
## Bridging Intercommunal Divides

—Ronald J. Morgan (Abilene Christian University, Abilene, Texas; ACU in Oxford)

1. Here, as in Chapter Eight, we employ the term "intercommunal" in reference to that which exists or occurs between communities. Indeed, the term is so often followed by words like "conflict" or "strife" that one wonders whether it enjoys any other connotation. The intercommunal gulfs described in Chapters Seven through Ten of this collection are varied in nature. They include rival nationalisms, U.S. "culture wars," and differences of class, language, or "civilization."

---

Chapter Seven: "With Open Eyes": Cultivating World Christians through Intercultural Awareness—Laura Montgomery and Mary Docter (Westmont College, Santa Barbara, California; Westmont in Mexico)

1. Milton J. Bennett, "Towards Ethnorelativism: A Developmental Model of Intercultural Sensitivity," in *Education for the Intercultural Experience*, ed. R. Michael Page (Yarmouth, ME: Intercultural Press, 1993), 24. We should note that we disagree with Bennett's implication that commitment to a "universalist" faith such as Christianity is incompatible with ethnorelativism.

2. Ibid., 53. The six stages (from the most ethnocentric to the most ethnorelative) are denial, defense, minimization, acceptance, adaptation, and integration. For a detailed discussion of the DMIS and each stage, see Bennett, "Towards Ethnorelativism: A Developmental Model of Intercultural Sensitivity," 21–71.

3. The authors have held a week-long workshop and provide ongoing individual consulting for prospective faculty leaders.

4. Students take the IDI online either prior to or during the first week of the semester. The IDI, developed by Mitchell R. Hammer and Milton J. Bennett, "measures an individual's (or group's) fundamental worldview orientation to cultural difference, and thus the individual's or group's capacity for intercultural competence. As a theory-based test, the IDI meets the standard scientific criteria for a valid and reliable psychometric instrument," Milton J. Bennett & Mitchell R. Hammer, "Interpreting your Intercultural Development Inventory (IDI) Profile," (Portland, Oregon: Intercultural Communication Institute, 2002), 1. For more information, see http://www.idiinventory.com.

5. Alternately, students sometimes place in a subcategory of defense called *reversal*, where "they" are superior and elements of the home culture are inferior. This often occurs with students who fall so much in love with the host culture that they "go native" and thereby fail to have a realistic view of either their own or the host culture. See Bennett, "Towards Ethnorelativism," 39–41.

6. Once in Mexico, if students are operating from this minimalist perspective, they are often perplexed as to why on some occasions they are chided by their host families or penalized by professors for "being late." The confusion comes from

their inability to tell time culturally: in this case, to recognize the contextual factors, such as relative social status or the type of event, activity, or interaction that determine the appropriate moments of arrival or departure. In our in-country seminar, we discuss these issues and attempt to move students to an ethnorelative level of cultural sensitivity where they can recognize these cues and shift their cognitive framework to act appropriately for the context.

7. Note that acceptance does not necessarily mean *agreement* with different cultural practices, nor does adaptation imply an assimilation which involves giving up one's own beliefs, values, and practices.

8. We would like to thank the Westmont in Mexico students who granted us permission to include their work in this chapter as well as all of those who we have had the privilege to accompany on their journey toward becoming world Christians.

9. One of our primary texts for this course is Craig Storti's *Figuring Foreigners Out: A Practical Guide* (Yarmouth, ME: Intercultural Press, 1999). We also use selections from Edward C. Stewart and Milton J. Bennett, *American Cultural Patterns: A Cross-Cultural Perspective*, rev. ed (Yarmouth, ME: Intercultural Press, 1991), L. Robert Kohl, *Survival Kit for Overseas Living*, 4th ed. (London: Nicholas Brealey, 2001) and Daniel J. Hess, *The Whole World Guide to Culture Learning* (Yarmouth, ME: Intercultural Press, 1994), among others.

10. This assignment, which requires extended time with another individual followed by written reflection, not only helps students get to know each other better but also provides practice in "reaching out" to new people, a skill they will need while abroad.

11. We discuss with students the scholarly debate regarding those elements of the Concheros' dance that may or may not be pre-Columbian. For an example, see Susanna Rostas, "The Concheros of Mexico: A Search for Ethnic Identity," *Dance Research: The Journal of the Society for Dance Research* 9 (1991): 3–18.

12. Although this two-unit course is optional, the great majority of students take it. At the end of the course, we re-administer the IDI to assess the degree of growth in intercultural sensitivity. In the four years we have done this, the results confirm that students have become more sophisticated in their conceptualization of cultural differences as measured by this instrument.

13. Other activities include regular reading of Latin American newspapers, increased involvement in the Latino Student Organization on campus as well as missions work abroad, the assumption of leadership positions in campus ministries, and research projects pursuing interests and questions raised during the semester abroad.

14. Interestingly, some in the WIM group—typically those who felt more disconnected prior to departure—actually felt more engaged upon their return. Note this student's reaction to a "major difference" in attitude: "Last year I felt like an outsider, so misunderstood. But now, in the day to day strolling about campus I felt happier, positive, confident. Walking through the Dining Commons was no longer scary, and my thoughts were no longer dedicated to analyzing why I felt

so miserable. Now, although things have changed here, I have embodied a new feeling: this is *my* school too."

15. This quote is from the same student who earlier reflected upon the Fiesta de la Cruz.

16. In the words of one student, campus workers from Mexico or other parts of Latin American "used to be invisible; now, though, I want to hear their stories and know them as people."

## Chapter Eight: Who Is My Neighbor? Forming Kingdom People in a World of Conflict—Ronald J. Morgan (Abilene Christian University, Abilene, Texas; ACU in Oxford)

1. Erich Maria Remarque, *All Quiet on the Western Front*, translated by A. W. Wheen (London: Putnam, 1929), 185–91.

2. The term "intercommunal" denotes that which exists or occurs between communities.

3. Philip Fountain and Chris Elisara, "Being is Believing? Out of the Box (Subversive) Education," *The Journal of Education and Christian Belief* 10.2 (2006): 63–90.

4. Miroslav Volf, *Exclusion and Embrace: A Theological Exploration of Identity, Otherness, and Reconciliation* (Nashville: Abingdon Press, 1996), 16–17.

5. Volf, *Exclusion and Embrace*, 17, emphasis in the original.

6. Volf, *Exclusion and Embrace*, 37, emphasis in the original.

7. Volf, *Exclusion and Embrace*, 51, emphasis in the original.

8. Lee C. Camp, *Mere Discipleship: Radical Christianity in a Rebellious World* (Grand Rapids: Brazos Press, 2003). As Camp acknowledges (p. 9), his thought on this point owes much to the work of his mentor, John Howard Yoder.

9. Volf, *Exclusion and Embrace*, 51. A few years ago I argued that evangelicals should acquaint themselves closely with spiritual models (or biographies) from the whole breadth of the Christian tradition, including the lives of Roman Catholic saints. Although I did not realize it at the time, my expressed "hope that a deeper knowledge of ancient spiritual models will broaden our understanding of what it means to be like Jesus" was an endorsement of what Volf calls "catholic personality." See "This Great Cloud of Witnesses: Evangelical Christians and the Lives of the Saints," *Fides et Historia* 35.2 (2003): 24.

10. One student admitted the value of reading Karl Marx with a more open mind:

> Previously, I had always had a very negative view of Marxism, seeing it as evil . . . After reading [*Communist Manifesto*], I have realized that Marxism actually has some similarities with the early church and the teachings of Christ . . . I found this remarkable and ironic, considering that Marx calls for the elimination of religion. [Though] I found enough ideas within the manifesto that I disagree with . . . it got me thinking about money, the poor, and social situations. [Here the student describes his family

background in business and banking.] Earning as much money as possible in business is what I have been taught and what makes sense to me.... But after reading Marx and grasping the connections to Christ's teachings, I began to question this a bit.... So I am faced with this dilemma, am I to give everything I have to the poor, or am I only called to give a percentage, or simply not to love my money?

11. See Alfie Kohn, "Human Nature isn't Inherently Violent," in *Detroit Free Press*, Aug. 21, 1988; Martin Luther King, Jr., "Love your Enemies," (Public domain sermon delivered at Dexter Avenue Baptist Church, Montgomery, Alabama, 17 November 1957); and Edward T. Linenthal, "The A-Bomb Controversy at the National Air and Space Museum," in *The Historian* 57 (Summer 1995). For the story of Le Chambon-sur-Lignon, see Colman McCarthy, "Nonviolent Weapons of the Spirit," in *Washington Post*, Feb. 25, 1990; and Philip Hallie, *Lest Innocent Blood be Shed* (New York: Harper Perennial, 1994).

12. Olivier Clément, *Taizé, A Meaning to Life* (Chicago: GIA Publications, 1997), 35.

13. For one of the seminal histories of the Churches of Christ in America, see Richard T. Hughes, *Reviving the Ancient Faith: The Story of Churches of Christ in America* (1996, reprint edition Abilene, Tex.: Abilene Christian University Press, 2007).

14. Happily, some voices within Churches of Christ and their affiliated academic institutions are returning to the unity values of their nineteenth-century roots. One important historical study from the late 1980s called for a new historical awareness among descendents of the Stone-Campbell movement. In *Discovering Our Roots: The Ancestry of Churches of Christ* (Abilene, Tex.: Abilene Christian University Press, 1988), C. Leonard Allen and Richard T. Hughes showed that the impulse to restore primitive Christianity was not unique to the Stone-Campbell movement, but was the aspiration for a whole range of restorationist projects. In so doing, Allen and Hughes demonstrated the kinship between Churches of Christ and many other Christian traditions. For recent calls to unity within Churches of Christ or among the denominations that trace their lineages to Barton W. Stone and Thomas and Alexander Campbell, see Jeff W. Childers, Douglas A. Foster, and Jack R. Reese, *The Crux of the Matter: Crisis, Tradition, and the Future of Churches of Christ* (Abilene, Tex.: Abilene Christian University Press, 2002) and Glenn Thomas Carson, Douglas A. Foster, and Clinton J. Holloway, *One Church: A Bicentennial Celebration of Thomas Campbell's Declaration and Address* (Abilene, Tex.: Abilene Christian University Press, 2008). Although such calls for unity are limited in scope, they represent a return to the earliest impulses to oneness in Christ that guided the early Stone-Campbell "restorationist" vision.

15. Volf, *Exclusion and Embrace*, 53–4, emphasis in the original.

16. John Barbour, "The Moral Ambiguity of Study Abroad," *Chronicle of Higher Education* 53.7 (2006).

17. James William McClendon, Jr., *Biography as Theology: How Life Stories can Remake Today's Theology* (Nashville: Abingdon Press, 1974), 101–2.

Chapter Nine: Middle Eastern Mirrors for the Children of Empire—David P. Holt
(CCCU Middle East Studies Program, Cairo, Egypt).

1. S. Huntington's *Clash of Civilizations and the Remaking of World Order* (Simon and Schuster, 1998) argued for the inevitability of war between Islam and the West, a thesis that has since resonated critically in both Western and Muslim discourse around the world. For recent views critical of Huntington and his supporters, see the collected essays in E. Qureshi and M. Sells, eds., *The New Crusades—Constructing the Muslim Enemy* (Columbia, 2003).

2. Third party mediators between conflicting parties often acknowledge the need for each side to express its narrative as an initial move in rebuilding relationships if any reconciliation is to occur. Dennis Ross makes this point in *The Missing Peace—the Inside Story of the Fight for Middle East Peace* (FSG, 2005).

3. McClelland, Smedley, and J. Morgan (in this collection) all discuss important aspects of how living with or through periods of dissonance, disorientation, and tension can prove spiritually and intellectually fruitful.

4. Oliver and Joan Lockwood O'Donovan, *A Sourcebook in Christian Political Thought—from Irenaeus to Grotius* (Eerdmans, 1999) provides a wonderful spectrum of Christian thinking about the requirements of faith in the face of political interest and necessity.

5. J. Morgan discusses Miroslav's Volf's idea of distance from culture as a prerequisite of faith. McClelland also deals with the struggle to live with "calmly held boundaries" in a "tension of opposites."

6. British scholar Hugh Goddard talks of his own struggles to compare Islam and Christianity fairly due to the beam in his own eye, so to speak, religiously, culturally, and historically. Goddard has two excellent resources for the student of Muslim-Christian relations, *Christians and Muslims—from Double Standards to Mutual Understanding* (Curzon, 1995) and *A History of Christian-Muslim Relations* (Edinburgh, 2001).

7. Like Barbour, I am agnostic on whether the study abroad experience is a vehicle of personal transformation, however understood. Generally, it is not my aim to tie up the loose ends of student discomfort, doubt, and confusion by attempting a formulaic 'integration of faith and learning' before students leave Cairo. In any case, such "wrap up" activities require an intentional reentry program presently not included in the MESP agenda.

8. In *Peace Be Upon You—the Story of Muslim, Christian, and Jewish Coexistence* (Knopf, 2007), Zachary Karabell illustrates this point by another great moment in history when Muslim, Christian, and Jew were forced to coexist and in the process, learned much about themselves and the other.

9. Most women in Cairo wear the veil today, a phenomenon that began in earnest after the Six Day War of 1967 when Israel's defeat of Egypt, Syria, and Jordan signaled the beginning of the end for secular Arab nationalism and the rise of Islam as a popular substitute.

10. This advice applies just as strongly to learning about their own culture—how many Christian Americans could teach Christianity or American history without

bias or other serious constraints? How many American students can explain the government, history, or culture of the United States?

11. Including lessons in dabka and belly dancing, tabla drum, and Egyptian style cooking.

12. Garbage City, otherwise called *Mokattam* or *Manshiet Naser*, is a rock quarry area located near Old Cairo where tens of thousands of poor Coptic Christians settled in the late 60s and filled a niche as trash collectors. While not officially on the tourist map of Egypt, students find its inhabitants wonderfully hospitable and the magnificent rock carvings of its local monastery and cave church, a veritable pilgrimage site for local Egyptian Copts, one of the best-kept secrets of Cairo. Garbage City is site to one MESP home stay and one service project.

13. This CLE grew out of the need for students to make contact with locals much sooner in the semester than the fourth or fifth week usually arranged for home stays. While less structured or immersed than home stays, it allows students more time with at least one circle of local contacts before travel component takes them out of Cairo.

14. One of the most important MESP goals is to create opportunities for students to return to the region after the semester. For this reason, MESP builds institutional relationships at places like the Arab League, language institutes, service project sites, and international schools where students can do internships or continue culture and language study in order to enhance vocational options.

15. Cf. M. Volf, *Exclusion and Embrace—A Theological Exploration of Identity, Otherness, and Reconciliation* (Abingdon, 1996), 21. R. Morgan deals with this issue more directly.

16. Goddard, *Christian-Muslim Relations*, 8.

17. One ubiquitous example of apple-orange thinking is to compare Jesus' life and teaching with the Islamic doctrine of Jihad. The idea is not to ignore unpleasant comparisons, but to compare ideals with ideals and practices with practices.

18. In part because of tendencies in the U.S. toward demonizing Islam as a whole, I find it necessary to discuss highly biased, hypercritical "expert analysis" on Islam directly, including select films depicting Islamic militancy.

19. Incarnational used here from Phil 2. The wider issue of incarnation as a model for cross-cultural experience is discussed much more directly in several essays in this volume.

20. See O'Donovan and O'Donovan, *Sourcebook*.

21. In the context of MESP, for example, I ask students to consider a sobering contrast between two Eastern Churches toward the use of violence. Historically, Egyptian Copts have adopted peaceful (non)resistance as a posture toward the dominant Muslim society. But if candid, street-level attitudes of Copts are any measure, this posture represents little more than a triumph of necessity over principle in recognizing that violent resistance by an insecure minority is as unwise as it is impractical. Lebanese Maronites by contrast, more evenly numbered among the their nation's mosaic of confessional groups, have few spiritual inhibitions to mobilizing for war in the name of defending the faith and its longstanding community. The implication of this comparison should be clear. Are Christian views

toward the legitimate use of violence merely contingent on history? If MESP advocates of nonviolent resistance were born in Beirut or Cairo, would they hold the same views they do today?

22. The tension inherent in the relationship between the requirements of ruling an empire and of complying with Christian teaching is a theme deeply rooted in Christian thought from the early Church to the present. In addition to O'Donovan and O'Donovan, *Sourcebook*, see Christopher Bryan, *Render Unto Caesar—Jesus, the Early Church, and the Roman Empire* (Oxford, 2005).

23. These policies involve a long list but include: U.S. invasion of Iraq and Afghanistan, bases in Saudi Arabia, U.S. support for militants during the Afghan war against the former Soviet Union, and U.S. support for Israel.

24. On the whole question of how study abroad experience relates to stages of spiritual growth, see various chapters in this volume.

---

## Chapter Ten: San Francisco Urban Program: Encountering America's Future-Tense—
Scott McClelland, Karen Andrews, and Brad Berky (Westmont College, Santa Barbara, California; San Francisco Urban Program)

1. Our U.S. equivalent to Shane Claiborne's call for us all to "Find your Calcutta," as he reminisced on his encounter with Mother Teresa, *Irresistible Revolution* (Grand Rapids: Zondervan, 2006), 89.

2. The term received large circulation with the ascendency of Nancy Pelosi to the position of Speaker of the House of Representatives. Its most recent incarnation comes from conservative commentators such as Bill O'Reilly and Newt Gingrich in 2006, but may have been originally coined by Rep. Frank Riggs in 1996.

3. Carl Nolte, "Freedom a Constant in Ever-Evolving San Francisco Values," *San Francisco Chronicle*, November 4, 2006.

4. LGBTQ is a preferred description by the community, for it delineates the categories "Lesbian, Gay, Bisexual, Transgendered, and Queer/Questioning."

5. Violet Blue, "San Francisco Values," *San Francisco Chronicle*, November 16, 2006.

6. Noted sociologist Christian Smith estimates only 15% of 18–29 year old Americans are "Committed Traditionalists," with the largest percentage (30%) now in a category he calls "Selective Adherents." Reported by Katelyn Beaty in "Lost in Transition," *Christianity Today* (October, 2009), 34–37.

7. Phyllis Tickle. *The Great Emergence: How Christianity is Changing and Why* (Grand Rapids: Baker, 2008), 16. Other writers are noting similar paradigmatic shifts within traditional Christianity, cf. Eric Elnes. *The Phoenix Affirmations: A New Vision for the Future of Christianity* (San Francisco: Jossey-Bass, 2006), xviii.

8. The reader is encouraged to investigate such works as Brian McLaren, *Everything Must Change: Jesus, Global Crises, and a Revolution of Hope* (Nashville: Thomas Nelson, 2007); Doug Pagitt, *A Christianity Worth Believing* (San Francisco: Jossey-Bass, 2008); Frank Viola and George Barna, *Pagan Christianity* (Ventura, CA: Barna Books, 2008); and Mark Scandrette, *Soul Graffiti: Making a Life in the Way of Jesus* (San Francisco: Jossey-Bass, 2007).

9. Eddie Gibbs, director of the Institute for the Study of Emerging Churches, notes the need for churches to consider a major shift in ministry structure and outlook in what he calls the "post Christendom context" of America. He writes, "Churches have to move from an attractional mindset to an incarnational mission model. In other words, churches must become the seekers." Quoted in John Bradon, "Crazy Passion," *Christianity Today* (Oct. 2009), 42–45. San Francisco could well be one of America's first "Post-Christian" cities. By this we mean a city where the gospel message has been represented and present within the city since its inception (the name itself implies it), and yet at this point of its history, the majority of citizens within the city have no positive relationship with Christianity. Leslie Newbigin points out how the "West" presents a special challenge to Christians. For the first time, the church has had to conduct missionary activity to a culture that was "previously Christian." This is summarized in Kevin J. Vanhoozer, Charles A. Anderson, and Michael J. Sleaseman, *Everyday Theology: How to Read Cultural Texts and Interpret Trends* (Grand Rapids: Baker, 2007), and Dave Kinnaman and Gabe Lyons, *unChristian: What a Generation Thinks About Christianity… and Why it Matters* (Grand Rapids: Baker, 2007). While some more conservative voices might find some degree of comfort in the "offense of the Gospel," it is often the style of presentation and alliances with particular political and social forces that offend our detractors more than any formulation of a theological understanding.

10. Note the tone of this brief survey of some recent articles such as Brad A. Greenberg, "'Get Out of San Francisco': City's Response to Christian Youth Event Poses Legal Question," *Christianity Today.org*, posted: June 1, 2006; "Anger Over Prop. 8 Erupts In San Francisco," *KTVU.com*, posted: November 14, 2008; and Barbara Anderson, "Does It Take A Jew, Michael Savage, To Defend Christians?" *American Chronicle.com*, posted: Oct. 1, 2007.

11. Brian McLaren, *Everything Must Change*, 280. He quotes "Graciela," an Argentine woman encountering the indigenous mountain people with a ministry of "presence." Her words are significantly relevant for ministry in our city: ". . . It wasn't the resources we brought that made a difference. It was our presence. We were simply among them as people with hope, among them as people with love, and that made the difference. They caught our hope."

12. Marilyn Chandler McEntyre is author of *Caring for Words in a Culture of Lies* (Grand Rapids: Eerdmans, 2009).

13. See Stanley Hauerwas and William H. Willimon, *Resident Aliens: Life in the Christian Colony* (Nashville: Abingdon Press, 1989).

14. A female student, Spring 2009, identified her new collaborations with the individuals behind Cora Jean's Old Skool Café (http://www.oldskoolcafe.org/) and Rapha House, a Holy Hip Hop Church (http://www.raphahouse.info/rh_prog.html).

15. Female student, Fall 2008.

16. Female student, Spring 2009.

17. Male student, Fall 2008.

18. Richard Rohr, in *Everything Belongs*, reminds us that we are all filled with contradictions needing to be reconciled. Rohr's concept of "calmly held boundaries, which neither need to be defended constantly nor abdicated in the name of 'friendship'" is to be appreciated here. This "Third Way" that "emerges only when you hold the tension of opposites" is what we try to model and encourage through living with the questions. Rohr, *Everything Belongs: The Gift of Contemplative Prayer* (New York: Crossroad Publishing Company, 1999), 23.

19. Female student, Spring 2009.

20. Janet O Hagberg and Robert A. Guelich observed: "We move from a posture of knowing to one of seeking. . . . We know we are no longer seeking *an* answer," *The Critical Journey: Stages in the Life of Faith*, 2nd Ed. (Salem, WI: Sheffield Publishing Company, 2005), 97.

21. Ephesians 2:10

22. Mark 9:38–40: "Teacher," said John, "we saw a man driving out demons in your name and we told him to stop, because he was not one of us." "Do not stop him," Jesus said. "No one who does a miracle in my name can in the next moment say anything bad about me, for whoever is not against us is for us."

23. Remembering C. S. Lewis' startling conclusions to his sermon, *The Weight of Glory,* where he stressed, "There are no *ordinary* people. You have never talked to a mere mortal . . . Next to the Blessed Sacrament itself, your neighbour is the holiest object presented to your senses" (*Theology* Nov. 1941), 9.

24. Female student, Fall 2008.

25. Female student, Fall 2008.

26. Formal collaboration with such internship/partner sites as The Not For Sale Campaign offer students an opportunity to be on the ground floor of this two-and-a-half-year organization, which describes its meteoric rise to influence in the anti-trafficking arena as significantly aided by "the Westmont interns" (quote from founder/president Dr. David Batstone speaking at Westmont College, September 30, 2009; cf. www.thenotforsalecampaign.org).

27. Fredrick Buechner, *Wishful Thinking: A Theological ABC* (San Francisco: HarperOne, 1993), 121. This well-known and often-quoted definition of "vocation" has long influenced what our program is about on the internship-practicum front.

28. This seminar class meets every Thursday from10:30 a.m.–12:00 p.m. and provides students with opportunities to critically reflect on their internship experiences, to hear the vocational journeys of selected guest speakers, and to explore any number of faith, ethical, and cross-cultural workplace issues.

29. Our experience has been that many of our Urban Program alums gain a deeper sense for the value of their encounters after leaving us and/or in the years afterwards. The regular visits and feedback times we receive on this front indeed suggests that a "something more" movement does eventually take place regardless of initial questions and doubts.

30. Christian-oriented development theorists such as Sharon Parks, Steven Garber, James Mannioa, and Parker Palmer all affirm the necessity of nurturing "crisis

moments" able to stretch the faith/worldview of students regardless of prior worldview commitments.

31. Excerpt from a Fall 2008 student internship evaluation.

32. David A. Hoffman builds upon Sharon Parks' work in his article *Reflections on the ACPA Spiritual Maturation Institute* (http://www.collegevalues.org/spirit. cfm?id=435&a=1). He calls upon us to "facilitate the learner's encounter with the relative nature of all knowledge, to free it from value neutrality, allowing it to serve and assist young adults in composing critically aware and worthy commitments to self and society within the context of a relativized world."

33. Sharon Parks, *The Critical Years: Young Adults and the Search for Meaning, Faith and Commitment* (San Francisco: HarperCollins, 1991), 52.

34. Excerpt from a Spring 2009 student internship evaluation.

35. Spring 2009 intern at the SF General Hospital Chaplaincy.

36. Supervisor comments, Spring 2009.

37. Female student, Spring 2009.

38. Parker Palmer, *To Know as We are Known* (San Francisco: HarperOne, 1993), 16.

39. Female student, Spring 2009.

40. Female student, Spring 2009.

41. Male student, Spring 2009.

42. Supervisor comments, Spring 2009 (reflecting on the student referenced in note 41, above).

---

Chapter Eleven: Learning from Slums: Study and Service in Solidarity with the World's Urban Poor—Richard Slimbach (Global Studies Program at Azusa Pacific University; India, Philippines, and Haiti)

1. E.J. Hobsbawm, *On the Edge of the New Century* (London: Little Brown and Company, 2000), 169.

2. Lester Brown of the Earth Policy Institute reports atmospheric CO2 discharges from fossil fuel burning (7.5 billion tons) and deforestation (1.5 billion tons) in *Plan B 3.0* (New York: W.W. Norton & Company, 2008), 50.

3. See Paul Collier, *The Bottom Billion* (New York: Oxford University Press, 2007).

4. United Nations Development Program, *Human Development Report 2007/2008* (New York: UNDP, 2008).

5. Some readers may find language like "third world," "slum," or "the poor" problematic for the pejorative or paternalistic meanings often associated associated with them. Language certainly matters: it can powerfully nourish race and class prejudices, and unwittingly contribute to the disadvantage of those of whom or with whom one is speaking. At the same time, the recommended "repair" of replacing a short, vernacular word with three or four more sensitive, and oftentimes obscure, words seems equally, if not more, irksome. For instance, substituting "lesser developed countries" for "third world," "materially deprived communities" for "slum," and "the economically disadvantaged" or "the otherly rich" for "the

poor" clarifies little. For this reason I've opted to retain the simpler, broadly used, and, at least in my mind, precise language. Ultimately, each group must decide how it wishes to be perceived and delineated. The reader is encouraged to enter empathetically into the lived reality of the peoples and places described in this essay, restraining the impulse to "patrol" descriptive language from a position of comfortable, arm's length neutrality.

6. United Nations Department of Economic and Social Affairs, *World Urbanization Prospects: The 2007 Revision* (New York: United Nations, 2008); and UN-HABITAT, *The Challenge of Slums: Global Report on Human Settlements 2003* (London: Earthscan, 2003).

7. Mike Davis, *Planet of Slums* (London: Verso, 2007), 19.

8. Robert Wuthnow, *Boundless Faith: The Global Outreach of American Churches* (Berkeley: University of California Press, 2009).

9. David Kinnaman, *unChristian* (Grand Rapids: Baker Books, 2007).

10. Among the works that have become *New York Times* bestsellers are Christopher Hitchens, *God Is Not Great* (New York: Hachette Book Group, 2007); Richard Dawkins, *The God Delusion* (New York: Houghton Mifflin Company, 2006); and Sam Harris, *The End of Faith* (New York: W.W. Norton & Company, 2004).

11. Jon Meacham, "The End of Christian America," *Newsweek* (2009): Retrieved June 21, 2009 <http://www.newsweek.com/id/192583>.

12. Ralph Winter, "Staggers, Stalls, and Sit Downs," *Mission Frontiers* (May-June 2008), 11.

13. See Brian McLaren, *Everything Must Change* (Nashville: Thomas Nelson, 2007); Jonathan Wilson-Hartgrove, *New Monasticism* (Grand Rapids: Baker, 2008); Scott Bessenecker, *The New Friars* (Downers Grove: InterVarsity Press, 2006); Tom Sine, *The New Conspirators* (Downers Grove: InterVarsity Press, 2008); and Shane Clairborne, *The Irresistible Revolution* (Grand Rapids: Zondervan, 2006).

14. UN-HABITAT, *The Challenge of Slums: Global Report on Human Settlements 2003* (London: Earthscan, 2003).

15. For program details, see www.apu.edu/explore/matul.

16. See Ashley, Roe, and Goodwin, *Pro-Poor Tourism Strategies: Making Tourism Work for the Poor: A Review of Experience* (London: International Institute for Environment and Development, 2001); and Regina Scheyvens, *Tourism for Development: Empowering Communities* (Harlow: Prentice Hall, 2002).

17. Within the Judeo-Christian tradition, numerous biblical passages indicate a world renewed, restored, and "made right." See, for example, Leviticus 26:4–6; Isaiah 2:2–4; 11:1–9; 32:14–20; 42:1–12; 65:17–25; Joel 2:24–29; 3:17–18; Jeremiah 29:7; Ezekiel 34:25–29; Micah 4:3–4; Psalm 19; Psalm 34:14; Psalm 72:2, 4, 13–14; Romans 8:19–23; Ephesians 2:12–22; and Revelation 21:1–5, 19; 22:1–5.

18. For example, in terms of a short-term missions project: Is a greater good achieved by sending a team of 15 North Americans to Ghana for three weeks of voluntary service at a local orphanage at a combined cost of $35,000 and 40 tons of $CO_2$ discharged into the sensitive upper troposphere and lower stratosphere when that

money could support six full-time nationals for an entire year without damaging the environment?

19. For a fuller treatment of "ecological love" and "biotic rights," see Ronald Nash, *Loving Nature: Ecological Integrity and Christian Responsibility* (Nashville: Abingdon Press, 1991).

---

## Chapter Twelve: The Phenomenology of a Christian Environmental Study Abroad Program—Chris Elisara (Creation Care Study Program; Belize, New Zealand, and Samoa)

1. The Maori are the indigenous people of New Zealand who discovered the "Land of the Long White Cloud," or "Aoetaroa," after navigating across the pacific in sea-going canoes.

2. I was introduced to the use of curation in worship, which I extend to this context, by Mark Pierson. For a brief exploration of this concept read the following blog by Mark at http://www.creativeworshiptour.com/profiles/blogs/curating-worship-what-does-it.

3. This prayer is read from a worship guide provided to students by the staff. This prayer (and the rest of the worship service) was written by CCSP staff and has been refined over time.

4. In other words, this service occurs right after students have separated from their former lives in the U.S. and are on the cusp of rebuilding their lives in a new home, in a different culture, and in a new country. If you conceive of a study abroad semester in terms of a rite of passage (which CCSP does), the very first night of the semester is a very powerful symbolic and ritualistic moment. CCSP does not let those rites of passage moments pass without bringing spiritual meaning and educational purpose to them. For more information on rites of passage, ritual, and liminality refer to works by Victor Turner.

5. Gloria Goris Stronks and Clarence W. Joldersma, eds., *Educating for Life: Reflections on Christian Teaching and Learning* (Grand Rapids: Baker Academic, 2002). Clarence W. Joldersma and Gloria Goris Stronks, eds., *Educating for Shalom: Essays on Christian Higher Education* (Grand Rapids: Baker Academic, 2004).

6. Nicholas Wolterstorff, "Teaching for Shalom: On the Goal of Christian Collegiate Education," in *Educating for Shalom: Essays on Christian Higher Education* (Grand Rapids: Baker Academic, 2004), 25.

7. Nicholas Wolterstorff, "Teaching for Justice," in *Educating for Life: Reflections on Christian Teaching and Learning* (Grand Rapids: Baker Academic, 2002), 282–283.

8. Nicholas Wolterstorff, "Teaching for Tomorrow Today," in *Educating for Life* (Grand Rapids: Baker Academic, 2002), 139.

9. Leonardo Boff, "Salvation in Liberation: The Theological Meaning of Socio-historical Liberation" in *Salvation and Liberation: In Search of a Balance Between*

*Faith and Politics,* Leonardo Boff and Clodovis Boff (Maryknoll: Orbis Books, 1979), 2.

10. Brenda Rockell, "Ritual, Church and World: Building up the Body of Christ, Connecting with the Culture Beyond the Church" (unpublished manuscript, Auckland, 2005).

11. Jim Wallis, *God's Politics: Why the Right Gets It Wrong and the Left Doesn't Get It* (New York: HarperOne, 2005).

12. Brian Walsh, *Subversive Christianity: Imaging God in a Dangerous Time* (Seattle: Alta Vista College Press, 1992), 45.

13. Eugene Peterson, *Leap Over a Wall: Earthy Spirituality for Everyday Christians* (New York: HarperCollins, 1997), 5.

14. We draw here primarily on the following two texts: Larry Rasmussen, *Earth Community, Earth Ethics* (Maryknoll: Orbis Books, 1998); and Steven Bouma-Prediger, *For the Beauty of the Earth: A Christian Vision for Creation Care* (Grand Rapids: Baker Academic, 2001). However, we also recommend the following for further exploration: Loren Wilkinson, ed., *Earthkeeping in the '90s: Stewardship of Creation* (Grand Rapids: Eerdmans, 1991); Calvin B. DeWitt, *Earth Wise: A Biblical Response to Environmental Issues* (Grand Rapids: CRC Publications, 1994); Fred Van Dyke, et. al., *Redeeming Creation: The Biblical Basis for Environmental Stewardship* (Downers Grove: InterVarsity Press, 1996); Calvin B. DeWitt, *Caring for Creation: Responsible Stewardship of God's Handiwork* (Grand Rapids: Baker Books, 1998); Brian Walsh and Sylvia Keesmaat, *Colossians Remixed: Subverting the Empire* (Downers Grove: InterVarsity Press, 2004).

15. Bouma-Prediger, *For the Beauty of the Earth,* 135.

16. Rasmussen, *Earth Community, Earth Ethics,* 76.

17. Walter Brueggemann, *The Land: Place as Gift, Promise, and Challenge in Biblical Faith* (Philadelphia: Augsburg Fortress, 1977); and also Christophor Wright, *Old Testament Ethics for the People of God* (Downers Grove: InterVarsity Press, 2004).

18. Rasmussen, *Earth Community, Earth Ethics,* xii.

19. Bouma-Prediger, *For the Beauty of the Earth: A Christian Vision for Creation Care,* 37.

20. These two Hebrew terms are taken from the creation account in Genesis chapter 2; *'adam* meaning human earth-creature and *'adamâ* meaning earth. See Bouma-Prediger, *For the Beauty of the Earth: A Christian Vision for Creation Care,* 74.

21. Brian Walsh and Steven Bouma-Prediger, *Beyond Homelessness: Christian Faith in a Culture of Displacement* (Grand Rapids: Eerdmans, 2008).

22. Today's CCSP is a distillation of the passion and dedication of its staff, faculty, and academic committee. Hence although I have the privilege of writing about CCSP, the good I describe is primarily attributable to the work of my former and current CCSP colleagues who have helped mold CCSP. I am gratefully indebted to them. To learn more about CCSP consult the following article co-written with Philip Fountain, a former CCSP Belize director. Considered with this chapter the reader will gain a more thorough understanding of CCSP. Philip Fountain

and Chris Elisara, "Being is Believing? Out of the Box (Subversive) Education," *Journal of Education and Christian Belief* 10.2 (2006): 63–90.

Chapter Thirteen: The Study Service Term: An Alignment of a Religious Tradition with an Academic Program —Thomas J. Meyers (Goshen College, Goshen, Indiana; Study Service Term, primarily working in developing countries)

1. More than seven thousand students have studied in twenty-two countries around the world. SST sites have included Belize, Cambodia, China, Costa Rica, Côte d'Ivoire, Cuba, Dominican Republic, El Salvador, Ethiopia, Germany, Guadeloupe, Haiti, Honduras, Indonesia, Jamaica, Mali, Nicaragua, Peru, Poland, Senegal, South Korea, and Tanzania. Goshen College has always had an alternative program that allowed a student who could not go abroad to complete the requirement by completing a set of specific courses in international education such as the History of Africa, Latin American Societies and Cultures or International Literature.

2. J. Lawrence Burkholder, "The Study-Service Term at Goshen College," in *The Role of Service-Learning in International Education: Proceedings of a Wingspread Conference*, ed. Stuart W. Showalter (Goshen, IN: Goshen College, 1989), 26.

3. Wilbur Birky, "Faculty Leader Manual" (Goshen College, Goshen, IN. 1997), 2.

4. The Anabaptists emerged in South Germany and the Netherlands in the third decade of the sixteenth century. They insisted on a radical break from the established church traditions. Among them was the practice of baptizing infants. They insisted that baptism must be a conscious choice, not a matter of tradition. Under the threat of death they began to re-baptize adults who had received infant baptism and hence the label Anabaptist was applied to them. They also insisted on a complete separation of Church and State and developed an understanding of Christianity that suggests that a believer must join with like minded individuals in a community that is distinct from the 'world.' Furthermore, the Anabaptists insisted that the essence of Christianity is discipleship. The believer's outward expression of the Christian life must be consistent with the inner experience.

5. The extent of Marpeck's important contribution to the Anabaptist movement has only recently been understood. Among the important recent works that focus on Marpeck are: Walter Klaassen and William Klassen, *Marpeck: A Life of Dissent and Conformity* (Scottdale, PA: Herald Press, 2008); Neil Blough, *Christ in our Midst* (Kitchener, ON: Pandora Press, 2007) and Stephen B. Boyd, *Pilgrim Marpeck, His Life and Social Theology* (Durham: Duke University Press, 1992).

6. Timothy W. Reardon, "Pilgrim Marpeck's Sacramental Theology Based on His Confession of 1532," *Mennonite Quarterly Review* LXXXIII (April 2009): 293–317.

7. Boyd, *Pilgrim Marpeck*, 170.

8. William Klassen, "The Legacy of the Marpeck Community in Anabaptist Scholarship," *Mennonite Quarterly Review* LXXVII (January 2004): 18.

9. Lydette Assefa, SST journal, Goshen College, 2009.

10. Ibid., 34.

11. Aletha Stahl, "A Turning Point on the Journey," *Goshen College Bulletin* (September 1998): 8.

12. Adam Nafziger, *God and Rhythmic Dust* (Goshen, IN: Goshen College, 1998): 17.

13. Lane Miller, unpublished paper, Goshen College, 2009.

14. Keith Graber Miller, "A One-Armed Embrace of Postmodernity: International Education and Church- Related Colleges," in *Professing in the Postmodern Academy*, ed. Stephen Haynes (Waco: Baylor University Press, 2002), 231.

15. Ruth Krall, "Leading SST Convinces Krall Relational Teaching is Best," *Goshen College Bulletin* (November 1988): 5.

16. Personal Interview, Keith Graber Miller, September 18, 2002.

17. Personal Interview, Ruth Krall, October 20, 2002.

18. Stuart Showalter, Nancy Ryan, Thomas J. Meyers, "The Study-Service Term at Goshen College and Its Long-Range Impact: a Cross-Sectional Survey of SST Graduates, 1968–97," 2006.

19. Ibid., 85.

20. Ibid., 89.

21. Ibid., 80.

22. Ibid., 78.

Conclusion—Ronald J. Morgan (Abilene Christian University, Abilene, Texas; ACU in Oxford)

1. Philip Fountain and Chris Elisara, "Being is Believing? Out of the Box (Subversive) Education," *The Journal of Education and Christian Belief* 10.2 (2006): 1–15 (1).

2. Nathaniel Taylor, "A Tale of Two Schools," *Books & Culture* (July/August 2005): 29.

Appendix: Liturgies for Study Abroad—Janine Paden Morgan (Abilene Christian University, Abilene, Texas; ACU in Oxford)

1. Abbey, *Iona Abbey Worship Book* (Glasgow: Wild Goose Liturgies 2001), 57.